Why America Can't Retrench
(And How it Might)

Why America Can't Retrench

(And How it Might)

PETER HARRIS

polity

First published in 2024 by Polity Press

Polity Press
65 Bridge Street
Cambridge CB2 1UR, UK

Polity Press
111 River Street
Hoboken, NJ 07030, USA

ISBN-13: 978-1-5095-6209-1
ISBN-13: 978-1-5095-6210-7 (pb)

A catalogue record for this book is available from the British Library.

Library of Congress Control Number: 2024932378

Typeset in 11 on 13 pt Sabon
by Cheshire Typesetting Ltd, Cuddington, Cheshire
Printed and bound by CPI Group (UK) Ltd, Croydon, CR0 4YY

The publisher has used its best endeavors to ensure that the URLs for external
websites referred to in this book are correct and active at the time of going to
press. However, the publisher has no responsibility for the websites and can
make no guarantee that a site will remain live or that the content is or will
remain appropriate.

Every effort has been made to trace all copyright holders, but if any have been
overlooked the publisher will be pleased to include any necessary credits in any
subsequent reprint or edition.

For further information on Polity, visit our website:
politybooks.com

For my family

Contents

Acknowledgments

I enjoyed writing this book. So much so, in fact, that I might have to write another one. When I do, I'll take care to share that manuscript with more people than I shared this one with—not least of all because then my acknowledgments section can be longer. This one will be short.

Louise Knight, Inès Boxman, and Olivia Jackson at Polity were tremendous to work with. I'm grateful to Louise for seeing the potential in this project and for her expert advice. I hope to have done her proud. Phil Dines paid enormous attention to detail when copyediting my work, adding immense value in the process, and Evie Deavall did the all-important work of shepherding the manuscript through the production cycle.

Two anonymous reviewers gave feedback on an earlier draft of the manuscript. I thank them for their generosity. As they will see, I've incorporated almost all of their suggestions in this final version. Truly, I am indebted to them for their care, attention, diligence, and astonishing depth of knowledge.

I've never been one for sharing ideas with close colleagues – much to my detriment, no doubt – but this book benefited from me being around a brilliant group of young scholars at Colorado State University. My thanks to JB Bae, Iasmin

Goes, Matt Hitt, Alexis Kennedy, Julia Lee, Kyle Saunders, Dom Stecula, and Daniel Weitzel in particular for making my workplace such a pleasant environment. Bob Duffy is a great chair.

Beyond CSU, I'm grateful to Defense Priorities for making me part of another intellectual community. Even though I don't identify as a realist, the DEFP team has been nothing but welcoming. I've learnt a lot about restraint from watching them go about their work. I respect their unwavering commitment to rigor and wish that every policymaker was exposed to their careful analyses.

Peter Trubowitz has been a strong source of encouragement for the past fourteen years. He probably won't agree with everything in this book, but he'll surely notice something familiar about the approach and argument. I hope that imitation is still the sincerest form of flattery.

Meriel Hahn provided outstanding research assistance and became a valued coauthor. Though we never actually met because of the COVID-19 pandemic, I appreciated Meriel's help and professionalism. Her work with me was supported by funds from CSU's College of Liberal Arts and Department of Political Science.

Two of my mentors sadly passed away during this book's evolution from proposal stage to finished product. In May 2019, just as I was developing ideas for how to spend my sabbatical year, my undergraduate adviser at the University of Edinburgh died unexpectedly. John Peterson was a terrific adviser. He had a big impact on me. I'm sorry that John didn't live to see this book come to fruition. I would've taken great delight in sending him a copy.

My friend Robert Lawrence died in October 2023, just weeks before I submitted the first draft of the manuscript to Polity. Bob was my predecessor at CSU. We discussed the thesis of this book more than a few times over burgers and coffee. I was always a bit embarrassed that progress was so slow. He

endorsed the broad contours of my argument and gave feedback on how to hone the contribution. I miss Bob very much. I
wish I could chat with him now.

The Charles Koch Foundation provided financial backing
for me to extend my sabbatical into a second semester. I thank
Andrew Byers for his support and kindness. Ted Tyler has
been great to work with, too. Portions of the book were written while I benefited from another grant, from the Carnegie
Corporation of New York. While this second grant funded a
separate research project, some of the ideas are connected. My
thanks to Karim Kamel, Noelle Pourrat, Hillary Weisner, and
the rest of the team in New York.

I hope my family in England, Scotland, California, and
Colorado enjoy the book. It is dedicated to them.

Introduction

The United States has pursued a grand strategy of military primacy since the end of the Cold War. Among other things, this has meant readying US forces to fight multiple, simultaneous overseas wars at a moment's notice; reassuring dozens of treaty allies that Americans will provide for their defense, whether in whole or in part; and trying to dominate rivals such that no challenger can hope to order international affairs in ways that cut against US interests. These are expansive foreign policies meant to serve expansive ends. In the words of historian Daniel Immerwahr, "The [US] federal government doesn't just run the United States; it seeks to run the world."[1] In this sense, America is truly exceptional. It is the only country that occupies dozens of foreign nations with its soldiers, sailors, and airmen. The US military accounts for around 40 percent of the international community's total defense spending, despite Americans constituting just 4.25 percent of the world's population. Simply put, no other government comes close to defining or acting upon its security interests as expansively as Washington. The United States is a *sui generis* world power.

But there is nothing inevitable about this world role. Indeed, it is doubtful that America's primacist approach to international affairs would be adopted today if leaders and the voting public were to redesign the nation's foreign policies from scratch. Over 800 overseas bases, approximately 170,000 active-duty military personnel deployed in more than eighty countries and territories (plus in excess of a million stationed at home),[2] a defense budget surpassing $850 billion, and treaty-based alliances with more than one quarter of the world's states – none of these statistics makes obvious sense in the absence of an existential threat to national security. Nor are they consistent with traditional tenets of US political culture like limited government, fiscal responsibility, and equality among nations. Worse still, there is compelling evidence that a grand strategy of military primacy makes Americans less secure, not more.[3]

Why is the United States such an outlier? Why are its foreign-policy leaders wedded to the pursuit of global military primacy? In this book, I pin the blame for America's stubborn attachment to primacism on its domestic political system. The simple version of my argument is that the United States can only adopt such foreign policies as its leaders dare to imagine – but that, for decades, members of the political class have been disincentivized from questioning the country's massive, indefinite overseas interventions. Indeed, some of the most celebrated US forward deployments in Europe and East Asia have ceased to be "interventions" at all – a word that connotes military missions of a temporary nature rather than the permanent garrisons that, by now, characterize much of America's forward presence in Eurasia.

It was not always so. Before World War II, it was common for leaders in Washington – including sitting presidents and their closest advisers – to articulate and implement "anti-interventionist" foreign policies.[4] Periods of expansion and activism were often followed by bouts of retrenchment and restraint. But the experiences of fighting World War II and the Cold War altered America's domestic politics in profound ways, gradually eroding the salability of noninterventionist ideas such that, eventually, outright primacism became cemented as the political center ground.[5]

It is difficult to overstate just how much the United States changed during the second half of the twentieth century. Between 1941 and 1991, persistently high government spending – especially on defense – became the norm, whereas before it had largely been shunned except during times of national emergency. The presidency expanded its powers at the expense of Congress, particularly over war and national security policy, with increasing numbers of decisions being taken in secret. Strict limits were set on the boundaries of acceptable political discourse. Antiwar positions – once noble, patriotic, and mainstream – became radical and, in some cases, were deemed "un-American." Cutting deals with America's adversaries became suspect, with arguments for retrenchment conflated with isolationism (now a slur), declinism, and dishonor. Militarism became a part of the US national identity. And of course, entire industries, towns, and cities became dependent upon a steady flow of defense dollars – what President Eisenhower unfavorably called the "military-industrial complex."[6]

These alterations to the fabrics of US government, politics, economics, and society were controversial at the time, emphasized by critics as evidence of a creeping "garrison state."[7] Even those most responsible for placing the United States on a permanent war footing often did so with a heavy heart. President Truman, for example, agonized about the trade-offs between containing the Soviet Union and preserving civil liberties and personal freedoms at home.[8] Eisenhower, too, sought to temper defense spending and used his Farewell Address (in vain) to caution against excessive militarism. By the end of the Cold War, however, such warnings had become fewer and farther between. The militarization of the United States was the new normal. The collapse of the Soviet Union left Washington without a peer competitor on the world stage

– but even though external conditions no longer *required* the United States to pursue primacy abroad and militarization at home, domestic politics strongly *encouraged* these things while discouraging efforts to return to a pre–World War II posture.

In short, the end of the Cold War revealed that the United States had become hardwired to favor the pursuit of global military primacy and all that went along with it. With the Red Army no longer posing a threat to Western Europe or East Asia, the United States could have adjusted to its new international environment – one defined by abundant security rather than intense rivalry with another superpower – by bringing home the forward deployments that had been sent overseas for the explicit purpose of deterring Soviet aggression. In the event, however, sizable drawdowns only occurred in Europe – and, even there, reductions in force strength were coupled with the expansion of US security commitments in the form of NATO enlargement and participation in the Yugoslav Wars. Everywhere outside of Europe, America's military footprint either remained static or grew larger. Meanwhile, the US state and its adjunct institutions continued to function just as they had during the Cold War: squarely focused on the question of how to mobilize national resources in service of sweeping international objectives. It went largely unquestioned that the United States ought to be involved in the political and security affairs of other regions; that overwhelming military power was an indispensable part of how the United States should interface with the rest of the world; and that a primacist approach to foreign policy would redound to the benefit of all Americans.

Today, a powerful bias in favor of militarized and interventionist foreign policies still exists across the full expanse of the US political system: in presidential politics, Congress, the news media, academia, think tanks, and beyond.[9] The gravitational pull of militarism is so strong that US leaders are almost always unable or unwilling to pare down America's overseas commitments while in office, regardless of whether they believe military primacy to be truly necessary as a means of securing US national interests. When they do engage in policies of retrenchment, presidents and their allies invariably face strong political headwinds.[10] This is true even though the original justifications for America's vast forward deployments have long since expired, a fact that ought to raise fundamental questions about why the United States has not adjusted its foreign policies accordingly. My argument, then, is that the US political system has become unfit for purpose – *unfit for peace* – because it disallows the types of discussion that are surely warranted given the gigantic changes that have taken place to the international system and domestic politics in recent decades. In the final analysis, this is why America has not retrenched: because its leaders operate inside a political system that comprehensively disincentivizes them from seriously considering such a course.

Can barriers to retrenchment and restraint be overcome? My answer is yes, it is possible to reform domestic politics to permit a move away from military primacy – and, moreover, that US leaders will be pressured to undertake exactly such a strategic adjustment under conditions of greater multipolarity. Just because Americans have become accustomed to waging a foreign policy of military primacy does not mean they cannot be jolted into accepting new and different imaginations of their country's proper world role. But such efforts must proceed from a sober reckoning of the domestic landscape as it currently exists. After all, more than eighty years have elapsed since America's entry into World War II, which means that the United States has been fighting for – or striving to preserve – something like global military primacy for a full third of its lifespan as an independent republic. The vast array of institutions, processes, habits, interests, ideas, and identities that have been inculcated during this time will not be easy to dislodge. Nobody under 30 years of age can recall a time when the United States was not at war in the Middle East. Hardly anyone alive can remember when their country's armed forces were not massively forward deployed in Europe and East Asia. The challenge for those who would have America relinquish its pretense to global leadership and indispensability, therefore, goes far beyond academic debates over the appropriate ends and means of US grand strategy. To dismantle the primacist superstructures of US foreign policy, critics must focus their attention on the base – that is, government and politics on the home front.

This is the second purpose of the book: to suggest ideas for how domestic-level stumbling blocks to military retrench-ment might be overcome. My goal is to complement the raft of scholarship that calls for a US grand strategy of "restraint."[11] Advocates of restraint have provided no shortage of persuasive arguments for why a turn away from military preponderance makes sense – for example, that America's external environ-ment no longer requires deep overseas engagement on par with what was viewed as necessary during the Cold War; that other countries are more than capable of providing for their own defense and for the collective security of key allies; that recent US-led military interventions seem to create more international turmoil than they resolve; and that a slenderer foreign policy would allow for social, economic, and demo-cratic renewal at home.

All these points have merit. But major strategic adjustments are difficult to bring about, even when the case for change is strong. America's current world role has put down deep roots in US domestic politics. Once new and extraordinary, the geopolitical reality of the United States being forward deployed across almost the entire planet is now sustained and supported by a powerful assemblage of domestic interests, from local communities that depend upon defense spending as an economic lifeline to national-level politicians who fear criticism for being "soft" on national security. This is why, if they are serious about changing foreign policy over the long haul, proponents of restraint must have a plan to change not just America's foreign relations but its domestic politics, too.

To restore flexibility and introspection to US foreign policy, I propose a two-pronged strategy of "domestic renewal" and "internationalism anew." In terms of the former, I suggest a series of political reforms that would level the playing field for those who believe the United States should pursue a more circumscribed world role. These include strengthening the Congress vis-à-vis the presidency, especially in terms of war powers but also over military policy during times of peace; disestablishing America's two-party duopoly through changes to the electoral system; and introducing new transparency measures so that a more diverse array of political actors can understand the impact of foreign relations on domestic society. If adopted, the domestic reforms introduced in this book would democratize US foreign policy and open the door to a more normal world role. The goal is not to replace America's primacist cartel with a restraint-oriented counterpart, but to imagine a more pluralistic political environment within which the American people might be exposed to a wider range of ideas about foreign policy. While others have made the case for domestic renewal before, my contribution is to argue that no such agenda will succeed unless it includes a proper diagnosis of militarism as a major feature (and cause) of America's ossified political system.

I recognize, of course, that no movement to replace the national security state will succeed unless it can recommend an alternative design for how to engage with the rest of the world. Americans cannot be expected to dismantle the domestic foundations of military primacy without a credible plan for what comes next. How will the United States ensure its external security without a massive military presence in Europe, East Asia, the Persian Gulf, and beyond? What would military retrenchment mean for the future of US prosperity? Will retrenchment jeopardize America's role as the lynchpin

of global governance? In short, what are the risks of retrenchment given the uncertainty that inheres in world affairs – and
how can these potential hazards be mitigated? My answer to
these questions is twofold.

First, the current strategy of military primacy has already
become ill-suited to prevailing international conditions. It will
become altogether unviable as a grand strategy once the international system completes its evolution toward multipolarity
in the coming decades. This means that maintaining the status
quo is simply not an option, a reality with which the American
people and their leaders must come to terms. Second, it is
essential that retrenchment and restraint are not mistaken
for retreat or isolationism. Proponents of retrenchment must
reclaim the mantle of internationalism from the militarists
whose one-dimensional view of international engagement has
served the United States so badly. The case must be made
that an astute blend of multilateralism, economic engagement,
diplomacy, and soft power can advance US interests far better
than today's overreliance on military force. Taken together,
domestic renewal and a nonprimacist version of internationalism anew have the potential to strengthen US democracy,
uphold national and international security, and provide a blueprint for values-based engagement with the outside world.

The Problems with Primacy

What, exactly, is military primacy? In the pages that follow,
I define military primacy as a grand strategy of maintaining
and exploiting America's military advantages over global and
regional competitors, with a view to leveraging these structural advantages in service of favorable political and economic
outcomes.[12] In the first instance, this means investing heavily
in the US military such that it remains a force that can fight
(and win) multiple, simultaneous wars around the world while

also deterring adversaries from attacking the United States or otherwise disturbing the peace. Primacy requires not just parity with adversaries, but a convincing level of military superiority in all relevant regions of the globe. The strategy only works if the US military is so far ahead of its nearest rivals that others are cowed into acquiescence. In short, primacy is a strategy of outpacing all of America's rivals in the military sphere. By establishing a wide gap between the United States and its competitors, the wager is that Washington can convince foreign governments to accept leadership in those issue areas that are of highest-order concern for the United States.

But primacy implies activism, not just readiness. Military primacy is rooted in a fundamental belief in the necessity and goodness of US overseas interventions.[13] Drawing on the lessons of Pearl Harbor, the Cold War, and the 9/11 terror attacks, proponents of military primacy argue that national security and global stability are goals best served when the United States projects power over and onto foreign soil. They caution that the outside world is a dangerous place full of autocrats, aggressors, and human rights abusers. If the United States has the material capacity to impose order beyond it shores, primacists argue, then it would be a derogation of duty to turn inwards.[14] To shrug off disorder abroad would be to court disaster, as major instances of global insecurity are bound to affect the United States sooner or later. At its heart, primacy is a strategy of moving preemptively and preventatively to neutralize threats abroad, preferably via deterrence ("peace through strength") but also via the adroit application of military power if necessary.

Global military primacy is an unusual ambition. Historically, few superpowers have viewed it as a practicable goal. Today, the United States is the only world power for which military primacy is an even semi-realistic grand strategy. Neither China, nor Russia, nor India – America's nearest peer competitors – can credibly aspire to military primacy in their own regions, let alone globally. The United States is alone in believing that it can assert military dominance across the world. But the uniqueness of America's aspiration to military primacy is not, by itself, a reason for opposition. Perhaps US exceptionalism is a good thing. Those who urge a move away from primacy must show that the strategy is pernicious or otherwise ill-suited to prevailing conditions.

Critics of primacy point to two main problems in this regard. First, they argue that the maintenance of military primacy will become increasingly fraught with danger in the context of a multipolar world.[15] Even if it is accepted that primacy made some sense during the so-called "unipolar moment"[16] (when the United States could deploy hard power overseas without placing the security of the homeland in obvious jeopardy), it cannot be argued that the same unilateralist policies are suited to a world that can punch back. Owing to the rise of China and the resurgence of Russia, in particular, the costs and risks of primacist policies are rising exponentially. Simply put, the US military cannot be deployed in or adjacent to flashpoints in Eastern Europe, Northeast Asia, and the Persian Gulf in perpetuity without significant risk of becoming embroiled in a devastating war. In this sense, primacy has already failed: the United States has not managed to cling onto military preponderance; it has not ordered world affairs in ways that guarantee lasting US dominance; it cannot reliably deter adversaries from pursuing bellicose foreign policies; and so, it should reconfigure its foreign relations to make sense of a new international environment.

Failure to adjust could be ruinous for the United States. The problem of hubris is real. President Biden, for example, has declared on multiple occasions that the United States would defend Taiwan against a Chinese invasion – despite the fact that the US military's own wargame exercises show that Beijing might well triumph in such a conflict, and that the use of nuclear weapons would be a high-probability event in any war over Taiwan.[17] President Trump, too, threatened war against both North Korea and Iran, despite the enormous death tolls that each of these regimes could inflict on the United States and its allies (North Korea, of course, is now a nuclear-armed state with the capacity to deliver nuclear warheads far afield).[18] After Russia's invasion of Ukraine in February 2022, some in the US media and politics called for the Biden administration to enforce no-fly zones over portions of Ukraine,[19] even if this meant destroying Russian air defenses and shooting down Russian airplanes. While these reckless ideas were not taken up by the White House, they reveal the extent to which some members of the US political class are willing to recommend the use of force even in circumstances that would ensure a confrontation with a nuclear-armed rival. How long before a sitting president acts upon advice that results in a major, uncontrollable conflagration? As Ben Friedman has cautioned in the context of Ukraine, "the longer you continue to roll those dice, even if the odds are low, the more likely you are to hit on a future disaster."[20]

Even if US leaders are inclined to stay out of foreign wars, a grand strategy of military primacy ensures that the decision will not always be theirs. Under primacy, the United States has deployed its forces overseas in dozens of foreign countries.[21] Including the members of the North Atlantic Treaty Organization (NATO) and the Rio Pact, the United States has fifty-one treaty allies, meaning that Washington is formally committed to the military defense of more than one quarter of the world's states.[22] These commitments date from eras when Washington thought it essential to provide a security umbrella to vulnerable allies, or else saw few risks in doing so. But US relative power has eroded since assuming these security obligations. The country's underlying interests have changed, too, and domestic politics have become more fractured. Under such conditions, it is plausible that a rival power might doubt the strength of US resolve and feel emboldened to attack an allied nation, engage in "gray zone" or "salami slicing" tactics, or even launch a preemptive assault on one of America's many overseas garrisons. Viewed from this angle, military primacy is a grand exercise in tempting fate. Thousands of forward-deployed US troops have been made vulnerable to attack from hostile forces, exposing the country to a perpetual risk of being ensnared in a foreign conflict at a time and place of another power's choosing. This is the exact opposite of promoting national security if defined as freedom from the threat of armed attack.

Beyond these security considerations, the second fundamental problem with primacy as a grand strategy relates to its patent unsuitability to US domestic politics today. As will be covered in chapter 1, the United States "went abroad" in World War II and the Cold War to ensure that the richest and most populous parts of Eurasia would not fall under the sway of a hostile powers. The goal was to safeguard national security but also to make the world safe for liberal capitalism, with US forces harnessed toward the end of ensuring the survival of an open world economy. This was viewed as a worthwhile undertaking because of the economic advantages that accrued to US firms and consumers across every region of the United States. But today, consensus has evaporated over whether economic openness and a stable international order more generally are goals worth fighting for. Many Americans are skeptical about the value of economic integration, blaming foreign trade and investment for a slew of social and economic problems at home. In this context, it is becoming less plausible for US leaders to defend military primacy as an extension of the US national interest. Especially now that US allies are powerful enough to provide for their own defense, some in the United States are asking pointed questions about why Washington remains the world's chief security provider.

There is even a strong case to be made that military primacy is actively harming US national interests. More than 7,000 active-duty personnel have been killed during America's wars since the terrorist attacks on 9/11, 2001. The Costs of War Project at Brown University estimates that a further 30,000 service members and veterans have died by suicide. The same researchers suggest that the federal government has spent or obligated more than $8 trillion toward warfighting over the same period, as well as passing legislation that has eroded civil liberties at home, harmed the natural environment, and adversely shifted the culture of the United States.[23] How much more democratic, free, harmonious, and prosperous might Americans be today if their government had not been wedded to military primacy for the past several decades? What social and economic problems might have been fixed if the federal government had been more focused on domestic issues rather than a globe-spanning array of international commitments? It is difficult to avoid the conclusion that the United States has suffered not just terrible costs but also staggering opportunity costs as a result of pursuing a grand strategy of military primacy. Whether this approach to international affairs continues to be "worth it" is hardly obvious.

The Alternatives: Restraint and Retrenchment

The opposite to military primacy is a grand strategy of restraint. In short, restraint is a blueprint for how to "do less" abroad in terms of military interventions.[24] Whereas primacy is a strategy of maintaining dominance, restraint is oriented toward more modest ends: the preservation of bare national security and an acceptable distribution of power among the United States and its chief rivals. The purpose of restraint is to reduce the likelihood of entering costly overseas conflicts while still maintaining the capacity to neutralize major threats to the homeland as they emerge – a much less ambitious set of objectives than ordering the entire world along lines favorable to US interests. Unsurprisingly, restraint requires far fewer resources than the strategy of military primacy. Restrainers thus call for much smaller portions of the economy and federal budget to be devoted toward national defense, and are far less likely to support military interventions abroad except when absolutely necessary to uphold national security in a strict sense of the term.

To be clear, a grand strategy of restraint would not require the United States to lessen its international engagement in terms of economic policy, diplomacy, contributions to multilateral organizations, or other forms of nonmilitary participation in global society. Restraint is not synonymous with isolationism. Rather, restraint is focused on reducing America's reliance on military tools of statecraft. In contrast to primacists, restrainers believe that international crises – including instances of severe regional or global instability – can often be addressed without the application of US military force. This might mean the United States using nonmilitary instruments of power to advance its interests, but it might also mean relying upon others to check aggressors, uphold international rules, stop civil conflict, defend human rights, and otherwise ensure the peaceful conduct of world politics. Indeed, restrainers point out that US interventions can often worsen security conditions abroad instead of improving them, outcomes that serve nobody's interests.[25]

It is important to distinguish restraint from retrenchment. Restraint is a grand strategy – that is, a coherent plan for connecting ends with means, and a guiding set of principles for how national resources should be harnessed toward achieving political objectives. Retrenchment, on the other hand, is not a grand strategy. It is a policy recommendation. All retrenchment means is the reduction of overseas forces and security obligations. For example, President Biden's decision to exit Afghanistan in 2021 was an instance of retrenchment because it involved the withdrawal of US forces from that country and a termination of Washington's commitment to the survival of Ashraf Ghani's government in Kabul. But Biden's implementation of this isolated policy of retrenchment said little about his overall grand strategy, which remained one of unabashed military primacy when viewed in the round.

Of course, it might be argued that a grand strategy of restraint would be easier to adopt if the United States would first implement wide-ranging policies of retrenchment. It might even be argued – as I do in this book – that meaningful retrenchment is a prerequisite for a sustainable grand strategy of restraint. But the two should not be confused or conflated. One is a grand-strategic design for how a state might go about achieving its goals on the world stage. The other is a policy; an injunction to downsize overseas military deployments in a specific case or as a general rule. In this book, I provide an argument for why the United States has not implemented policies of retrenchment in the recent past, and how US government might be altered to become more friendly to such policies in the future.

Outline of the Book

The rest of the book is organized as follows. In the first chapter, I place America's contemporary overseas deployments in historical context. I trace how the United States has undergone six distinct waves of overseas expansion, from early annexations of island territories in the mid-nineteenth century to the assumption of global military obligations in the late twentieth century. The point of this chapter is to show that the United States has retrenched before, but that instances of retrenchment have become less common and consequential as time has worn on. Part of the explanation is that, in the past, US forward deployments were justified with reference to a range of different logics – commercial, logistical, humanitarian, and

so forth. Today, almost all of America's overseas commitments are justified in terms of national security, a rationale for
interventionism (and military primacy) that is much harder to
argue against in domestic politics.

Chapter 2 canvasses the various arguments that have been
made in favor of military primacy since the end of the Cold
War. I point to two stylized sets of arguments in particular:
one centered on the idea that the outside world is an uncertain, insecure, and dangerous place, and so the US military is
required to be vastly forward deployed as insurance against
unpredictable foreign forces; and another that emphasizes
more idealistic (even utopian) ideas about US power and purpose, arguing that America has a noble role to play in ushering
the world toward something resembling a Kantian perpetual
peace. I show that, in the 1990s and 2000s, these two rival
camps disagreed mightily on the purpose of military primacy
but largely agreed on the premise that US dominance ought
to be maintained and extended as far as possible into the
future. Today, most members of America's political class blend
insights drawn from both schools of thought. Chapter 2 also
discusses contemporary arguments in favor of retrenchment,
drawing attention to the many dimensions along which these
various camps (I identify five) differ from one another even
as they agree on the basic idea that the United States should
shrink its overseas military presence.

Chapter 3 introduces some concepts from political science
to help explain why America's grand strategy of military primacy has become so hard to dislodge. These are: stateness,
path dependence, exogenous shocks, and temporal sequencing. Of these, the concept of stateness is perhaps the most
important. Stateness helps to capture the idea that the US
government has, historically, varied in terms of its size, capacity, and legitimacy in the eyes of the people. When the United
States had a low degree of stateness, it underextended on the
world stage. Now that the United States has a high degree of

stateness in the realm of foreign policy and national security, it is much more active and harder to restrain. The concept of stateness is central to the argument of the book: my contention is that the United States government has taken on a particular size, shape, and set of standard operating procedures such that a grand strategy of military primacy has become hardwired into the US state itself.

The concept of path dependence is also of critical importance. It describes in a generic sense how political actors can find themselves trapped by decisions made by people in the past. Even powerful leaders cannot escape the influence of institutional contexts that are passed down from one generation to the next. Over time, ways of doing politics – including on the scale of grand strategy – become routinized and hard to overturn. This is especially true when "business as usual" serves the interests of the powerful within society. In this book, I argue that path dependence helps to explain why the US state is organized in such a way as to reward adherence to military primacy while discouraging (and punishing) actors who articulate alternative paths.

Exogenous shocks are external events that impose some sort of stress upon the US polity; they are instances that test the resilience of prevailing norms and institutions, force political leaders to reveal and articulate their preferences, and provide openings for political entrepreneurs to propose reorganizations of politics and government or else recommit themselves to prevailing orthodoxies. I argue that several exogenous shocks help to explain the ossification of America's national-security state over the past century, the attack on Pearl Harbor and the 9/11 terror attacks chief among them. However, the concept of temporal sequencing helps to clarify the idea that the political significance of any given event is always contingent upon the historical context within which that event takes place. While this is a basic insight, perhaps, temporal sequencing is essential for understanding not just *how* but also *when* and *why* the

United States might be able to break free from the strictures of military primacy in the future.

In chapter 4, I turn to discuss the domestic groups who have a vested interest in the continuation of military primacy as a grand strategy. The purpose of the chapter is to illustrate that path dependence is not automatic. On the contrary, a network of political agents is tightly involved in the perpetuation of primacy as America's operational code. These actors include lobbyists for certain economic sectors, bureaucrats, policy experts, think tankers, and various advocacy groups who have grown to rely upon US power abroad as a means of promoting their preferred set of values on the world stage. The chapter categorizes domestic support for primacism in terms of those who have a material interest in primacy's endurance as a grand strategy; those who have ideational reasons to support military primacy; and a more diffuse set of actors for whom primacy has become interwoven with their sense of national identity and ontological security.

Chapter 5 demonstrates how the national-security state and its votaries work to block any moves toward retrenchment. This is an important chapter, serving to illustrate my argument that domestic politics truly is to blame for America's weddedness to military primacy. What evidence is there for the US political system getting in the way of policies of retrenchment? Are there plausible counterfactual scenarios in which the United States could have retrenched under some different set of domestic conditions? Drawing upon vignettes of US foreign policy over the past thirty years, I argue that there is compelling evidence that leaders in Washington would now be overseeing a very different set of foreign policies if the US political system had been calibrated differently at critical junctures. As will become clear, there is not just one process via which domestic politics tends to upend even small movements toward restraint; there are several such mechanisms, with veto points existing across the major organs of government and wider society. But there is nevertheless a recognizable and coherent political ecosystem at play – one that is heavily biased against policies of retrenchment, and which must be reformed if the goal is to bring about substantial changes to US foreign relations.

In chapter 6, I begin to explain how and why leaders in Washington might yet come to recognize advantages in ending military primacy as the default grand strategy of the United States. I argue that there is a disconnect between what a proper grand strategy should do for ordinary Americans and what the grand strategy of military primacy can provide. I agree with others that the United States needs a period of domestic renewal, reform, and realignment, but argue that this can only happen in conjunction with a major strategic adjustment abroad. In this chapter, I offer prescriptions for how US politics could be restructured to make alternative grand strategies more feasible. The point is not to argue for whatever set of domestic reforms would make restraint more likely to obtain, but rather to insist upon a democratized political system in which all options for engagement with the outside world are given a fair hearing and chance of success. Some of my suggested reforms are difficult to imagine today – my call for a radical overhaul of the electoral system, for example – but others are more modest in nature.

Finally, chapter 7 concludes with a discussion of what form of grand strategy should replace the ailing edifice of military primacy. My main goal is to articulate a set of foreign policies that are suitable for the coming multipolar world, and which have the potential to deliver tangible benefits to the American people. My secondary goal, however, is to advance a proposal for US foreign policy that stands a chance of withstanding domestic scrutiny. One premise of the chapter is that the US political system will not endorse a move away from military primacy unless there are alternatives in place to guarantee national security and promote economic prosperity while remaining faithful to core US values. What I propose meets these standards: military retrenchment but with caveats that Washington should continue to invest in a strong national defense, especially in terms of nuclear forces, intelligence capabilities, and cybersecurity; "offshore balancing" as a means of securing critical overseas regions from hostile powers, coupled with vigorous participation in multilateral organizations; and a greatly expanded focus on humanitarian and economic aid, along with robust support for free trade and an open world economy. This version of restraint is a far cry from isolationism – but it is much preferable to the wrongheaded and increasingly unsustainable policies of military primacy.

The book has been written for policy audiences as well as informed general readers. But it is also a work of political science. Throughout, I will draw insights from International Relations theory and the literature on American political development. My scholarly interest is to clarify the two-way relationship between international affairs and the evolution of US domestic politics, including the shape, size, and purpose of the US state.[26] The intuition here is that, while Robert Kagan is surely right that America "made" the modern international system,[27] the reverse is also true – that the world beyond America's shores has played an enormous role in molding the modern United States. What I hope to show is that at least some of these "outside-in" changes to US domestic politics have outlasted their usefulness and should now be viewed as instances of institutional maladaptation. In the past, it might have made sense for the US state to be ordered toward the end of permanent warfighting. During World War II and the Cold War the United States faced bona fide threats to national security, forcing America's leaders to construct a political system at home that would allow for the defeat of tyranny abroad. Today, however, the US government has become so accustomed to fighting wars and preparing for future conflicts that its leading officials cannot imagine doing their jobs in the absence of war; the state and its permanent warfighting activities have become conjoined and codependent, with "specialists in violence" dominating the US government's foreign-policy bureaucracies even during eras when peace has been within grasp.[28] This is a phenomenon that must be studied, explained, and understood if it is to be undone.

I will make these arguments in social-scientific terms, but the normative implications are enormous and run like a leit-motif through the entire book: Americans will never enjoy the sort of "peace dividend" they so richly deserve until domestic reforms can proceed in tandem with changes to defense policy. Indeed, my analysis suggests that only radical reforms to US government and politics will be enough to allow antimilita-rist, anti-interventionist, and antiprimacist ideas to receive an equal hearing in the organs of state – something they have not enjoyed since the attack on Pearl Harbor in December 1941.[29] Retrenchment, restraint, and national renewal will have to come from the inside out.

1

Waves of Expansion, 1857–Present

The United States today is a "beached superpower."[1] At least in Eurasia, its immense forward presence is a holdover from the World War II and Cold War eras, when US military personnel were sent in their millions to Europe and the Asia-Pacific to defeat fascism and then deter communist expansion. When World War II ended in 1945, the Army alone had around 2,327,000 troops in Europe and the Mediterranean, with an additional 1,791,000 in the Asia-Pacific. Over 450,000 soldiers were deployed overseas in other locations – i.e., the Americas, and Africa, or else were "in transit."[2] Millions more served in the Navy. Few in the US government expected that these would be permanent garrisons. On the contrary, having vanquished the Axis Powers, President Truman moved quickly to bring home as many US troops as possible. Toward the end of 1945, his administration was discharging up to 1.2 million personnel per month from all branches of the military – the quickest demobilization in history.[3] Even during the early Cold War, as US leaders accepted the need to retain a significant military presence in Europe and East Asia, officials in the executive branch assured Congress that stationing troops in allied nations was a temporary measure that could and would be reversed once those living in the shadow of the Soviet Union were able to provide for their own defense.[4]

Yet more than three decades after the Soviet collapse, the United States remains in occupation of around eighty foreign countries and territories. To be sure, the total number of US military personnel based overseas is much smaller today than during the second half of the twentieth century (in the region of 170,000 compared to an average of around 535,000 during the period 1950–2000).[5] But at the same time, the geographic expanse of America's security obligations has increased dramatically in the post-1991 period, with the United States adding bases large and small to its already gigantic military footprint in Europe, East Asia, the Persian Gulf, Africa, and elsewhere. On its face, it is something of a puzzle why the United States chose to remain vastly forward deployed after the Cold War. Why did US officials never make good on their promises to retrench once conditions in Eurasia became more favorable? Why, instead, has the US military footprint expanded? What has been the justification for America's overseas presence in the absence of a hegemonic competitor?

To answer these questions, it is helpful to view America's contemporary forward deployments in historical context. For today's permanent overseas garrisons are only the latest manifestations of US interventionism. Since the mid-nineteenth century, the United States has undertaken at least six waves of overseas expansion, which I define here as programmatic attempts to project power and influence over foreign lands in furtherance of perceived national interests. These waves occurred for a variety of reasons: commercial, strategic, ideological, imperialistic, domestic-political, and defensive. Some resulted in the annexation of new territories, leading to the permanent stationing of forces abroad. Other waves were characterized by interventions of a temporary nature; politico-military actions that, once completed, were followed by the total withdrawal of US military personnel. Still other waves of expansion looked likely to be temporary at the outset but morphed into a constellation of indefinite occupations with the passage of time – the World War II and Cold War–era deployments to Europe and East Asia being the most obvious cases in point.

In this chapter, I categorize the six waves of US expansionism as follows. The first wave occurred between 1857 and 1897 and was defined by the seizure of relatively small and predominantly unpopulated island territories in the Caribbean and Pacific. These acquisitions were undertaken for instrumental purposes, such as narrow commercial gain or to meet an obvious logistical need, and were performed by private citizens as well as the US military. A second wave took place between 1898 and 1917, during which era the United States annexed its first populated overseas territories – the Philippines, Guam, Puerto Rico, Panama Canal Zone, and US Virgin Islands – and thereby came to resemble a colonial empire. Of these, only the Philippines and Panama Canal Zone have since been decolonized. This era also saw the United States launch a number of military interventions-cum-occupations in Latin America, the Caribbean, and China. The third wave of overseas expansion happened during World War I and the interwar period (1918–1940), when the US military intervened decisively in European affairs to defeat Imperial Germany and assist in the imposition of a postwar settlement at Versailles, only to withdraw its military forces from the troubled continent. The fourth wave occurred during World War II and its immediate aftermath (1941–1949) and saw the United States undertake a globe-spanning effort to defeat the Axis Powers, then wrestle with the questions of whether, how, and how quickly to retrench from Europe and East Asia amid uncertainty about the threat posed by the Soviet Union. The fifth wave happened during the Cold War (1950–1989), when US leaders accepted the need to occupy parts of Western Europe and the Asia-Pacific (and later the Persian Gulf) on a permanent basis. The Cold War was defined by massive US military interventions abroad, with the United States fighting two devastating hot wars against communist rivals – in Korea and Vietnam – and electing to wage proxy wars in places such as Angola, Mozambique, and Afghanistan. The sixth and final wave of overseas expansion has lasted from 1990 to the present day, as the United States has chosen time and again to wield the mammoth forward deployments inherited at the end of the Cold War in service of expansive aims: an enlarged NATO alliance in Europe; near-permanent warfighting in the Middle East, North Africa, and Central Asia; and an ambitious military-strategic "pivot" to the Indo-Pacific, all justified as necessary to uphold US national interests and the associated rules-based ("liberal") world order.

The chapter concludes by making two descriptive points: (1) that the United States does have some experience of retrenchment following waves of expansion, and has exercised meaningful restraint at various points in its history as a great power; but (2) the tendency for Washington to resist retrenchment and instead preserve (repurpose) its overseas military deployments has become more pronounced with the passage of time. To be sure, the exceptions to this general trend toward permanent military deployments should not be minimized – the withdrawal of forces from Taiwan in the 1970s, the handover of the Panama Canal Zone, the downsizing of US forces in Europe during the 1990s, and the exit from Afghanistan in 2021, for example, were all appreciable instances of retrenchment. Each offers clues regarding the conditions under which the US political system is capable of supporting drawdowns in overseas forces. But the broad pattern described in this chapter is striking, and important: viewed in the *longue durée*, the United States has been gathering overseas security commitments since the 1850s – and it has become much less adept at shedding these obligations as time has worn on.

Commerce, Coal, and Colonization: 1857–1897

The United States has always been an expansionist power.[6] When the Thirteen Colonies declared independence from Britain in 1776, they did so claiming jurisdiction over the Northwest Territory, an enormous expanse of land that was subsequently settled by US citizens and became incorporated into the United States proper as the present-day states of Ohio, Indiana, Illinois, Michigan, and Wisconsin, as well as parts of Minnesota. In 1805, the United States almost doubled its land area when President Jefferson agreed to purchase the Louisiana Territory from France. This was followed by the acquisition of the Floridas (1819), Texas (1845), and the Oregon Territory (1846). In 1848, the United States defeated Mexico in the Mexican–American War and annexed around 55 percent of Mexico's prewar territory as part of the treaty of peace. With this gargantuan act of conquest, the United States completed a westward continental push that few could have anticipated at the time of its founding. In just over half a century, the United States had grown to encompass the entire middle portion of the North America – from "sea to shining sea."

America's overseas conquests unfolded on a different timeline, however. The origins of this story can be traced to the Guano Islands Act of 1856, which authorized private citizens to seize islands on behalf of the US government, so long as the islands in question were unclaimed, unpopulated, and contained deposits of guano (bird excrement).[7] With the passage of the Act, enterprising US citizens moved to claim several small island territories in the Pacific Ocean, including Baker Island, Howland Island, Jarvis Island, Kingman Reef, Swains Island, and the Johnston Atoll. All these islands were later made into unorganized, unincorporated US territories and remain so today. In the Caribbean, the United States claimed sovereignty over the Swan Islands, Roncador Bank, Navassa Island, Bajo Nuevo Bank (Petrel Island), Quita Sueño Bank, and Seranilla

Bank – all tiny island outcrops of little economic potential beyond guano harvesting. Washington relinquished its claims to most of these Caribbean islands (all except Navassa and the Seranilla Bank) in the twentieth century.

In 1867, the US government purchased the Alaska Territory from Russia, which added another 586,412 square miles to the United States. Notably, the Alaska Territory included the Aleutian Islands, an archipelago of around seventy islands that stretches 1,000 miles into the Northern Pacific from the southwest tip of the Alaskan mainland. Upon their annexation, these islands became the first inhabited islands in the Pacific Ocean to be under US administration. More expansion soon followed. In 1872, the eastern Samoan islands sought military protection from the United States in return for basing rights on their largest island of Tutuila. Washington accepted the proposal, and funded the construction of a port at Pago Pago – now the capital of American Samoa – in 1878. At the same time, large numbers of American settlers began to colonize Hawaii, with wealthy US citizens – plantation owners, especially – coming to dominate the islands' economy and politics. There were serious debates over whether to annex Hawaii as a US territory, and although leaders in Washington demurred on the question of annexation, they concluded a treaty with Hawaii in 1875 that gave the United States rights to build a port at Pearl Harbor.[8]

For the most part, these early instances of expansion were driven by instrumental considerations, especially commercial and logistical imperatives. The guano islands, for instance, were prized for their guano – a type of fertilizer that commanded a high price at the time – and their potential to serve as waystations for whalers and fishermen, who found it expedient to utilize US-controlled islands rather than depend upon the goodwill of others. Other annexations were driven by the growing desire among private firms and the US government to expand trade relations, particularly in East Asia. In

1844, the US government signed the Treaty of Wanghia with China, which aimed to foster strong commercial ties; in 1853, Commodore Perry sailed his "black ships" into Tokyo harbor in an effort to convince the Japanese to open their islands up to American traders; and in 1876, the United States signed a treaty of friendship and commerce with Korea. With opportunities for international trade burgeoning, people in the United States viewed island bases as essential logistical hubs to facilitate commerce. Nobody wanted to be dependent upon indigenous peoples or, even worse, Europeans for coaling facilities, and so a consensus emerged that trade with East Asia would be most secure if there was a chain of US-controlled islands to connect America's west coast with ports across the Pacific.[9] More than anything else, this helps to explain why the US government authorized the acquisition of new territories and naval bases in the late nineteenth century, whether by leasing land or annexing islands outright.

It is worth noting that the United States might well have acquired even more overseas territories during the period 1857–1897 if not for the politics of race and racism. As Richard Maass has shown, there were lively debates in the US Congress about whether to annex Santo Domingo (the Dominican Republic) during the 1860s and 1870s – but the US government declined to absorb the territory and its people even though leaders in Santo Domingo expressed a clear interest in the idea. In 1893, President Harrison similarly declined to support the annexation of Hawaii.[10] These instances of restraint or underexpansion can appear puzzling at first. But the historical record seems to be clear: before 1898, the US political class was divided on questions of territorial expansion, not least of all because they could not agree on the wisdom of absorbing nonwhite populations into the United States.

Imperial Apogee: 1898–1917

National-level indecision about imperial expansion came to an end in December 1898, when the United States defeated Spain in a war nominally fought over the fate of Cuba, but which resulted in the military occupation and annexation of Guam, the Philippines, and Puerto Rico – all former Spanish-held territories seized during the conduct of the war. Five months earlier, Congress had finally authorized the annexation of Hawaii as a US territory. The following year, Washington annexed the eastern Samoan islands as American Samoa. In 1903, the Panama Canal Zone was annexed (after Washington backed secessionists in what had been the northernmost region of Colombia) and the United States secured an indefinite military presence on the island of Cuba, at Guantánamo Bay. Despite some debate on the question, the United States declined to annex Cuba itself – although the island was placed under informal US "protection" via the so-called Platt Amendment to the Cuban constitution, which placed limits on the island's sovereignty and afforded the United States certain rights of intervention in Cuba's domestic affairs.[11]

The years 1898–1903 were the apogee of US colonial expansion. In a succession of rulings known as the *Insular Cases*, the Supreme Court grappled with vexing questions regarding how America's new imperial acquisitions could be governed in a manner consistent with its republican constitution. For the most part, the Court held that the federal government could administer nonsovereign territories in ways that limited the application of the Constitution – decisions that firmly etched into public law a distinction between the United States proper and its colonies ("insular areas").[12] While many in the United States rejected the label of empire, it was becoming increasingly difficult to describe US expansionism in terms other than colonialism and imperialism. Not only were millions of noncitizens brought under the sovereign control of the federal government, but the United States also asserted a formal right of intervention in neighboring countries (the so-called "Roosevelt Corollary" to the Monroe Doctrine).

To be sure, commercial and logistical considerations still weighed heavily on the minds of US decision-makers. The Panama Canal, for example, was primarily valued for commercial reasons. By extension, so was the base at Guantánamo, which was meant to help provide for the canal's defense. The Roosevelt Corollary was aimed at ensuring the "correct" economic management of Caribbean states, both because US firms had an interest in protecting their overseas investments and because Washington was eager to ensure that Caribbean governments would pay their debts so as to placate the Europeans. And as trade with East Asia continued to grow, the need for island bases hardly abated; fleets of commercial vessels crossed the Pacific each year, all of them requiring coaling stations and places to reprovision. Toward this end, Wake Island and the Palmyra Atoll were annexed to the United States in 1898 and 1899. But there is no mistaking that, after the Spanish–American War of 1898, the United States was a colonial empire. For the first time in its history, the federal government in Washington was responsible for governing territory and peoples far removed from the North American continent.[13]

Not everyone supported America's emergence as an imperial power. The Anti-Imperialist League was founded in June 1898 (just weeks before Congress voted to incorporate Hawaii as a US territory) for the express purpose of opposing the annexation of the Philippines and overseas expansion more generally. The League's opposition to imperialism was rooted in traditional American values of republicanism, self-government, and equality among nations.[14] It was an elite-level organization in the sense that its members included ex-presidents Grover Cleveland and Benjamin Harrison, the industrialist Andrew Carnegie, social reformer John Dewey, and writer Mark Twain; but the League's mass membership was hardly trivial, peaking at around 25,000. In the event, however, the League failed to win over political or public opinion to the anti-imperialist cause. It disbanded in 1920 having had little tangible effect on US foreign policy.

On the contrary, the United States during the period 1898–1917 began to wage overseas military interventions with increasing regularity. In 1900–1901, the US military helped to put down the Boxer Rebellion in China as part of the broader American effort to promote "Open Door" trade relations. The Army and Marine Corps established a garrison in the Chinese city of Tientsin (now Tianjin) that would last until 1941. In 1914, President Wilson ordered the US military to occupy the Mexican city of Veracruz – partly a punitive expedition in response to Mexico's detention of nine US sailors, but also a deliberate attempt to influence the outcome of the ongoing Mexican Revolution. In 1915, Wilson authorized the occupation of Haiti, which would last until 1934. The following year, Wilson ordered the occupation of Dominican Republic. Troops would only leave there in 1924. Meanwhile, US forces occupied Cuba on several occasions: 1898–1902, 1906–1909, and 1917–1922. In Central America, US troops occupied Nicaragua from 1912 to 1933[15] and conducted several discrete military expeditions in Honduras between 1903 and 1925. In 1917, Wilson negotiated the purchase of the Danish West Indies (the US Virgin Islands) amid concerns that Denmark and its territories might fall to Germany in the context of World War I.

Needless to say, all of these interventions and territorial acquisitions required military backing. Members of the Army and Marine Corps were deployed overseas on an almost continuous basis. In the Philippines alone, over 4,000 US troops died during the campaign to suppress nationalist fighters. Vast sums of money were spent so that the United States could deploy a world-class navy in both the Pacific and Atlantic oceans. These were costly endeavors, which forced Americans to confront the hypocrisy of being a self-styled democratic republic that also administered – by force of arms – an overseas colonial empire. But during the years 1898–1917, political leaders from both parties judged the fiscal, military, and political costs of an imperial world role to be a tolerable exchange. Now dominant in the Caribbean, the United States could be assured that its southern shores and trade routes were secure; as a resident power in East Asia, Washington gained a toehold in lucrative overseas markets as well as influence over European policy in the region; and on the international stage, America's growing clout could no longer be ignored by capitals in the Old World. In 1907, President Roosevelt dispatched sixteen battleships – the so-called Great White Fleet – on a circumnavigation of the globe, the purpose of which was to telegraph the significance of US sea power to foreign governments. It was a message that the rest of the world received loud and clear.[16]

Age of Ambivalence: 1917–1941

President Wilson was an unabashed interventionist, but even he had grave reservations about entering World War I – so much so, in fact, that Wilson famously made nonparticipation in the war a central feature of his reelection campaign in 1916. But in 1917, the United States joined the Great War on a grand scale, partly in response to German attacks on transatlantic shipping, and partly because of Berlin's secret offer to Mexico of military support for the reconquest of formerly Mexican territories (the Zimmermann Telegram). Around 4,800,000 men served in the US armed forces during 1917–1919, playing a decisive role in defeating Germany and its allies. The United States emerged as the leading power at the peace conference in Versailles, with President Wilson the single most influential statesman in the world at that time.

After the war, it seemed likely that the United States would entrench its political and military presence in Europe. American forces occupied the Rhineland until January 1923, and might easily have stayed longer had the Democratic nominee, James Cox, won the 1920 election. President Wilson dispatched US troops to participate in two theaters of the Russian Civil War between 1918 and 1920, doomed attempts to influence the government and politics of Europe's largest country. And with his proposal for a League of Nations, Wilson looked certain to cement America's place as the preeminent diplomatic power and security provider in international politics – a position that, if assumed, would have matched the reality of the United States as the world's most important economic center.

However, support for US membership of the League of Nations was lacking at home, with the US Senate ultimately declining to approve membership of the organization. In 1920, Wilson's preferred successor, Cox – who endorsed the League of Nations, and broadly shared Wilson's international-ist proclivities – was defeated by the Republican candidate, Warren G. Harding, who campaigned on the opposite political platform of a "return to normalcy." To be clear, the interwar presidents – Harding, Calvin Coolidge, and Herbert Hoover – were not isolationists. They engaged in an ambitious program of international treaty-making, for example, especially in the realms of arms control and dispute resolution, and contin-ued to oversee military interventions in Latin America and the Caribbean. But during the 1920s and 1930s, US foreign policy was characterized by a powerful aversion to military engagement beyond the Western Hemisphere (the continued occupation of the Philippines and the small garrison in Tientsin notwithstanding). The withdrawal from the Rhineland was emblematic: what had been a 250,000-strong force occupying Germany in 1919 dwindled to around 20,000 by late 1922. By the end of January 2023, all US troops had left Europe.

What caused the United States to relinquish its ambitions in Europe and farther afield? What explains its ambivalence toward global leadership and interventionism? In other words:

Why did America retrench? The answer has to do with domestic politics. Simply put, America's political and economic elites were divided over questions of overseas involvement during the interwar period. Their ambivalence had economic roots.[17] Some sectors of the economy benefited from international trade and investment opportunities and therefore pressured elected representatives in Washington to implement a foreign policy of overseas activism that would protect their interests. Other sectors, however, saw few advantages from an open world economy and chafed at the costs of an assertive foreign policy. These groups lobbied the US government to shun overseas engagement and focus instead on domestic priorities (the politics of "normalcy," as Harding had put it). Because these two stylized coalitions – the "internationalists" versus the "nationalists" – were roughly evenly matched in terms of domestic power and influence, the result was national-level equivocation and indecision regarding America's world role.[18]

During the late 1930s, these divisions among the political class were pronounced. As president, Franklin Roosevelt recognized the threat posed by the rise of Nazi Germany and Imperial Japan to America's national (and economic) security. He tried in vain to move public opinion toward accepting the need for rearmament, and used his executive powers to prepare the country for its eventual entry into World War II. But Roosevelt persistently ran up against entrenched opposition to overseas interventions. Via the Neutrality Acts, in particular, an anti-interventionist majority in Congress put a significant brake on what the President could achieve.[19] It is possible, perhaps, that Roosevelt would have found a way to secure US entry into the war without the attack on Pearl Harbor. But as of December 6, 1941, it was difficult to envisage exactly how this outcome could have come about. Public opposition to the war was strong, the United States and its territories seemed to be secure, and anti-interventionists held key positions in

Congress and across the executive branch. Where the Anti-Imperialist League had failed, the isolationist America First Committee succeeded – that is, at winning the hearts and minds of ordinary voters and convincing a broad slice of the political class that overseas interventionism would not serve core US interests.

World War II and Its Aftermath: 1941–1949

After the Japanese attack on the United States Pacific Fleet at Pearl Harbor, serious opposition to US entry into World War II became untenable. It was self-evidently imperative that the United States must defend itself against Japan and its Axis allies in Europe (Hitler and Mussolini each declared war on the United States on December 11, 1941). Even the America First Committee, an anti-interventionist pressure group that represented 800,000 fee-paying members,[20] voted to disband. Its leader, Charles Lindbergh, threw his personal support behind the war effort and even enlisted in the military. The attack laid the foundations for bipartisanship over foreign policy for the first time in decades – not just broad agreement during wartime that the Axis Powers must be vanquished, but also the postwar consensus in favor of defeating communism. President Roosevelt was right when he told Congress on December 8, 1941, "I believe that I interpret the will of the Congress and of the people when I assert that we will not only defend ourselves to the uttermost but will make it very certain that this form of treachery shall never again endanger us."[21] This sentiment could have dissipated during the course of the war, but in fact it remained a lodestone to orient the nation's institutions of government even after World War II's conclusion. Having experienced the trauma of Pearl Harbor, the United States did not just mean to win a defensive war against its immediate enemies; its leaders were determined to prevent the emergence of any world power that could threaten the homeland again.

During the war, President Roosevelt and his closest advisers imagined that a concert system of sorts might be established to uphold international tranquility once the Allies had established victory. FDR pinned his hopes on a group he called the Four Policemen – the United States, British Empire, nationalist China, and the Soviet Union – working in close collaboration to maintain global order, all under the auspices of a new League of Nations-style organization.[22] But such hopes were dashed almost as soon as World War II was over. The Soviet Union and the specter of international communism, in particular, appeared to pose grave threats to the security of Europe and Asia – and, by extension, the United States. In Europe, Stalin refused to honor his promises at Yalta to hold elections in countries under Soviet occupation. In 1946, the Soviet Union appeared to abrogate its earlier agreements to vacate Iranian territory, even looking poised to annex parts of northern Iran.[23] Fraudulent elections in Poland in January 1947 were followed by a communist takeover. Months later, Soviet agents organized a coup in Czechoslovakia.[24]

In private, the White House was being briefed about the Soviet threat by diplomat George Kennan, who in 1947 urged that a policy of "containment" would be necessary to discourage Soviet expansionism.[25] With fears growing that Greece and Turkey might fall to communism, Truman was eventually persuaded to act by announcing the Truman Doctrine – an expansive commitment to aid any world government facing a communist takeover.[26] In 1948, closed-door discussions began about the formation of a military alliance in Western Europe. NATO was formed the following year. Meanwhile, events in the Far East heightened anxieties about international communism. In August 1949, the Soviet Union detonated its first atomic bomb. Less than five weeks later, Mao Zedong proclaimed the People's Republic of China – an event that placed almost the entirety of the Eurasian interior from Berlin to Beijing under communist control.

It warrants emphasis that the people setting US policy during this period were not the same as those who had been in charge before World War II. The experience of fighting a global conflagration had altered minds about the proper relationship between America and the outside world. In the war's wake, even Senator Arthur Vandenberg – previously a staunch isolationist voice in Congress – became a convert to the idea of US power projection, famously arguing in January 1945 that "Our oceans have ceased to be moats which automatically protect our ramparts." His point was that Americans would have to grudgingly accept the need for deep overseas engagement – including membership of the newly proposed United Nations – given that national security was now so obviously intertwined with international conditions. In time, Vandenberg and his colleagues in the political class came to embrace other tenets of an interventionist program for the postwar world, too – not just the formation of inclusive international institutions, but also the forward deployment of US garrisons, binding mutual defense treaties with allies in Europe and East Asia, and the construction of an open world economy.

To be clear, the attack on Pearl Harbor and the experience of World War II did not entirely banish anti-interventionist ideas from the US political system. On the contrary, powerful voices – not least of all Robert Taft, a senator from Ohio and leading figure in the postwar Republican Party – railed against interventionism for years after World War II. As noted above, President Truman was eager to demobilize US forces after 1945 and, if external conditions had been different, he might well have ordered full withdrawals from Europe and East Asia once the war had ended. But in the top echelons of US government, the effect of Pearl Harbor proved to be enduring. Military and civilian bureaucrats alike were firmly of the opinion that isolationism, noninterventionism, and a lack of military preparedness had cost the United States badly in the interwar years. They were not willing to be caught unprepared again, especially as geopolitical conditions in Europe and East Asia appeared to worsen. To be secure going forward, it was resolved, the United States would have to project power abroad, over and onto foreign soil, instead of leaving the fate of international security to others.

The Cold War: 1950–1989

By the late 1940s, hopes of a placid postwar environment lay in tatters; everyone in Washington concurred that the Soviet threat in Eastern Europe and the Asia-Pacific constituted a major challenge for US foreign policy. The Cold War was in full swing. Taking stock of this new geopolitical context, in January 1950 President Truman ordered a review of US defense and security policy. This process produced the NSC-68 planning document – a sweeping set of policy proposals for containing the Soviet Union via the application of US power across almost the entire Eurasian rimland. NSC-68 called for the tripling of planned defense outlays and included language to reassure anyone nervous about high levels of military spending that such investments would spur economic growth, generate national prosperity, and help the United States to eclipse the Soviet Union over the long term.[27]

The contents of NSC-68 represented a major break with how the United States had historically behaved following its wars. But Truman was persuaded that national and economic security depended upon a global strategy of the sort envisioned by the authors.[28] The President's calculus was simplified by the economy sliding into recession, which challenged the long-standing assumption of a slender foreign policy (and a balanced budget) being best for US prosperity at home. Looking to reverse the economic downturn, Truman became susceptible to arguments for increased defense spending ("military Keynesianism") for reasons of political self-interest.[29] But international events were of overriding importance, with North Korea's invasion of US-backed South Korea in June 1950 seeming to lay bare the threat posed by world communism.[30] Three months after the Korean War broke out, and with political and public opinion having turned decisively in favor of fighting communist expansion, Truman signed NSC-68 into policy.

Between 1950 and 1953, the Truman administration significantly increased defense spending and ordered a massive rearmament program. Not only did the United States enter the Korean War – at the cost of over 36,000 American lives[31] – but in 1951, more US troops were sent to Europe in order to assuage NATO allies' fears that the Korean emergency would come at the expense of America's transatlantic commitments. The President and his team worked assiduously to put together a coalition of domestic interests that would support high levels of investment in foreign and defense policy. Such coalition-building was essential to the success of containment given that, to no small degree, additional spending on the military came at the expense of domestic programs – universal healthcare, infrastructure, and social welfare payments, for example – that had previously ranked high on the national agenda.[32]

As the Cold War began in earnest, the United States accumulated ever more overseas obligations. The Rio Pact was established in 1947 and the NATO alliance founded in 1949, committing Washington to the defense of most countries in the Western Hemisphere plus ten European nations. Greece and Turkey joined NATO in 1952. Also in the 1950s, the United States signed mutual defense pacts with several East Asian governments – the Philippines, Australia and New Zealand, Japan, South Korea, and Taiwan – as well as forming the Southeast Asia Treaty Organization ("Manila Pact"). In 1957, President Eisenhower undertook to provide US military and economic support to any country facing external threat (the "Eisenhower Doctrine"), which paved the way for an inauspicious military intervention in Lebanon. Eisenhower also began the process of intervening in the Vietnam War, a conflict that would be expanded under JFK, LBJ, and Nixon – only to be ended under President Ford in 1975, and not before 58,000 US troops had been killed in action. Nuclear weapons were placed in South Korea in 1958, Taiwan in 1960, and throughout Western Europe.[33]

All told, the Cold War was an era of massive overseas expansion for the United States. Over 1,700,000 Americans served in the Korean War. An additional 3,500,000 military personnel were dispatched to Southeast Asia from 1964 to 1975. Troop numbers in Vietnam peaked in 1968, with nearly 550,000 stationed in the country. While there were no shooting wars in Europe during the Cold War, the United States at one point placed as many as 400,000 of its own troops on the continent.[34] The US military and Red Army almost came to blows on several occasions (especially during the Berlin crises of 1948 and 1958–1961). In effect, Americans mortgaged their own national security as a means of securing others from the threat of Soviet predation. The wager was that, if the United States made credible commitments to fight World War III on behalf of its allies, then Moscow would be deterred from attempting further expansionism. It was an audacious gamble – one that saddled the United States with an enormous amount of insecurity in exchange for the hope of stability abroad, and which left US leaders with the unenviable task of upholding a number of simultaneous extended deterrents.

To be sure, strategic retrenchment was *possible* during the Cold War. After all, the United States did not win the war in Vietnam – it exited the country in 1975, abandoning the South to communist control. In 1977, President Carter agreed to hand the Panama Canal over to the government of Panama, with the Panama Canal Zone ceasing to exist as a US territory two years later. Also in 1979, the United States terminated its defensive relationship with Taiwan upon the normalization of diplomatic relations with Beijing. More broadly, the United States made serious efforts to accommodate the Soviet Union under the Johnson, Nixon, Ford, and Carter administrations – the set of policies known as *détente*. These efforts resulted in several arms control agreements such as the Outer Space Treaty, the Nuclear Non-Proliferation Treaty, the Anti-Ballistic Missile Treaty, the Biological Weapons Convention, and the two sets of Strategic Arms Limitation Talks. In 1975, the United States and Soviet Union – together with their respective allies – concluded the Helsinki Accords to finalize the borders of Eastern Europe and put East–West relations on a firmer footing. At least two Cold War–era presidents – Eisenhower and Nixon – managed to bring down defense spending by considerable amounts during their time in the White House.

But events during the latter portion of the Cold War put strict limits on the extent to which presidents could entertain anything approaching broad-based retrenchment. President Carter, for example, tried to reorient US foreign policy away from the East–West struggle and toward a focus on North–South relations and global development. But two events – both taking place in 1979 – forced Carter to relent.[35] In January, the Shah of Iran fled the country amid domestic unrest and opened the door to the return of exiled Shia cleric Ayatollah Khomeini, who took advantage of the Shah's absence to lead the establishment of an Islamic Republic. Not only did the Iranian Revolution result in the infamous hostage crisis – and the ill-fated Operation Eagle Claw to rescue the hostages, in which eight US servicemen died – but it also provoked an energy crisis and raised fears in the United States about the wider stability of the Persian Gulf region. The second event was the Soviet invasion of Afghanistan in December. In short order, the President enunciated the "Carter Doctrine" in January 1980, placing the Persian Gulf at the heart of national security policy by declaring that an "attempt by any outside force to gain control of the Persian Gulf region will be regarded as an assault on the vital interests of the United States of America, and such an assault will be repelled by any means necessary, including military force."[36]

Even though Carter abandoned the policy of *détente* in response to the events of 1979, his opponent in the 1980 presidential election – Ronald Reagan – wasted no time blaming Carter for the failures associated with the strategy. Reagan accused Carter of allowing a missile gap to emerge between the United States and Soviet Union, complained that the US military had been underfunded despite Soviet advances abroad, and vowed to roll back communist influence across the globe – what the conservative columnist Charles Krauthammer would later call the "Reagan Doctrine."[37] When Americans went to the polls in November 1980, President Carter carried just six states (plus the District of Columbia) and garnered only 41 percent of the popular vote.

It would be wrong, of course, to attribute Carter's electoral defeat in 1980 to foreign policy alone. Domestic issues – especially economic indicators – are almost always more important determinants of election outcomes in the United States than a president's handling of international affairs. But the mythology surrounding Carter's defeat and Reagan's political rise has become part of US political lore. One lesson of the 1980s, the argument goes, is that strength, hawkishness, and a willingness to intervene abroad will pay handsome political dividends at home, whereas the accommodation of hostile powers and inaction in the face of national-security threats will lead to calamitous results. This lesson was reinforced once the Cold War ended and the Reaganite mantra of "peace through strength" appeared to be vindicated. The Reagan presidency seared into the minds of Democrats that they must never again allow themselves to be portrayed as "weak" on national security, a liability blamed for Carter's loss in 1980 and Walter

Mondale's similarly devastating electoral defeat in 1984. Put simply, every Republican candidate in recent history has wanted to be associated with President Reagan and his legacy. Few Democrats want to be viewed as the next Jimmy Carter or Walter Mondale.

The Beached Superpower: 1990–Present

By the time the Berlin Wall came down in 1989, heralding the end of the Cold War in Europe, the United States had been implementing its worldwide strategy of containing communism for over forty years. Including the World War II years, the United States had spent nearly half a century engaged in global struggles against foreign powers. These decades of maintaining a constant military presence in Eurasia had required millions of American troops to cycle through hundreds of overseas bases. Defense outlays had remained at high levels throughout the period, during which time local communities across the United States became dependent upon military spending for their economic fortunes.[38] Nor did the United States show any signs of fatigue: the Reagan years had been defined by jingoism, international activism, and unabashed militarism – qualities that seemed to serve America well in the sense that they coincided with growing prosperity at home as well as ultimate victory in the Cold War.

It was against this backdrop that the United States began the 1990s as a beached superpower. Its forces had been sent abroad during the Cold War for the explicit purpose of containing the Soviet Union, but they did not come home once this initial justification for their forward deployment had expired. Instead of being withdrawn, America's garrisons in Europe, East Asia, the Persian Gulf, and elsewhere were given new *raisons d'être*. In Europe, the US military slashed troop numbers and closed a significant number of overseas bases but compensated for these drawdowns with a succession of primacist policies – namely, war in Bosnia (1995) and Kosovo (1999), and the almost doubling in size of NATO (which grew from having sixteen members in 1989 to thirty-one members by 2023).[39] After 2014, the United States began to deploy forces in the Baltic States and Poland as a means of deterring further Russian aggression in the wake of Moscow's annexation of Crimea – and, in February 2022, Washington rushed to provide massive military and economic aid to Ukraine in support of its fight against Russia's full-scale invasion of that country.

In Asia, too, the number of US troops deployed to the region fell after the collapse of the Soviet Union. But the Clinton administration was keen to reassure East Asian governments that the United States would not be undertaking anything close to a withdrawal. Writing on behalf of the administration, Joseph Nye explained in 1995 that the United States considered itself a force for stability in the Asia-Pacific.[40] America's "deep engagement" in the region would help to forestall a dangerous arms race between Japan and China, he argued, and would discourage the rise of a destabilizing regional hegemon. Nye announced that US foreign policy would rest upon three pillars: renewed alliances, large forward deployments, and stronger regional institutions. It was hoped that such a "leadership strategy" would create the stable conditions necessary for Beijing to be eased into the US-led international order. Subsequent administrations have come to rethink whether China can be integrated into existing institutions, viewing China as more of a threat to regional security (and, by extension, US interests) than a potential partner. But these changing views on China did nothing to precipitate an overall shift in policy: forward deployments, strong alliances, and active regional leadership have remained the basic ingredients of US foreign policy in Asia since the end of the Cold War.

Indeed, hardened views on China only encouraged the United States under both George W. Bush and Barack Obama to double down on deep engagement. Each president pursued a broad policy of ringing China with US alliances, partnerships, and forward deployments (albeit alongside some nontrivial efforts to conciliate Beijing).[41] Both sought to expand economic ties with the region, resulting in a free trade deal with South Korea and plan to envelop the entire Asia-Pacific (excluding China and North Korea) in an ambitious free trade deal that would later become known as the Trans-Pacific Partnership (and ultimately, after the United States had withdrawn from negotiations, the Comprehensive and Progressive Agreement for Trans-Pacific Partnership). Under President Trump and President Biden, the United States expanded the geographic scope of its efforts to contain Chinese power from East Asia to a larger (if somewhat ill-defined) "Indo-Pacific" megaregion. While Trump and later Biden backed away from free trade as a cornerstone of Asia policy, what all post–Cold War presidencies have had in common is a firm commitment to maintaining the alliances and forward deployments inherited from the World War II and Cold War eras.

In the Middle East, there were no withdrawals of US forces in the 1990s to match the early post–Cold War drawdowns in Europe and Asia. On the contrary, America's military footprint expanded. The purported reasons for continued US engagement remained the same as during the Cold War – that is, to stabilize global energy markets and to keep the region from falling under the domination of a single hostile power – but the primary target(s) of US foreign policy switched from the Soviet Union to Iraq and Iran, giving rise to the policy known as "dual containment."[42] To contain both of these so-called "rogue" regimes in a post–Cold War context, the United States found that it must carry a heavy burden. Between 1991 and 2003, the US Air Force flew almost daily sorties over Iraq to enforce the two no-fly zones imposed after the first Persian Gulf War. In 1995, the US Navy reconstituted the Fifth Fleet and based it in Bahrain, anchoring a large and permanent naval presence in the region. Troop numbers were bolstered in Kuwait, Qatar, and elsewhere. In 1998, President Clinton ordered the bombing of targets in Sudan, Afghanistan, and Iraq as part of a broad-based campaign to defeat international terrorism and subdue those few remaining regional governments that refused to acquiesce in US regional dominance. In reality, none of these were actions designed to keep the Middle East free from domination, the nominal purpose of US foreign policy since the Cold War. They were the actions of a would-be hegemon, an order-builder; a state that saw itself as having a controlling stake in the region's political configuration – in other words, the actions of an activist "resident power."

After the terrorist attacks of September 11, 2001, of course, there was a renewed impetus for US intervention across the Greater Middle East, from North Africa to Central Asia. Neoconservative leaders in particular blamed the success of al-Qaeda on policy failures emanating from Washington.[43] It had been wrong to disengage from Afghanistan after the Cold War, went the conventional wisdom. Rogue regimes could not be left in power, religious extremists must be confronted and defeated, and the social rot created by failed states ought not be allowed to fester. From this view, anti-American extremism would thrive in the Middle East so long as the region remained unfree and undemocratic. These diagnoses were internalized by the Bush administration and other key actors in the US political system, leading to a swift decision after 9/11 to invade Afghanistan; the subsequent choice to invade Iraq; and the initiation of an indefinite "global war on terrorism" with major theaters in the Middle East, North Africa, Central Asia, and South Asia.[44]

The rationale for the War on Terror was expansive: to defeat political and religious extremism, deprive terrorists of safe havens, export democracy, secure territory from great-power rivals, and defend human rights (the "freedom agenda"). The battlefield was expansive, too, with the US military and intelligence agencies seeing action (of various sorts) in Afghanistan, Iraq, Pakistan, Syria, Libya, Somalia, Yemen, Kenya, Niger, the Central African Republic, Uganda, and elsewhere. As before, these interventions were not envisaged as temporary actions fought to keep the Greater Middle East free from external predation or to protect the United States from imminent attack. They were, instead, accepted as open-ended military engagements meant to suppress terrorist activity, check the future emergence of threats to US security (the doctrine of "prevention"), as well as ensure favorable political outcomes long into the future. In 2008, Senator John McCain (then a candidate for the presidency) argued that the US military might have to remain in Iraq for "maybe 100" years.[45] In 2019, President Trump's Defense Secretary, Mark Esper, invoked the euphemistic phrase "mowing the lawn" to describe the indefinite nature of America's counterterrorism policy in the Middle East.[46] The columnist Max Boot put the situation in nakedly imperialistic terms, calling US policy in places like Afghanistan and Syria an exercise in "policing the frontiers of the Pax Americana."[47]

To this day, America seems to struggle with retrenchment. Even after the global financial crisis of 2007–2008, which put a heavy strain on the public purse, the United States never seriously considered reducing its overseas obligations as a way of economizing. This surprised at least some US-based analysts, who assumed that runaway budget deficits and soaring national debts would force Washington to trim defense spending.[48] Instead, successive US leaders have simply refused to reckon with the problem of crippling debt. The killing of Osama Bin Laden in May 2011 and the pullout from Iraq in December 2011 presented different sort of offramps – that is, moments at which the United States could have declared victory in the post-9/11 wars as a prelude to wide-ranging retrenchment. Again, however, it was revealed that America's leaders were not looking for excuses to bring US forces home.

Overseas deployments are not just normal, they are seemingly sacrosanct. Even President Trump, who once told a graduating class at West Point that his administration was dedicated to the task of "ending the era of endless wars,"[49] made no meaningful progress toward retrenchment while in the White House.

Conclusion

Several lessons can be drawn from these six waves of expansion, all of which provide essential context for the rest of the book. First, the overall trend has been unmistakable: since the mid-nineteenth century, the United States has been an expansionist power in the sense that its government has steadily worked to project power *over* and *onto* foreign lands. Even though the United States has practiced retrenchment at times, at no stage has Washington undertaken an obvious net decrease in its overseas commitments. The decolonization of the Philippines in 1948 was dwarfed by the assumption of Cold War–era commitments around the same time (including to the newly independent Republic of the Philippines); withdrawals from Panama, South Vietnam, and Taiwan were followed by the massive Reagan-era military buildup; drawdowns in Europe during the 1990s were outstripped by the expansion of NATO and the onset of permanent wars in the Middle East; and the retrenchment from Afghanistan was overshadowed by the largest US military budget in history, the persistence of a widened global War on Terror into sub-Saharan Africa and elsewhere, and a clear push to retain military primacy in the Indo-Pacific. Simply put, the United States has been expanding its overseas commitments – territorial, political, and military – for 165 years. The trend has not been linear, but it has been pronounced.

This is not to dismiss the fact that the US political system is (or has been) capable of producing policies of retrenchment.

It is important to acknowledge that the United States decolonized the Philippines and the Panama Canal Zone, exited the
war in Vietnam, withdrew troops from Taiwan, cut the size of
US forces in Europe after the Cold War, and ended the wars
in Iraq and Afghanistan. Such histories suggest that the puzzle
is not just "why can't America retrench?" but also "when and
why can America retrench?" The rest of the book will try to
develop clear answers to both questions. But for now, it is
worth highlighting several factors that seem to correlate with
US retrenchment.

For one thing, it appears that whenever the United States
has intervened for purely (or mostly) commercial reasons, it
has eventually come home. This suggests that Washington is
no mere handmaiden to domestic capital. The United States
has also retrenched when the costs of undoing retrenchment were low or manageable. This helps to explain why the
United States disengaged from Cuba, Haiti, the Dominican
Republic, and elsewhere in the Western Hemisphere during
the so-called "Banana Wars" – because the US military could
have quickly and easily redeployed to these places if it was
deemed necessary.[50] Another cause of retrenchment seems to
be massive domestic opposition to foreign wars. Thus, while
the smallish-sized Anti-Imperialist League failed to curb imperial expansion in the late 1800s and early 1900s, the much
larger America First Committee was remarkably successful at
delaying US entry into World War II. Public opposition also
helps to explain the US pullouts from Vietnam in the 1970s,
Somalia in the 1990s, Iraq in the 2010s, and Afghanistan in the
2020s. To be sure, public opinion is never a perfect predictor
of foreign policy, but it does seem capable of influencing war
policy at critical moments.

In contrast, America seems to have stayed abroad for two
reasons: (1) whenever political annexation has taken place;[51]
and (2) whenever a compelling security rationale is prof-
fered for an overseas occupation. Annexations stopped in the

twentieth century, the Northern Mariana Islands (1986) being the last territory brought under US sovereign control. But the logic and language of national security are now ubiquitous when justifying forward deployments. More than anything else, this seems to be why America's overseas deployments since 1945 have been so hard to kill – because they have been justified in the domestic political imagination on national-security grounds, using arguments that tie the hands of future leaders and thus make retrenchment treacherous to attempt in political terms.

How can a president contemplate withdrawing from Europe, for example, when deployments there are portrayed as essential to transatlantic security, or even "sacred" (to use President Biden's words)?[52] How could any US leader advocate for a drawdown of forces in East Asia without inviting the criticism that they were complacent about Chinese expansionism? Similarly, no president can safely consider a wide-ranging exit from the Middle East without being tarred as "soft" on terrorism and blind to the threat posed by Iran and its proxies. Put simply, America hardly ever chooses to withdraw from a country or territory once it has been occupied by US troops because the very fact of an occupying force is usually evidence enough that domestic actors have engaged in something like threat inflation, deploying the logic and language of securitization to justify an overseas military presence. To voluntarily retrench today is to contradict the narrative that has been given to justify almost all of America's existing forward deployments: that overseas military primacy is essential to US national security.

While isolated instances of retrenchment continue to take place on a case-by-case basis, they almost never amount to anything like a shift away from global military primacy in grand-strategic terms; they are recalibrations, not revolutions. In fact, there is hardly any serious discussion of a programmatic move away from primacism in US politics today. It is vanishingly rare for anyone in a position of power to imagine aloud that the United States could or should cease to be a massively forward-deployed military power – a subject which the next chapter will discuss in more detail.

2

The Restraint Debate

The early 1990s were a watershed in the history of US foreign relations. The Soviet Union formally ceased to exist in December 1991. Two years earlier, ordinary East German citizens breached the Berlin Wall and tore down that hated symbol of the Cold War. Elections were held across the states of Eastern Europe, most of which resulted in the defeat of communist parties and the creation of democratic governments.[1] In August 1994, the Soviet Union's successor state, Russia, finalized the withdrawal of Soviet-era forces from Eastern Europe. As early as 1990, opinion polls showed that half of the US public viewed Russia as either "neutral" or "friendly" toward the United States – a far cry from how the Soviet Union had been regarded in the previous decade.[2] Without question, the Cold War was over and the United States had won. Yet as described in chapter 1, the geopolitical changes unleashed by the Soviet collapse did not prompt the United States to withdraw from Eurasia. On the contrary, large military deployments in Europe, the Asia-Pacific, and the Middle East remained firmly in place – and, in some cases, expanded.

Why were proponents of retrenchment unable to secure a major shift in US grand strategy? One way to answer this question is to explore the arguments that were made during the 1990s in favor of military primacy. As will be explained, there was no single justification given for why the United States ought to retain military preponderance over its long-term potential challengers. America's political leaders, top scholars, and analysts made several distinct (if overlapping) arguments in favor of maintaining the status quo. Some insisted that the post–Cold War international environment could not be trusted to remain tranquil, and that only US hypervigilance could ensure national security in an uncertain world. Others made the case for something approaching a Kantian peace – the idea that, if only the United States would provide the overall security conditions, the world could be ushered into an era of perpetual concord as it became more democratic, liberal, and joined together by international organizations. At home, meanwhile, there were more parochial interests at play: those who had spent decades benefiting from the steady flow of defense dollars had an obvious interest in resisting any changes to US foreign policy that would entail smaller military budgets.

To be sure, some argued forcefully against the status quo and dared their fellow Americans to entertain the idea of broad-based retrenchment; another "return to normalcy." But in the final analysis, opponents of military primacy were too few in number, too short on political influence, and too badly hamstrung by going up against a foreign policy orthodoxy that had been in place for four decades. During the 1990s and early 2000s, the broad center of American politics was firmly of the opinion that the preponderant position inherited at the end of the Cold War ought not to be given up, and that the United States should take advantage of the unipolar moment to ensure favorable international conditions. Major policy disagreements concerned only the *purpose* of US military primacy, not the wisdom of primacy as a *means* of achieving foreign-policy ends.

By and large, these dynamics have persisted into the present day.[3] Politicians and their advisers on both sides of the aisle mostly converge on the idea that it would be wrong to dismantle the global garrison state put in place between 1945 and 1991. As before, there are still those who make cogent, persuasive arguments against US military primacy – but the "restraint" community remains sorely disadvantaged in the sense that it is arguing for the destruction of a foreign-policy edifice that has been part of US national identity for around eighty years. A preponderant slice of the political class is wedded to the idea that military primacy can be utilized to bring about a more propitious external environment, even if they disagree over how the outside world should be made to look.

Why do arguments for retrenchment continue to fall flat? The second half of this chapter moves to focus squarely on what these ideas are. I describe five stylized "camps" that argue in favor of retrenchment today: academic realists, libertarians, nationalists, progressives, and leftists. One obvious point is that these various positions against military primacy are, at present, difficult to arrange into a coherent movement for a more circumscribed world role. But this observation should not be allowed to overshadow the fact that antiprimacy groups are tangible, well-established, and perhaps growing – despite not being ascendant. Either way, the purpose of the present chapter is this: to establish that America's grand strategy of military primacy has always been controversial and is still contested in contemporary politics – even if, for whatever reason, critical perspectives have tended to be less influential than voices in favor of the status quo. Understanding how this dynamic has played out over the past thirty years is an essential prerequisite to mounting a more effective challenge going forward.

Why America Didn't Retrench:
Primacy as Geopolitical Insurance

During the 1990s, there were two main arguments in favor of the United States staying forward deployed at the end of the Cold War: strategic uncertainty and liberal utopianism. Each of these arguments arrived at the same conclusion, however, which was that the United States should not give up the privileged geostrategic position inherited at the end of the Cold War and should instead use its favorable distribution of power assets toward a particular set of ends. President Clinton captured the essence of the strategic uncertainty argument in his first inaugural address, cautioning that despite the collapse of the Soviet Union, new threats had already emerged to make the world a dangerous place. "Today," he said, "a generation raised in the shadows of the Cold War assumes new responsibilities in a world warmed by the sunshine of freedom *but threatened still by ancient hatreds and new plagues.*"[4]

The following year, this sort of pessimism about world politics was crystallized into article form by Robert Kaplan, whose "The Coming Anarchy," printed in *The Atlantic*, described a world beset by civil conflict, demographic problems, disease, environmental breakdown, and collapse of political order.[5] Perhaps tellingly, Kaplan's article – in all its fatalistic glory – was circulated among Clinton administration officials at the behest of the President himself. Not long after, the Harvard political scientist Samuel Huntington would publish his landmark text, *The Clash of Civilizations* – another gloomy analysis of geopolitics, which argued that the relative stability and predictability of the Cold War era was being replaced by volatility and bloodshed as ethnoreligious divisions returned to the fore of world politics.[6]

In this context of uncertainty and perceived geopolitical instability, some in Washington warned against retrenchment. It would be imprudent, they argued, to relinquish political and military control over global affairs without knowing what sort of international system would come next. The columnist Charles Krauthammer offered perhaps the clearest version of this argument, insisting even before the Soviet Union had dissolved that the United States should use its preponderant power abroad to *create* international security rather than *hoping* for placid conditions to remain in place absent US engagement. "International stability is never a given. It is never the norm," Krauthammer argued. "If America wants stability, it will have to create it."[7] As the 1990s wore on – a decade blighted by war in the Persian Gulf and genocide in the former Yugoslavia, Rwanda, and Congo – few could object to Krauthammer's claims about the intractability of global disorder. The outside world was *not* safe and secure, it seemed, and nor would it become so if left to its own devices.

In government, the view that US military primacy was a necessary insurance policy against international instability was best encapsulated in the 1992 defense planning guidance, a document authored at the direction of Paul Wolfowitz, Under Secretary of Defense for Policy under President George H.W. Bush. This document called for the United States to maintain military superiority so that Washington might deter the emergence of a global peer competitor, as well as deterring smaller regional powers from behaving in incendiary ways. Wolfowitz and his coauthors acknowledged a role for global rules and international organizations, and even betrayed a modest desire for US-led coalitions of democratic and like-minded states where appropriate. But fundamentally, their vision was of a world order underpinned by US hard power. From this view, the unipolar moment was a windfall – an unexpected gift, which gave the United States an opportunity to fashion an international environment that would keep its people safe in perpetuity. Certainly, untrammeled military primacy was not something to be given up for nothing in return.[8]

When it was leaked to the press, the defense planning guidance caused outrage, with critics seizing upon the document
as a crass statement of imperial ambitions. In public, President
Bush repudiated the guidance and renewed his support for a
more multilateral vision of international order.[9] In practice,
however, US foreign policy during the 1990s came to resemble the Wolfowitz Doctrine in important respects. Certainly,
intellectuals and policymakers would later echo much of its
core content and assumptions. With regards to US policy in
Asia, for example, Joseph Nye – then a high-ranking official
in the Clinton administration – wrote in 1995 that "among the
important and often neglected reasons for East Asia's success
are American alliances in the region and the continued presence of substantial U.S. forces."[10] What was this if not a claim
that US military dominance was a cause of peace in Asia?

The same arguments were made with respect to NATO
expansion in Europe and in defense of US forces in the Middle
East, where US pilots were then flying daily sorties over Iraq
to enforce no-fly zones over the country's north and south. In
Europe, the Clinton administration pushed ahead with NATO
enlargement despite fifty national-security experts and former
high-ranking officials penning an open letter to slam the policy
as a needless provocation of Russia.[11] Justifying the administration's position, Deputy Secretary of State Strobe Talbott argued
that NATO's expanded presence would strengthen democracy
abroad and provide an international forum for dispute resolution.[12] Again, the dominant narrative was that US overseas
deployments were necessary to suppress insecurity – a basic
tenet of the original Wolfowitz Doctrine.

To be clear, it is not hard to intuit why arguments in favor of
US military primacy might have made sense during the initial
post–Cold War period. Forty years of tense geopolitical rivalry
with the Soviet Union had conditioned Americans to believe
that the outside world was a foreboding place, and that military strength had a major role to play in ensuring the country's

national security. And as described above, the 1990s were
hardly a time of peace and tranquility. Iraq's invasion of Kuwait,
North Korea's pursuit of nuclear weapons, the bloody breakup
of Yugoslavia, civil war in Somalia, genocide in Rwanda, and
an expansive conflict centered on the Democratic Republic
of the Congo – all of these events and more served to remind
Americans that their external environs harbored innumerable
potential threats to national and international security. Calls
for the United States to remain vigilant and forward deployed
made some logical sense. Arguments in favor of retrenchment,
on the other hand, could easily come across as ill-suited to a
world in turmoil.

Liberal Utopianism: Constructing a New World Order

Distinct from these arguments about security in an uncertain
world, others in the foreign policy establishment insisted
during the 1990s that US power was essential to upholding
something more noble than the bare suppression of conflict:
a "liberal" and progressive international order. In 1990, even
President George H.W. Bush – someone who, by his own
admission, did not "do" the "vision thing" – declared that his
objective was to create a "new world order" from the rubble
of the crumbling Cold War. This new order would be rooted
in international law, Bush explained, and would be overseen
by a revitalized United Nations – but the application of hard
military power would also serve as a key component.[13]

The New World Order concept was test driven during the
1990–1991 Gulf War, sparked by Iraq's invasion of neighboring
Kuwait. In response to Iraqi aggression, President Bush mobilized around 540,000 US troops and deployed them in Saudi
Arabia and elsewhere in the Gulf as a means of deterring an
attack on the oil-rich kingdom (Operation Desert Shield). In
January 1991, the United States attacked Iraqi positions inside

Kuwait and launched a full-scale invasion of Iraq (Operation Desert Storm). The war was over in six weeks and resulted in the liberation of Kuwait. For many reasons, the Gulf War was an extraordinary conflict.[14] A coalition of thirty-nine countries participated in the war against Iraq, and even the Soviet Union agreed to support the US-led intervention by permitting UN Security Council authorization. It was the quintessential "good war" in that it was lawful, fought in the name of collective defense against a clear aggressor, and supported by a broad cross-section of the international community. At home, analysts declared that the war had put paid to the "Vietnam Syndrome" and heralded a return to confidence in the US military.[15] President Bush saw his approval rating soar to 89 percent in March 1991, and Democrats in Congress who had voted to condemn the war came to rue their decision. For years afterwards, popular video games and movies used the Gulf War as a setting for normalizing and glorifying the exercise of US power abroad.[16]

In operational terms, the Gulf War demonstrated the utility of a global garrison state. Once political leaders in Washington had determined that an intervention in the Gulf would be required, the Pentagon was able to use its forward-deployed assets in the region to execute this plan within a remarkable timeframe. No other country in the world would have been able to mobilize and deploy more than half a million troops in a matter of weeks. The United States was (and remains) the only global power with the worldwide infrastructure of military bases and logistical hubs necessary for such a massive endeavor. The lesson, it seemed, was that US forward deployments were not just consistent with international law and order but might even be essential to upholding a rules-based system in the unipolar world.

When President Clinton came to office, his approach was one of continuity with the Bush years in terms of foreign policy – that is, broadly maintaining America's global military footprint.[17] But if anything, Clinton's team placed a heavier emphasis on justifying US primacy in idealist terms. No phrase encapsulates this attempt to render military primacy in a liberal-internationalist light than Madeleine Albright's description of the United States as the "indispensable nation." Albright first used this phrase in February 1998, in the context of speculation that the Clinton administration would order a bombing campaign against Saddam Hussein's Iraq.[18] "It is the threat of the use of force and our line-up there that is going to put force behind the diplomacy," Albright explained. "But if we have to use force, it is because we are America; we are the indispensable nation. We stand tall and we see further than other countries into the future, and we see the danger here to all of us." She went on: "I know that the American men and women in uniform are always prepared to sacrifice for freedom, democracy and the American way of life."[19]

This was a thoroughly liberal justification for US power abroad. According to Albright, the United States was not engaged in overseas warfighting for selfish reasons; its forward deployments were not meant to serve national security, narrowly defined. Rather, the United States used its military power across the globe for the good of all humanity. Viewed from this perspective, it would be an unconscionably selfish and irresponsible act for the United States to retrench. Without the United States to enforce international rules and punish acts of wrongdoing, who else would nurture the causes of freedom and democracy worldwide? Overseas police actions were part of America's job description as the sole superpower – and it was a job worth doing well and with pride.

Clinton tended to agree with Albright's narrative. He was an optimist, arguing strenuously that economic integration would lead to liberalization and democratization in places like China, Russia, and elsewhere. Clinton led NATO into the Kosovo War in 1999 even though the US Congress refused to give its consent. He embraced the label of "enlargement" to describe his commitment to democracy promotion abroad, a word meant to convey an intent to expand US power and influence but without negative, imperialistic connotations.[20] This was the liberal world order in action – ambitious, universalizing, devoted to humanitarianism, and underpinned almost entirely by American power.

Some, such as Krauthammer, were cynical about the emerging liberal order, and especially the role of international organizations and consensus-building. "Why it should matter to Americans that their actions get a Security Council nod from, say, Deng Xiaoping and the butchers of Tiananmen Square is beyond me," he wrote in 1990. "But to many Americans it matters. It is largely for domestic reasons, therefore, that American political leaders make sure to dress unilateral action in multilateral clothing. The danger, of course, is that they might come to believe their own pretense."[21] In other words, Krauthammer was saying, the narrative of a liberal-democratic world order was merely a cover for power politics, window dressing to disguise the raw self-interest that truly (and in Krauthammer's view, quite rightly) drove US foreign policy.[22]

But even if they started out as cynics, it seems clear that US leaders *did* come to believe their own pretense about liberal internationalism, just as Krauthammer had feared that they would.[23] Leaders who were repulsed by the brash and unapologetic primacism of neoconservatives such as Krauthammer and Wolfowitz nevertheless embraced the justifications for military primacy put forth by more idealistic leaders such as Clinton and Albright. The outcome was the same, perhaps, given that both ideational frameworks provided rationales for continued US occupation of Europe, the Asia-Pacific, and the Middle East, and lent a logic to military interventions large and small. But the intellectual cores of each perspective were rooted in fundamentally different theories of international politics.

The Liberal–Primacist Fusion: Today's Consensus

To be clear, not all US leaders during the 1990s were sincerely motivated by geopolitical uncertainty or liberal utopianism. Many did not hold any strong views about international relations. But politicians usually find it difficult to publicly contradict narratives that have become conventional wisdom even when they harbor severe doubts about US foreign policy in private. George H.W. Bush, for example, was the consummate pragmatist, yet always took care to cloak his foreign-policy pronouncements in idealist language. Clinton, on the other hand, does not seem to have been much interested in foreign policy at all upon becoming president – at least, not interested in the articulation of grand strategies. He was, instead, focused mostly on domestic priorities, especially the economy, and his foreign policy positions – such as they were – derived from his laserlike focus on the home front. But it did not take long for Clinton to realize that US foreign policy could not run entirely on autopilot; he was criticized in the early 1990s for his actions and nonactions in Haiti, Somalia, and elsewhere, as well as for his record on Chinese human rights. The military revolted against several of Clinton's preferred policies, such as his support for the inclusion of gays in the military and for winding down the Reagan-era Strategic Defense Initiative.[24] Finding himself bogged down by the protestations of primacists and liberal internationalists in government and broader society, Clinton eventually just embraced elements of both camps.

The point is that even self-interested US leaders who do not care much about foreign policy tend to recognize, in due course, that they reap political benefits from pursuing militarist foreign policies.[25] This was one of the most obvious lessons of the First Gulf War, given how high George H.W. Bush's approval rating soared as a result of the war (opponents of the war, on the other hand, found it difficult to justify their reluctance to use force in defense of international law and order once the war had been won in short order). President Clinton similarly saw his approval ratings "bounce" after interventionist actions such as the 1998 bombing of Iraq (Operation Desert Fox) and the dispatch of two aircraft carrier battle groups to the Taiwan Strait in 1996. By contrast, few politicians in the 1990s recognized a clear self-interest in proposing wide-ranging policies of retrenchment. And, of course, security-dependent allies in Europe, Asia, and the Middle East lobbied hard throughout this period for the US defense umbrella to stay in place.[26] Coupled with a permissive international environment that allowed for expansionist foreign policies without endangering too much the security of the US homeland, it was perhaps overdetermined that Washington in the 1990s would not join Russia in withdrawing its troops from the independent states of Eurasia. For America's leaders, maintaining military primacy was the path of least resistance.

Today, almost all US leaders have followed the same trajectory as Clinton: even if they were once ambivalent about US primacy (or hostile to it), politicians in the United States almost all seem to coalesce eventually around the idea that either Krauthammer or Albright – or both – were right: the world is unsafe, and so requires US domination; but the world can be made tame, albeit only with the application of US force. Perhaps nobody blended these two logics better than President George W. Bush, who argued after the 9/11 attacks on New York and Washington, DC that the world was full of potential threats to US safety and security, but that these challenges could be overcome through the suppression of tyranny and the export of democracy.[27] But even President Obama – a president so closely associated with liberal internationalism that he was awarded the Nobel Peace Prize in 2009 *in anticipation* that he would behave justly in office – was always clear that US military primacy had an important role to play in ordering international affairs. On accepting the Nobel Peace Prize, Obama said:

[I]n many countries there is a deep ambivalence about military action today, no matter what the cause. And at times, this is joined by a reflexive suspicion of America, the world's sole military superpower. But the world must remember that it was not simply international institutions – not just treaties and declarations – that brought stability to a post-World War II world. Whatever mistakes we have made, the plain fact is this: The United States of America has helped underwrite global security for more than six decades with the blood of our citizens and the strength of our arms. The service and sacrifice of our men and women in uniform has promoted peace and prosperity from Germany to Korea, and enabled democracy to take hold in places like the Balkans.[28]

In effect, this speech was a defense of America (the "world's sole military superpower") and its right to use military force abroad. And the basis of Obama's defense was simple: that the ends (global security, peace, prosperity, and democracy) justify the means (military primacy), even if others around the world are skeptical. To be sure, Obama lamented that the United States ever had to send troops into battle, but he reassured his audience that America's goals were always to spread freedom and uphold international law and order. Moreover, he took exception to the idea that there was a viable alternative to US dominance. From this view, primacy is not just good – it is natural.

Even President Trump, a politician known for questioning and even outright condemning interventionist foreign policies, seemed to agree once ensconced in office that the United States must play a role in guaranteeing international security. Not only did Trump elevate a number of neoconservatives to high office in his administration (as well as establishment figures from the military, business, and think tank worlds),[29] but early on in his presidency Trump effectively admitted to delegating decision-making power to "generals" when it came to military actions abroad.[30] Following the counsel of his military and civilian advisers, Trump ordered an expansion of the US presence in Afghanistan, sent lethal aid to Ukraine, bombed Syrian government forces on two separate occasions, assassinated the Iranian general Qasem Soleimani, and threatened to attack North Korea with overwhelming force. It was revealing, perhaps, that when Trump spoke to explain his decision to bomb targets in Syria, in particular, he explicitly focused on the importance of punishing rogue regimes for breaking humanitarian law – a rationale drawn straight from the liberal internationalist playbook.[31]

President Biden, too, committed his administration to defense of the "rules-based" international order soon after becoming president. Biden focused his rhetoric on the threats posed by Russia and China in particular, the world's leading authoritarian powers. Moscow and Beijing clearly represent challenges to international and national security in a traditional sense – the invasion of Ukraine and fears about a Chinese invasion of Taiwan being the two obvious cases in point – but, in Biden's telling, they also constitute a broader threat to democracy as a form of government and the "rules-based order" as a feature of the international system. At least rhetorically, Biden committed the United States to meeting this challenge and overcoming it – including via the projection of force abroad if necessary. In this respect, Biden is like all of his post-Cold War predecessors in supporting what realists like Stephen Walt have called "liberal hegemony" – a grand strategy of using military power to advance democratic values, deter would-be aggressors, and strengthen the circle of liberal polities.[32]

Why America Should Retrench:
Arguments Then and Now

For the past three decades, arguments in favor of continued forward deployments have been compelling in part because they have justified a long-standing status quo. The insight here is that it is always easier to argue in favor of stasis – that is, *not* changing something – than to argue for radical transformation. Yet even in the early 1990s, not everyone agreed that the status quo inherited at the end of the Cold War ought to be maintained. Some were bold enough to argue in favor of America undertaking a wide-ranging strategic adjustment in response to new circumstances. In a symposium for *The National Interest*, for example, Jeane Kirkpatrick wrote:

> Most of the international military obligations that we assumed were once important are now outdated. Our alliances should be alliances of equals, with equal risks, burdens, and responsibilities. It is time to give up the dubious benefits of superpower status and become again an unusually successful, open American republic.[33]

With just these three sentences, Kirkpatrick summed up several of the primary arguments in favor of retrenchment during the post–Cold War era: (1) the international system had changed, and so US foreign policy ought to change along with it; (2) allied nations could afford to provide for their own defense, and should do so; and (3) that domestic renewal could not be achieved without cutbacks to international obligations. There was much to recommend these arguments, which were rooted in a sober calculation about changing external circumstances, updated material interests, and an appeal to US history and political culture. Kirkpatrick's plea for retrenchment was all the more notable given that it came from her – a socialist-turned-neoconservative and renowned "cold warrior" who had served as Ambassador to the UN under President Reagan.

But there was also a fourth – more nationalistic – argument for retrenchment put forward during the 1990s: the idea that (4) the United States was being humiliated by nominal "allies" who benefited from US military protection but provided nothing in return. Patrick Buchanan, an ex-speechwriter for President Reagan and a candidate for the Republican Party nomination in 1992, was an early adopter of this line of thinking. He memorably called for "America First – and Second, and Third" instead of using US power to advance the interests of foreign countries.[34] In doing so, Buchanan deliberately invoked the memory of Charles Lindbergh and the America First Committee, whose members had opposed US entry into World War II before the attack on Pearl Harbor. The language of "America First" was also used by Paul Tsongas, who campaigned against US primacy from the left but with strong nationalistic overtones.[35] Although he was not a major political figure at the time, Donald Trump – then a New York businessman and minor celebrity – also argued that the post–Cold War arrangement was a humiliation for the United States. Why should the US taxpayer underwrite the defense of Germany and Japan, these populist agitators cried, when those countries were America's main economic competitors? Why should the United States not retrench instead, and devote scarce national resources toward domestic projects and priorities? In effect, the complaint was that the United States was being abused by its allies and partners, and so should regain a sense of national self-interest as well as basic self-respect.

For the most part, however, opposition to US military primacy ended here: with retired officials, intellectuals, the occasional celebrity, and minor players within the two political parties. The broad center of US politics remained committed to the long-standing consensus that military primacy was good for America and the rest of the world. As a result, the national security state remained intact at home, and the global garrison state was preserved abroad. Public opinion remained supportive of America's defense establishment, with trust in the military almost always registering at higher levels than trust in other organs of government.[36] Some anthropologists even expressed fears that the United States had developed a cultural disposition toward war and conflict; that the country's identity had shifted such that engaging in violence abroad was no longer a necessary evil for America but a consumption good – something that the United States as a society could not easily do without.[37]

But despite its relative lack of success in the early post–Cold War period, the movement for retrenchment has persisted and evolved over the last thirty years. In some ways, it has grown stronger and better organized – although few would argue that it has become more coherent. Today, there are at least five distinct "camps" within the proretrenchment community: academic-realist, right-leaning libertarian, right-leaning nationalist, left-leaning progressive, and hard left. In what follows, I provide a thumbnail sketch of each camp.

The Realist Critique

First, there are scholarly arguments in favor of retrenchment that emanate from the Ivory Tower. Prominent members of this camp include John Mearsheimer, Stephen Walt, Barry Posen, Charles Glaser, Eugene Gholz, and Patrick Porter – all self-described "realist" scholars of International Relations.[38] Their arguments against primacy tend to be rooted in academic theories about how the international system works – for example, the idea that unipolar systems are inherently unstable, that the United States should expect other powers to balance against it and need not necessarily struggle against such behavior, and that foreign policy blunders are most likely to occur whenever leaders adopt a misplaced focus on ideals and values rather than raw power politics. From this perspective, military primacy leads to hubris and temptation to overreach, thus inviting disaster in terms of national security. Realists blame the failed policies of primacism for catastrophic mistakes such as the Iraq War and the stubborn refusal to withdraw from Afghanistan long after the war there became evidently unwinnable in a conventional sense.

Academic proponents of retrenchment and restraint are not shy of entering the public square to make recommendations regarding US policy.[39] Among other things, prominent realists opposed the 2003 invasion of Iraq; called for the war in Afghanistan to be wound down once al-Qaeda bases had been destroyed; have argued for NATO to disband or consolidate; recommend that the United States retrench from the Middle East; and float the idea of striking a grand bargain with China. Some of these policy prescriptions are highly controversial. John Mearsheimer's strident attacks on NATO expansion, which extends to blaming the United States for provoking Russia into invading Ukraine, has been roundly criticized as apologia for Vladimir Putin.[40] Similarly, Charles Glaser's proposal to rethink US commitments to Taiwan has been lambasted by critics of restraint as little better than appeasement.[41]

In fact, it is difficult to think of any major policy debate where the realist school of thought has "won the day" in Washington, DC. The general pattern seems to be that academic realists have a hard time influencing US foreign policy. In part, this might be a function of academia's general irrelevance from the perspective of policymakers; at least, there is a cottage industry of books and articles that lament the distance between scholarship and policymaking.[42] But as William Walldorf and Andrew Yeo have shown, the realists' political impotence might also be because they are simply too far removed from the median views of the US political class and public.[43] For one thing, realists do not buy into the essential goodness of US forward deployments and interventions, and so are freer to make the case that such foreign policies are imprudent, counterproductive, or even immoral (in the sense that they unnecessarily place the lives of US service personnel in harm's way). These are defensible positions to hold, but they differ wildly from the foreign-policy orthodoxy to which most policymakers ("the Blob") adhere. This basic lack of intersubjectivity over US forward deployments is a recipe for marginalization.[44]

The Libertarian Critique

Second, there are political groups who advocate restraint from a right-leaning, libertarian perspective. The Cato Institute is perhaps the most high-profile of these organizations, and the Charles Koch Foundation is a major funder of projects in this area. Prominent analysts and scholars in this tradition include Chris Layne, Clyde Prestowitz, Justin Logan, John Glaser, William Ruger, Ted Galen Carpenter, and others. Analysts in this camp share the realists' assessment that unipolarity has led to greater insecurity for the United States (as well as people around the world), but also emphasize the negative effects of military primacy for US domestic politics and fiscal policy. Unlike the realists, libertarian restrainers have managed to accrue a small number of allies in Congress in recent years – mostly in the Republican Party. To greater or lesser degrees, these allies include (or included) politicians like Rand Paul, Ben Sasse, Mike Lee, Cynthia Lummis, Justin Amash, and Thomas Massie. Some of these legislators made names for themselves by opposing interventionist foreign policies. Rand Paul, for example, engaged in a high-profile filibuster in 2013 to demand that the Obama administration agree to greater oversight of its drone war in the Middle East.

Among other things, libertarian-leaning critics of primacy point out that permanent militarism has had a corrupting effect on the US republic, worsening the nation's finances, eroding effective civilian control of the military,[45] weakening the role of the legislature, encroaching upon civil liberties,[46] and misallocating fiscal resources toward unproductive ends. This gives them some things in common with what Walter Russell Mead once called "the Jeffersonian tradition" of US foreign policy – a tradition that emphasizes the preservation of democracy at home rather than abroad.[47] The only difference is that, unlike Jeffersonians, today's right-leaning libertarians are usually supportive of freer trade, whereas Thomas Jefferson was distrustful of America's merchant class.

The Nationalist Critique

Third, there is a right-leaning push for retrenchment that is more nationalistic than libertarian. This group is close to what Mead labels the "Jacksonian tradition,"[48] and is exemplified today by Donald Trump. Nationalists support restraint in the narrow sense that they often regard overseas commitments as useless, indulgent, or even betrayals of US interests. But they are not generally opposed to high military spending and the maintenance of a strong national defense, a point that distinguishes them from Jeffersonians. When perceived threats to national security emerge, erstwhile restrainers in the Jacksonian tradition transform into vociferous proponents of using military force to crush America's enemies. Jacksonians are warlike, says Mead; it is just that they are selective about the wars they choose to fight.

President Trump has been the most prominent representative of the nationalistic school of retrenchment in modern times.[49] After announcing his bid for the presidency in the summer of 2015, Trump consistently criticized the costs of US foreign policy. As a candidate, he claimed that $6 trillion had been spent on wars in the Middle East, arguing that these resources should have been invested in domestic infrastructure rather than foreign wars. "With this $6 trillion we could have rebuilt our country – twice," he insisted. "And maybe even three times if we had people who had the ability to negotiate."[50] Once in the Oval Office, Trump repeatedly criticized US allies for not doing enough to provide for their own defense and raised the possibility of withdrawing US troops from South Korea, Japan, Germany, Syria, and Afghanistan. He suggested that, if US forces were to be stationed abroad, then host countries should pay the United States for protection – a worldview that portrayed the US military as a mercenary force rather than a beneficent provider of global public goods.

In reality, however, members of the nationalistic camp are often inconsistent with their support for retrenchment and restraint. This was certainly the case with Trump, who increased troop deployments in Afghanistan, launched two sets of airstrikes against the Syrian regime, risking provoking a major regional war with his assassination of Iranian general Qasem Soleimani, and threatened "fire and fury" against North Korea over its nuclear program. But these apparent inconsistencies are features of the nationalist camp of restraint, not bugs, with even Pat Buchanan arguing in 1990 that the "strength of the U.S. navy should be non-negotiable."[51] The point, again, is that nationalists are distinguished from libertarians by a full-throated support for a strong national defense. What makes them restrainers is their insistence that America's military be deployed only when the US homeland is threatened in some way.

The Progressive Critique

Fourth, calls for restraint also come from the left. This includes most progressives, who favor reductions in defense spending and articulate a values-based foreign policy that elevates concern for human rights, environmentalism, and economic justice over militarism. Progressives argue for a diversion of fiscal resources from the defense budget toward social spending, averring that this *could* be done without jeopardizing national security and *should* be done as a way to counter corporate greed and to compensate long-suffering ordinary Americans. Ro Khanna (D-CA) might be considered an archetypal proponent of this version of restraint in the US Congress, while academic supporters of progressive grand strategies include Stephen Wertheim,[52] Peter Beinart,[53] and Van Jackson.[54]

Much of the progressive case for antimilitarism derives from an understanding that the economic and social costs of maintaining America's global garrison state are enormous. The annual defense budget is now over $850 billion. Including funds for the State Department and other agencies responsible for America's foreign policy, the United States spends over $1 trillion on international affairs on a yearly basis. This works out as $8,143 per household.[55] For comparison, in 2018 the average US household paid $15,748 in federal, state, and local taxes.[56] The National Priorities project estimates that annual US defense spending could fund nearly 17 million jobs paying $15 per hour, over 9 million elementary school teachers, or 20 million Head Start slots for the nation's children.[57] These are crude estimates, of course, and nobody seriously argues that the United States should spend nothing on defense, but such comparisons make the essential point that high levels of defense spending entail not just significant costs but also pointed opportunity costs that must be borne by members of domestic society.

Critics accuse the progressive left of being light on detail, especially with regard to their positions on military force and authoritarianism abroad.[58] In response, supporters of progressive grand strategy have offered the idea of military "sufficiency" instead of "superiority," as well as plans to form democratic alliances (as opposed to dealmaking with authoritarian regimes), commitments to international institution-building, and calls for defense policy to be reoriented toward the end of mutual threat reduction instead of zero-sum security-seeking.[59] There is also a distinct political-economy element to progressive grand strategy, which emphasizes the importance of inclusive growth, labor rights, strengthened environmental standards, and the wresting of power away from transnational capital.[60]

The Left Critique

Fifth and finally, there are also calls for retrenchment and restraint from the socialist left in the United States. Members of this camp take a more hardline (and fringe) view than progressives, viewing US primacy as part and parcel of American neo-imperialism that cannot properly be dismantled without broader, societal-level changes. Whereas progressives seek to reform US foreign policy and turn it toward domestic ends, the socialist left is pessimistic that America's world role can be altered without massive (revolutionary) restructuring of US foreign and domestic policy. This faction is anticapitalist, anti-imperialist, and almost entirely rejects the idea that power projection by the US state can ever be a good thing. Versions of this critique have been made by Jill Stein, the Green Party's presidential candidate in 2016; intellectuals such as Noam Chomsky; and 2024 presidential candidate, Cornell West.

Socialists view US foreign policy as the product of a neoconservative and liberal nexus, often casting progressives in the role of "useful idiots" or enablers.[61] Indeed, some of the socialist left's most stinging vituperation is often reserved for liberals in the Democratic Party and its satellite institutions, whom leftists accuse of possessing political power but not using it for the purpose of dismantling US militarism.[62] In Daniel Bessner's words, "the [liberal-internationalist] vanguard . . . has become startlingly backward-looking and incapable of charting a new path for the United States in the twenty-first century."[63] What should this new path look like? For scholars and activists like Bessner, it must include radical antimilitarism and working-class politics – that is, a thorough overhaul of US politics, economics, and societal relations, not just foreign policy.

Conclusion:
Is There a Coherent Movement for Restraint?

This chapter has described – in brief – the contours of America's post–Cold War debate about power and purpose. As is clear, there have been vibrant debates over the direction of US grand strategy. But it has not been a debate between equals. Primacists of various stripes have greatly outnumbered their restrainer adversaries. Today, primacists tend to blend ideas of neoconservatives like Paul Wolfowitz and liberal internationalists such as Madeleine Albright to form a palatable narrative about why the United States occupies so many foreign countries and why America's long-running experience of overseas interventions should continue uninterrupted. Meanwhile, the politics of antiprimacism is divided into at least five discernible blocs, none of which has managed to capture a decisive portion of the US political elite.

An obvious question arises: can a coherent movement be forged from the five proretrenchment camps described above? There have been signs in the recent past that this might be possible. In 2018, for example, the leading realist scholar Stephen Walt called for a left–right alliance against the foreign policy "establishment" that, he suggested, might be possible given the common ground that existed between them.[64] In 2019, the Quincy Institute for Responsible Statecraft was created to bridge the gap between right-leaning and left-progressive proponents of retrenchment, benefiting from seed funding provided by the Soros Foundation and the Charles Koch Foundation – two philanthropic organizations at polar opposites of the ideological spectrum.[65] And of course, the distinctions made above are somewhat artificial and stylized; in reality, there are overlaps between all pro-restraint groups, with some prominent restrainers – such as Andrew Bacevich, for example – not fitting into any single category. It might well be possible, then, for a bipartisan (or "trans-partisan") movement for restraint to emerge and cohere.

The problem, however, is that ideas must be translated into policy – and for this to happen, ideas require their adherents to occupy actual positions of power.[66] There are few grounds for optimism that this can happen in the present context. This is the subject of the next chapter, which will begin the process of explaining in detail why primacist ideas tend to hold sway in the United States while proretrenchment policies mostly fall flat. The answer, in short, is that the debate described in the foregoing chapter does not unfold on a level playing field. On the contrary, the political context is heavily biased in favor of primacists – the result of a decades-long process of state-building and political rewiring performed in response to perceived international exigencies.

3

Making the Militarist State

In the previous chapter, I suggested that arguments in favor of retrenchment have tended not to hold sway in Washington during the past thirty years. Why not? One explanation, of course, is that they are inferior arguments when judged against those put forward by primacists. This is a tempting conclusion – that US foreign policy is made by people who carefully weigh logic and evidence before choosing to implement whatever ideas seem best suited to serving America's national interests. But in this chapter, I lay the groundwork for another explanation: that the US foreign-policy ecosystem is heavily tilted in favor of primacist policies, with proposals for wide-ranging retrenchment facing a stiff uphill battle in Washington. From this view, America's international policies suffer from a poorly functioning marketplace of ideas. Decision-makers only ever consider a truncated set of options, most of which take military primacy as a given. Arguments in favor of retrenchment are sometimes made, but they are rarely given a full hearing along the corridors of power. The US political system is designed to reject them.

How did we get here? When and why did the United States become hardwired in favor of military primacy? What explains the lack of collective imagination about alternative approaches to international affairs? In this chapter, I introduce four concepts from political science – stateness, path dependence, exogenous shocks, and temporal sequencing – that will help to explain how the US government came to favor military primacy so heavily over policies of retrenchment and restraint. Taken together, these concepts focus attention on the institutional and historical context within which US leaders contemplate foreign policy, helping to provide insight as to why presidents often find it difficult to initiate major drawdowns of America's overseas presence. What becomes clear is that today's elected officials and national-security bureaucrats are operating inside a political system that was arranged in the latter half of the twentieth century for the explicit purpose of managing vast forward deployments and overseeing a never-ending series of military interventions. In other words, broad-based policies of retrenchment are nothing short of repugnant to the type of state that US leaders have built and maintained for the past eighty years.

One theme of the chapter is that international events have played a major role in catalyzing the political development of the US state. In this sense, I draw on a tradition in the International Relations literature known as the "second image reversed." This is an approach to studying the domestic–international nexus that grew out of pioneering work done by Peter Gourevitch in the 1970s and 1980s.[1] Gourevitch was influenced by Kenneth Waltz, who had argued that international politics could be studied at three different levels of analysis (or "images"): the individual level ("first image"), which encouraged paying analytic attention to the behavior of individual leaders; the national level ("second image"), which emphasized the importance of national political systems; and the systemic level ("third image"), which elevated the international-level interactions between nation-states above any domestic-level factors.[2] But Gourevitch's insight was that the second image cannot be divorced from the third; what happens inside states is often a function of what happens among them. In this chapter, I argue that the second image reversed is invaluable for telling the story of state-building in the United States since 1945. In Bat Sparrow's words, government and politics in the United States have been made "from the outside in,"[3] with major crises – exogenous shocks – doing much of the heavy lifting.

Breaking with America's primacist past would be a radical move, a rejection not just of shared ideas about US power and purpose but also a repudiation of the sort of government that generations of Americans have viewed as essential to their national security. This point requires some emphasis: *almost all of the organs of government relevant to foreign policy were designed for the explicit purpose of implementing policies of military primacism in response to perceived international exigencies.* Neither the institutions themselves nor the people staffing them are accustomed to orchestrating or even imagining the meaningful reduction of America's overseas commitments. Even if they hold sincere doubts about the strategy of military primacy, then, high-level leaders in the United States are pressured by the country's domestic political topography to put aside any thought of retrenchment once in office. The upshot is that the United States remains forward deployed in Europe, the Western Pacific, the Middle East, and elsewhere for reasons that long ago became obsolete – but individual leaders are almost powerless to do anything about it. In the final analysis, these domestic-level pathologies constitute the most fundamental barrier to the United States implementing policies of retrenchment or a grand strategy of restraint.

The Changed American State

The world is divided into around 195 sovereign states. These states are the same in the bare sense that they each enjoy formal sovereignty and thus full membership of the international community. But along a host of other dimensions, the world's states are utterly unalike. Some are strong, some are weak, and some hardly exist at all in practical terms. As the political scientist J.P. Nettl once put it, the state should be considered a "conceptual variable."[4] His insight was that states can be evaluated and measured in terms of their state*ness*. States enjoy a high degree of stateness when they are (1) de facto and *de jure* recognized as being "in control" of a jurisdiction's territory and people (the "summating" dimension); (2) highly capable of regulating their domestic population and economy via public institutions; (3) featured prominently in a nation's cultural life, with the state being central to the prevailing political culture in particular; and (4) unquestioned as an actor in world affairs.[5] By contrast, states with a low degree of stateness are devoid of power and legitimacy, incapable of enforcing policy solutions upon domestic actors, uncoupled from or unimportant to the dominant political culture with which they are geographically coterminous, and contested as sovereign actors on the international stage. Most states, of course, fall somewhere in between these two extremes. Indeed, it is common for states to have high degrees of stateness along some dimensions but not others. But either way, a state's degree of stateness will say something about its likely behavior. In this sense, stateness can be considered an independent variable – a shaper of what states can and cannot do.

During the first century of its existence, the US state was limited in capacity and constrained by narrow conceptions of what constituted the legitimate functions of the federal government. For one thing, the power of the state was hampered by geography as leaders in Washington found it difficult to project authority over America's ever-expanding frontiers. As a result, the US government was, at first, a state of "courts and parties."[6] It did not enjoy a public mandate to intervene much in the affairs of ordinary citizens, with antifederalist beliefs commanding widespread adherence among the population and political elites from the very beginning.[7] Even in the realm of taxation, the federal government was limited in contrast to the state governments. Congress had the power to levy tariffs (customs duties) on imported goods as well as indirect taxes (excise duties), but it lacked authority over direct taxation (income tax). For all these reasons, most ordinary citizens had little reason to interact with Washington except when voting and facing justice. As others have written, this diminutive size and shape of the US state – and the sort of politics fostered by America's low degree of stateness – provides an important explanation for a slew of political and policy outcomes in US history.[8]

In the realm of foreign policy, the smallness of the US state made a significant difference during the nineteenth century. Despite growing in terms of its geographic expanse and underlying material endowments – that is, *potential power* – the United States pursued a relatively circumscribed role on the world stage until the late 1800s. The reason, as Fareed Zakaria has explained, is that the hobbled US government was mostly unable to convert latent domestic resources into concrete instruments of influence (*usable power*) on the world stage.[9] Had the US state enjoyed higher administrative capacity and greater domestic legitimacy, the United States could feasibly have become a regional or global power much earlier in its history. Instead, Washington was slow to acquire the bare capabilities – that is, the requisite degree of stateness – necessary for overseas power projection.[10] In this sense, the structure and relative underdevelopment of the US state at home was a major factor in constraining US policy abroad.

According to Stephen Skowronek, the industrial revolution provided both the opportunity and the impetus for the development of a strong national state.[11] Industrialization brought with it social problems for which citizens expected the federal government to devise solutions. Progressives like President Theodore Roosevelt and Woodrow Wilson took on these challenges with zeal, expanding the power of the state to regulate large corporations, ensure food safety, conserve vast tracts of the natural environment, and more.[12] As the nation matured, a national political culture began to emerge, with the burgeoning state afforded a central role in the public imagination. Advances in transportation technology gave Washington a major part to play in facilitating transcontinental commerce, such as by financing the construction of roads, canals, and railways.[13] The Federal Reserve was created in 1913, the same year that the Sixteenth Amendment went into effect, which gave Congress the power to levy an income tax. The federal government began to assert itself in several other domestic policy areas, too, such as by adopting the Eighteenth Amendment and Volstead Act in 1919 (banning the sale of alcohol) as well as the Nineteenth Amendment to ensure a woman's right to vote. In the 1930s, of course, Washington's role underwent another major expansion in response to the Great Depression, with Congress creating the Social Security program and other New Deal initiatives that enormously increased the presence of the federal government in peoples' everyday lives.

By the mid-twentieth century, then, the American state had expanded in line with a broad, intersubjective understanding that the era of minimal government (*low stateness*) was over, and that national officials in Washington required a well-staffed, well-funded, and well-managed administrative state at their disposal (*high stateness*) if they were to undertake all of the business now deemed essential for governing a modern society. The executive branch, in particular, had become bigger, more intrusive, and more legitimate in the eyes of the people. These things were prerequisites for America emerging as a global power.[14] In the second half of the twentieth century, however, the causal arrow began to point in the other direction – that is, the experience of being a global power started to precipitate an expansion of the US state at home, rather than the other way around. In this book, the focus will be on the development of those organs of government that are dedicated to the development and implementation of foreign and defense policy (the "national security state"), which were remade almost entirely during the 1940s and 1950s in response to international events. But it is important to note that, beginning in World War II, US foreign relations restructured all aspects of domestic politics, not just the state's national-security apparatus. As Bat Sparrow puts it, "The *intra*national American state, thought to be the legacy of the New Deal, was systematically affected by the *extra*national factors of World War II and its aftermath; the American state was built [during this period] from the outside in."[15]

After the defeat of the Axis Powers, the federal government adopted a series of reforms designed to make the US state more capable of meeting future threats to national security. The National Security Act of 1947 was the centerpiece of this initiative, broadly defining the presidency's power over defense and intelligence. The 1947 Act created the Central Intelligence Agency; merged the Department of the Army, Department of the Navy, and Department of the Air Force into the new National Military Establishment (later renamed the Department of Defense); and created the office of National Security Adviser, a high-ranking official responsible for coordinating national security policy but which did not require Senate approval. Ever since 1947, the National Security Adviser has overseen the National Security Council – the locus of decision-making when it comes to security policy – and provided almost daily advice to the president on matters of national security.[16] By design, the executive branch was handed a vast advantage in terms of access to expert information. From Harry Truman onwards, every US president has been able to count on thousands of advisers in the White House, Department of Defense, National Security Council, and intelligence community who operate with only inconsistent oversight from the legislature or judiciary (both Congress and the Supreme Court – each of which are meant to provide checks and balances against the executive branch – tend to show a great deal of deference toward the presidency when it comes to national security). Over time, this has led to a one-way "ratchet effect" as the presidency has arrogated new powers to itself without the other branches of government doing much to claw those powers back.[17]

Over the course of the Cold War, the US state changed beyond all recognition in comparison to the state that the Constitution had brought into existence in 1789. While the basic constitutional framework was left mostly untouched, the actual state apparatus that stood atop the Constitution's articles and clauses underwent a radical overhaul. As one indicator, consider that, in 1940, the federal budget constituted around 9.6 percent of gross domestic product (GDP). By 1991, the federal budget had more than doubled to around 21.7 percent of GDP.[18] Consider, too, that in 1940 the executive branch employed just 699,000 civilians but that by 1991 that number had tripled to 2,243,000.[19] These statistics imply a massive increase in the size and scope of the US government during the course of World War II and the Cold War. Of particular relevance for this book's argument, the Pentagon appears to have benefited disproportionately from the expansion in federal manpower. Between 1940 and 1991, there was a nearly fourfold increase in civilian employees working for the Department of Defense (256,000 to 1,013,000), which outstrips the tripling in manpower seen across the executive branch as a whole. At the end of the Cold War, roughly half of all civilian employees in the executive branch were dedicated to serving the US military, a figure that does not even include those working in the Department of State, Department of Energy, and other agencies that have a role to play in developing US foreign policy.

The tilting of the American state in favor of the executive branch and its national-security apparatus did not go unnoticed, but nor was it effectively challenged. In 1966, the political scientist Aaron Wildavsky noted with some equanimity that American presidents seemed to have more power and policy success in foreign policy than domestic policy – his so-called "two presidencies thesis."[20] By 1973, scholars such as Arthur Schlesinger, Jr., were even discussing the existence of *extraconstitutional* powers in the realm of national security – a dramatic undercutting of supposed republican and constitutionalist norms.[21] In the past, prerogative powers to act in contravention of the Constitution had been exercised by presidents in times of crisis – President Lincoln during the Civil War and FDR during World War II, for example – but had always "snapped back" once an emergency had passed. In the Cold War, however, the national-security emergency in question never passed, and instead came to define daily life in the United States – the result being that the government became ever more powerful and ever more secretive in terms of security policy, with no end in sight.[22] The progressive Marcus Raskin wrote in 1975 that the maintenance of the national security state went so far as to risk "fascism" or "Bonapartism."[23] But despite some pushback from Congress after the Vietnam War – including the passage of the War Powers Resolution – today, the "imperial presidency" is alive and well in the realm of national security.[24] What is more, almost all actors within the US political system seem to support the presidency having preponderant power over foreign policy due to a well-worn assumption that the United States would be weaker, less agile, and more vulnerable if its foreign and defense policies were taken out of the hands of a single, unitary actor.

Indeed, recent decades have seen the federal government – and especially the executive branch – arrogate even more powers over national security than were afforded during the Cold War. After the terrorist attacks of September 11, 2001, for example, Congress passed the Homeland Security Act and Patriot Act, which expanded the national-security bureaucracy and strengthened the role of the intelligence community at home.[25] Lawmakers also authorized the use of military force to respond to 9/11, granting President George W. Bush sweeping powers to use "all necessary and appropriate force" to bring the perpetrators to justice – a decision that, as Karen Greenberg has argued, set in motion the erosion of certain elements of American democracy and civil liberties as well as beginning a decades-long era of warfighting in the Middle East, Central Asia, and North Africa.[26] The authorization for the use of force (AUMF) passed on September 18, 2001 remains in force today.

Then there is the social and economic rewiring of the US heartland, which has brought the national-security state closer to the everyday lives of ordinary Americans than ever before. Today, the Department of Defense owns or leases 26.1 million acres of land – roughly the same size as Kentucky, Virginia, or Ohio. This is a vast complex of bases, barracks, proving grounds, test sites, and other military installations – all manned by personnel who are under the near-total control of the executive branch. The Department of Defense is the largest employer in the United States, with nearly 3 million Americans on its payrolls. At the same time, the Pentagon spends hundreds of billions of dollars per year on research and development – a steady flow of outlays that has led the US government to become firmly entwined with the arms and aerospace industries, tech sector, higher education, and other branches of the economy. When the Department of Defense closes a base or ends a large contract, the implications for local communities can be devastating – so much so that the Pentagon has established an Office of Economic Adjustment to help local economies transition away from reliance on defense dollars whenever they face being cut off.[27]

Of course, most communities would prefer never to lose defense spending once they have become accustomed to receiving it. In 2015, researchers from the RAND Corporation estimated that the Army alone was pouring around $121 million per year into the median congressional district, supporting around 4,200 jobs in each area.[28] In light of such huge sums of money being at stake, it is easy to intuit how a powerful military-industrial complex has taken hold across the United States: a large number of local communities and their elected representatives – a plurality, perhaps – view themselves as having a direct economic stake in the continuance of high defense spending. For the most part, these "military towns" tend to have good relations with the armed forces.[29]

Over the course of the past eighty years, then, the military has become one of the most obvious ways that ordinary citizens interact with their government. Military bases are everywhere – and so are active-duty personnel and veterans. From 1940 to 1973 (when the military became an all-volunteer force), millions of US citizens were drafted into service. Even after the draft ended, the Department of Defense continued to be a major employer, with numbers of active-duty personnel peaking in the late Cold War at around 3.2 million in 1987. In 1980, veterans of the armed forces accounted for around 18 percent of the adult population. Today, the figure is around 7 percent – still a high proportion given that compulsory military service ended half a century ago.[30] Alongside voting, facing justice, paying taxes, and receiving entitlements, rubbing shoulders with active-duty personnel and veterans has become one of the most visible ways in which Americans interface with their government.

Path Dependence

Why has the US state grown along the lines described above? One plausible answer is that this is the size and shape of state that the United States needs to be secure. This would be a functionalist argument – an inference about the US state's purpose made with reference to the simple fact of its existence. But in reality, the national security state has not always made Americans more secure. What was once necessary during World War II and the Cold War is now ill-suited to a new and vastly different international context. The expansion of the US state in the realm of national-security policy has eroded civil liberties at home, devoured resources that could have been devoted toward human development, and plunged the US military into an endless series of wars and interventions.[31] Nor has the national-security state even kept America safe from external attack, as the 9/11 terrorist attacks laid bare. Viewed in this light, a functionalist explanation of the US state's political development would seem to fall short.

The concept of path dependence offers an alternative narrative of the national-security state's persistence. This is the idea that political actors are, to a significant degree, prisoners of past decision-making. While national leaders have real agency to make decisions over foreign policy, the set of options available to them – or that they perceive to be available to them – is always determined by what came before, including the sort of state that they find themselves steering.[32] From this view, what was once a grand strategy formulated to suit a specific set of external circumstances – namely, the geopolitical threat posed by the Soviet Union during the Cold War – has become a default setting, a language and logic for engaging with the rest of the world that is set in stone rather than subject to real scrutiny. It is the product of inertia rather than inspiration; a permanent feature of US government and politics rather than a policy that the people's representatives have arrived at through a process of careful deliberation.

As Paul Pierson has noted, "single institutional arrangements, or sets of rules, often have a *monopoly* over a particular part of the political terrain."[33] In other words, it is simply not the case that Americans choose from a menu of options when it comes to organizing their foreign-policy bureaucracy. There is only one practicable option available to them – the one that has been in place for the past eighty years. Indeed, US citizens and their elected representatives are not even presented with alternative modes of organizing the foreign-policy bureaucracy, let alone estimates of whether these alternatives would be better suited to prevailing conditions at home and abroad. If they were, it might be expected that the size of the US state would contract as well as expand in line with changing international conditions – but this is not what happens.

But how does path dependence happen? Why do political actors find themselves locked into availing themselves of existing institutions and processes instead of feeling empowered to reshape their political environment? First, it is important to recognize that the designers of institutions purposefully make their preferred institutional arrangements hard to reform.[34] They make it costly for future actors to redevelop the institutional context, creating incentives for their successors to buy into the status quo. Pierson puts it well: "Actors do not inherit a blank slate that they can remake at will when their preferences shift or unintended consequences become visible. Instead, actors find that the dead weight of previous institutional choices seriously limits their room to maneuver."[35]

To be clear, change *can* and *does* happen under conditions of path dependence. But it tends to unfold slowly and in ways that do not disturb the underlying substrate – that is, reformers find themselves having to graft new structures and processes onto old ones. Scholars of American political development call this "layering."[36] When it comes to foreign policy, it is easy to identify this sort of layering having happened since 1991: bases get closed, but often in ways that protect local economic interests; Congress sometimes moves to exercise oversight over the intelligence community, but never challenges the fundamental principle of executive branch control; the defense sector has consolidated rather than shrunk in overall size; and drawdowns of overseas deployments sometimes happen, but affected troops are often relocated to other overseas bases rather than brought home. In layman's terms, political actors have managed to tinker with the national security state – but never have they come anywhere close to overhauling or overturning it.

Second, state institutions select for aspirants to public office that possess certain interests, ideas, skills, and capabilities. Thousands of people enter the US government each year. They have often spent years training for the opportunity to do so – as undergraduates, graduate students, interns, early-career professionals, and so forth. Over time, these public servants are socialized to appreciate the system that they have worked toward joining. Otherwise, they are "organized out" of the system and into some other profession. It would be irrational for public servants to go about dismantling the national-security state having spent so long working to gain entry. Only individuals comfortable with the broad contours of US foreign policy are likely to seek out a career as part of its operationalization and delivery. Those who are overtly hostile to militarism never choose public service as a career path.

Third, institutions generate narratives to justify their existence that can be hard to break with. The longer a set of institutional arrangements endures, the harder it is for actors within (and even outside) the system to countenance ideas that cut against those institutions' right to exist. Such ideas are especially powerful when they are professed by people whose personal and professional fortunes are tied to its continuation, or who are otherwise zealous about its cause. This is certainly the case with the national security state, which boasts no shortage of "true believers" who are willing to defend US militarism and challenge those who call for major reforms. As Richard Barnet observed in the 1980s, "One way to keep the policy choices within narrow limits is to challenge the motives of those who put forward alternatives." He went on: "In an atmosphere of permanent threat the distinction between dissent and disloyalty is often blurred in such a way as to set the limits of 'responsible' debate and to discredit ideas that veer too far from the orthodox consensus."[37]

To sum up, my argument is that domestic actors have created a set of institutions within the United States – initially in response to external conditions – that are now proving difficult to undo. It strains credulity to imagine that the United States would develop the same institutional structure all over again if the federal government were to be designed from scratch. America's national-security state persists not because it works, but because it would be enormously difficult to change. Perhaps even more fundamentally, many government insiders cannot even imagine what could possibly replace it.

The Role of Exogenous Shocks

The development of the national security state has not been linear, however. Even path dependent outcomes can happen in fits and starts, often as the result of unexpected events. Scholars of political science use the concept of "exogenous shocks" (and the related concept of "critical junctures") to make sense of this nonlinear, punctuated, and contingent evolution of institutional arrangements. Whereas path dependence explains why institutions and policies remain constant over time, the language of exogenous shocks and critical junctures provides a way to understand when and why big changes sometimes happen.[38]

Essentially, exogenous shocks are unexpected events that create openings for a certain historical trajectory to be disrupted. They lend political actors not just a *reason* to question established trends but also a *vocabulary* and sometimes a sense of *urgency* for ensuring that change happens. Sometimes, exogenous shocks are so severe that they upend what came before in a total sense, forcing political entrepreneurs to establish entirely new and different institutional arrangements. Usually, however, exogenous shocks are not quite so disruptive and, at most, provide leverage for political actors to push an agenda that they already wanted to pursue but which could not have attempted absent an exogenous change in circumstances.[39]

This was the case with the Japanese bombing of Pearl Harbor, for example, arguably the most important exogenous shock that affected the United States during the twentieth century. Some scholars suggest that FDR wanted to bring the United States into World War II even before the attack on Pearl Harbor and had been angling in this direction for several years.[40] It is possible to imagine a counterfactual scenario, therefore, whereby the United States entered the war even absent the Japanese attack on the Pacific fleet. But in the actual event, it was the attack on Pearl Harbor that gave FDR the justification he needed to declare war and mobilize the nation. It *matters* that Pearl Harbor happened. The precise contours of the Japanese attack impressed upon America's populus the absolute importance of being proactive in dealing with emerging threats, making it implausible to argue in US domestic politics that instability abroad could be ignored without risk accruing to the United States. As well, a fixation on "preparedness" was internalized across the US political system – part of the explanation for why the postwar National Security Act was so sweeping in its changes.[41] Without Pearl Harbor, these ideas might never have taken hold and the US state would have been dramatically different as a result.

The 9/11 terrorist attacks had a similar effect six decades later. President Bush did not provide any obvious indications that he would pursue an activist foreign policy prior to September 11, 2001. As Colin Dueck notes, the Bush administration spent the first part of 2001 moving US foreign policy away from the liberal internationalism of the Clinton years and toward a grand strategy of "realism."[42] But when the attacks happened – a violent shock to the US polity – they created a set of conditions that forced administration officials and ordinary citizens alike to reconsider their approach to international affairs. In theoretical terms, Dueck shows that Bush and his team *could* have responded to 9/11 in several different ways; there was nothing intrinsic about the terrorist attacks that mandated a particular strategic response. It was important, therefore, what administration insiders were saying and thinking – that is, *it mattered who they were*. As it turned out, those advocating for a muscular grand strategy of military primacy were especially well positioned to influence the President in the wake of 9/11. They had experience, positional power, and claimed to have compelling answers to the immediate problem facing America.[43] Ultimately, this is why Bush chose to invade Afghanistan, pursue regime change in Iraq, boost security assistance to regional partners in the Middle East and North Africa, and begin an era of "forever wars" that has yet to conclude – because his advisers and others in the political system were forceful in recommending such a course of action in response to the horrific tragedy of 9/11. As with the attack on Pearl Harbor, the point is that these sweeping changes to US foreign policy might not have happened without an exogenous shock to the domestic system; international events strengthened the hand of some actors while undercutting the arguments being made by others.

The 1948–1950 period can be considered another critical juncture, during which time US leaders – including President Truman – genuinely wrestled with the best approach to handling the Soviet Union.[44] If international conditions had been different, it is eminently possible that Truman might have withdrawn all or most of the forward deployments inherited at the end of World War II. But a series of external events conspired to make retrenchment impossible – or, at least, dangerous to attempt in geopolitical and domestic-political terms. As discussed in chapter 1, the United States faced a barrage of exogenous shocks in 1948–1950: a *coup d'état* in Czechoslovakia, the proclamation of the People's Republic of China, the Soviet detonation of an atomic bomb, and North Korea's invasion of South Korea. It is now known that President Truman had decided to authorize the NSC-68 strategy document, which laid out the broad contours of a grand strategy of containment, sometime before the North Korean invasion of South Korea. But Truman nevertheless waited until after the outbreak of the Korean War before signing NSC-68 into policy because he judged this to be the most propitious time to sell the strategy to a political class and general public that might otherwise have been skeptical. The bottom line is that, absent external events – which, taken together, amounted to a *significant* worsening of the international environment – it is questionable whether Truman would have chosen a grand strategy of broad-based containment or authorized the continued development of a national security apparatus capable of waging a global contest for supremacy against the Soviet Union. He might, instead, have continued with demobilization or pursued some other means of engaging with the outside world. America would have been different as a result.

Other exogenous shocks do not so much cause a change in US political behavior as they serve to "discipline" or "condition" political actors, reminding them to stay on the beaten path of primacy. This was true in 1957 with the launch of Sputnik, which provoked a wave of anxiety in the United States and served to caution the Eisenhower administration against any policies that might be construed as being "soft" on the Soviet Union. It was also the case in 1979, when the Soviet invasion of Afghanistan and the Iranian Revolution seemed to demonstrate the folly of *détente* with Moscow, providing a compelling rationale for why a military buildup was essential to secure US national interests and preserve global stability.

Other examples might include Islamic State terrorist group's march on Baghdad in 2014, which forced President Obama to recommit troops to Iraq (having exited the country in 2011); the Taliban takeover of Kabul in 2021, which served to remind US leaders of the domestic-political risks associated with withdrawing from warzones; and the Russian invasion of Ukraine in 2022, which seems to have impressed upon Americans just how dangerous the international environment can be – and just how real are the prospects of one day facing off against a nuclear-armed rival like Russia.

Temporal Sequencing

The final concept introduced in this chapter is that of temporal sequencing. In short, temporal sequencing draws analytic attention to the fact that timing matters – that the same event will have a different social and political impact depending upon the historical context.[45] As a general rule, for example, it becomes harder to veer from path-dependent trajectories the longer the path is trodden; being driven toward a path-dependent outcome can be avoided early on, but ruts are difficult to escape after a lengthy period of time has elapsed. Even exogenous shocks can have less of a disruptive effect upon path-dependent trajectories once the equilibrium has been firmly established and domestic actors lose a sense of imagination for how things could be done differently. In other words, it matters when things occur – when crises happen, when ideas are advanced, and when efforts are made to reform political institutions.

Pearl Harbor would not have elicited the same response from US decision-makers if it had happened in 1901 instead of 1941, for example. The context mattered. In 1901, it is plausible that the United States might have retrenched from East Asia in response to an external attack – that is, it could have been beaten back by a hostile power. By 1941, however, this was unthinkable. Similarly, it mattered that the 9/11 terrorist attacks happened in 2001 and not some earlier time in US history. In 2001, the United States was already vastly forward deployed across the Greater Middle East, with decades of experience fighting in the region. There was no Soviet Union to deter the United States from pursuing wars of regime change, and the US military was not concurrently fighting any other major wars that might have divided the nation's attention and resources. For these reasons, invading and occupying Afghanistan and Iraq were practicable options in 2001–2003 in a way that should not be taken for granted. The United States could not have launched these wars of choice at an early time in history, and it may not be able to pursue similar such policies in the future.

One specific way that temporal sequencing matters is with regard to the development and coherence of groups who are invested in the preservation of the status quo. In this sense, temporal sequencing is similar to what Skowronek calls "political time" – the idea that a political actor's room for maneuver is heavily conditioned by the context within which they operate.[46] For example, during the late 1930s and early 1940s, President Roosevelt found himself surrounded by a political class that was split between interventionists and noninterventionists. He could count on the support of most interventionists when trying to engineer America's entry into World War II, but he could expect nothing but obdurate opposition from the anti-interventionist bloc, who worked assiduously to prevent FDR from steering the nation toward war. This affected how the President proceeded – quietly, subtly, and sometimes in absolute secrecy. By the early 2000s, by contrast, almost the entirety of the US political class was well used to primacy as an operational grand strategy. After 9/11, it was not a hard sell for President Bush to convince Congress of the need to invade Afghanistan. Even the invasion of Iraq, which had little to do with the 9/11 attacks, enjoyed considerable support in Congress and the public at large.

Other examples of the importance of temporal sequencing abound. Consider the effect that the so-called "loss" of China in 1949 had upon US politics. Scholars argue that it likely taught Eisenhower, JFK, and LBJ – especially the latter two, perhaps, as fellow Democrats – that they must never allow themselves to be accused of "losing" a country to communism. This played a role in Cuba policy and conditioned American participation in the Vietnam War.[47] But the perception of having "lost" China would not have been as important if it had happened in the 1910s or 1920s; nobody accused President Harding of having "lost" Russia to the Bolsheviks, for example, even though he was president in 1922 when the Russian Civil War finally came to an end. Or consider the examples of Reagan's withdrawal from Lebanon (1983–1984) and Clinton's exit from Somalia (1994). These were two instances of retrenchment from active warzones that were undertaken with low political costs at home – and, indeed, were quite popular domestically – yet in the decades that followed, US leaders have become much more reluctant to pull the plug on failing or costly interventions. The concept of temporal sequencing can help to account for why similar events can have such drastically different impacts upon domestic politics at different junctures.

Viewed through the lens of temporal sequencing, the task facing restrainers in the United States today is foreboding. As has been discussed, the United States has been accustomed to military primacy for decades; few Americans alive can remember a time when their country was not fighting wars overseas. To suggest a programmatic foreign policy of retrenchment to Americans today is to suggest a new and radically different approach to foreign affairs than any of them have ever experienced, a dramatic departure from a long-standing status quo. Calls for retrenchment can therefore come across as anachronistic and divorced from the reality of America's contemporary experience, throwbacks to a bygone era (the pre–World War II world) that is difficult to imagine today. In other words, restrainers are making their arguments at a disadvantageous political time.

One implication is that restrainers must not be fooled into believing that America can simply turn back the clock to an era in which the country pursued a more circumscribed world role. It is true that US history provides instances of leaders who warned against excessive militarism and practiced forms of anti-interventionism – Thomas Jefferson, John Quincy Adams, Calvin Coolidge, and Herbert Hoover, for example. But restraint is not a strategy that the United States can simply revert to implementing. The point about path dependence is that you cannot easily go backwards to explore paths that were once available. The only way is forward. The past can be invoked for illustrative purposes, but it does not provide anything useful in terms of a blueprint for how to implement retrenchment today or in the future. The country has changed since then. For retrenchment to be made viable, it must change again.

Conclusion: The (Militarist) State We're In

Applying the concepts of stateness, path dependence, exogenous shocks (and critical junctures), and temporal sequencing to the US case can help to clarify the chances of America undergoing a strategic adjustment in favor of retrenchment and restraint. For the most part, the concepts seem to clarify that military primacy is a fairly stable grand strategy that will not easily be budged. After all, the US state was built for the purpose of implementing military primacy; path dependence has proven to be a strong, stabilizing force in US foreign policy; powerful exogenous shocks such as 9/11 have conditioned America's political class to "stay the course" in terms of a primacist grand strategy; and the country seems to be only remotely connected to earlier periods in its history when retrenchment was a more viable policy choice.

But describing the situation in the terms above, though dire at first blush, can actually serve to alter the political status quo, not just capture it. For as John Gerring has pointed out, descriptive inference is a value-laden exercise.[48] To describe the world as being a certain way is to insist on clarity about *what is* and what *is not*. By deduction, good description invites readers – scholars, analysts, concerned citizens – to draw implicit comparisons with how the world could otherwise be. In this sense, informed and analytical description can be a clarion call for others to evaluate the status quo when otherwise it might have gone unchallenged or even unnoticed.

What can be learned from rendering America's national security state as an artifact, something that endures for reasons other than its suitability for current conditions? There is at least some potential that such an exhibition could resonate with reformist groups inside the United States today. The failures of the so-called forever wars – the debacles of Afghanistan and Iraq, for example – have fostered deep skepticism about overseas intervention. Younger generations of Americans in particular seem to be disillusioned with global leadership as a national ambition, and appear primed to imagine a less activist foreign policy. Moreover, the international context is changing to become less hospitable to policies of overseas intervention. It might soon become impossible (if it has not already) for US leaders to order the sort of military missions that were carried out during the 1990s and early 2000s. Combined, these discernible trends in domestic and international politics create conditions that are arguably propitious for a major strategic adjustment. Telling the truth about how and why the US state exists – and how it could be made differently – will be essential for such a transformation to unfold.

Of course, there is good reason for pessimism – not least of all because America has been here before. In the wake of the

Vietnam War, the public similarly turned against a failing war and Congress wrested some powers back from the presidency when it came to foreign policy. But the so-called Vietnam Syndrome did not result in a major reorientation of US grand strategy. On the contrary, it was followed by the Carter and Reagan buildups (responses, in part, to the international conditions of the late 1970s and early 1980s). And in any case, the Vietnam Syndrome – if it was ever real at all – was comprehensively exorcised from the US polity after the First Gulf War. This means that proponents of retrenchment should be cautious about overinterpreting apparent trends in conditions at home and abroad. Even if there is an opening to push for a major strategic adjustment, it must be attempted in a thoughtful and whole-of-society manner. As argued at the outset of the book, alterations to American grand strategy will have to be made in conjunction with reforms to domestic politics. This is the only way to avoid the United States reverting to what has become its default mode of operation: military primacy.

But if Americans are ever going to imagine and implement a new grand strategy, they must begin by developing a conceptual understanding of how and why they have become encumbered with the present one. The concepts outlined in this chapter go some way toward assisting in the development of such an understanding. The concepts are helpful because, without them, it would be difficult to make sense of the dramatic changes that have been wrought on the US political system since 1941. The rest of this book will do two things. First, it will explain in more detail how domestic inflexibility and myopia have combined with international conditions to produce the situation whereby the US state has been hardwired to pursue military primacy. Second, however, it will provide an argument for how the country might be jolted or persuaded to take a different path.

4

America's Primacists

States do not run all by themselves. They are run by people. It matters who these people are, what beliefs they hold, and which domestic constituencies they tend to represent. In the previous chapter, I argued that much of the US state's foreign-policy architecture is the product of path dependence; a constellation of institutional holdovers from past eras, which current officeholders are dissuaded from attempting to overturn. But path-dependent explanations of politics and foreign policy do not dismiss the role of human agency. Far from it. On the contrary, the concept of path dependence draws attention to the ways in which people – whether acting as individuals or in groups – make strategic decisions under conditions of inherited constraints. In this chapter, I begin the work of cataloguing the various groups that stand to benefit from US primacy and who either mobilize in support of overseas military dominance or else quietly acquiesce in the primacist project.

I begin by analyzing those groups in domestic society that have *material* interests in the continuation of primacy as a grand strategy. These include local communities that have grown dependent upon military spending; arms manufacturers and aerospace firms; sectors of the economy that profit from international commerce, such as export-oriented industries; and the legions of bureaucrats whose livelihoods are tied to a continuation of the status quo. The point is not that these groups have illegitimate or cynical reasons for supporting primacist foreign policies. In a democracy, it is entirely reasonable for groups to advance their own interests. It becomes a problem, however, if vested interests are *too* successful at shaping politics – that is, if groups with rival material interests are excluded from the policy process entirely. Alas, something close to this has happened to the United States in the realm of foreign policy.

Moving beyond the material foundations of primacy, I also survey the role of *ideas* in pushing domestic groups to support interventionist foreign policies. I begin by discussing how the concept of "security" has evolved as an idea for making sense of the US relationship with the outside world. In the past, ideas about security were narrow in scope, focusing attention almost exclusively on the relationship of the United States to its military competitors. Today, however, ideas about security have stretched such that American foreign policy is supposed to manage any number of "threats" to the United States, its people, and its values. At the same time, campaign groups have emerged to encourage the US government to use its preponderant power for the purpose of exporting certain values. I call these groups "moral movements" because they are animated by ideational or ideological commitments rather than pure material self-interest. The section concludes with a discussion of ethnic lobbies – groups that often hold strong opinions about how and where the United States should use force abroad, even if their influence on foreign policy is sometimes exaggerated.

Next, I describe how support for militarism seems to have seeped into the broader public consciousness. The point here is that the main tenets of military primacy as a grand strategy enjoy widespread support across the political system, not just among those people who have the most obvious stake in its continuation. Stable pluralities of ordinary Americans view militarism as compatible with – and, in some cases, essential to – their national identity. The sacrality of defensive obligations to allied nations, deference to military leaders and veterans, and a firm (if selectively applied) belief in the capacity of the United States to "save" the world's downtrodden can now be considered core aspects of America's political culture. In this context, it is difficult for leaders to advance agendas of retrenchment for fear of looking out of step with society.

Taken together, these features of US domestic politics constitute the (micro)foundations of a militarized and interventionist foreign policy. They explain why individuals – leaders and laypeople – continue to tread the path of primacy instead of resolving to do the hard work of fashioning a different world role for the United States. Simply put, programmatic attempts at retrenchment are doomed to failure in the present context because there are too many Americans who profit from militarism, who regard primacy as a means of promoting their values abroad, or who would view across-the-board retrenchment as an assault on their sense of national identity.

The Profits of Primacy

America's grand strategy of military primacy is a gargantuan effort, requiring over $850 billion in annual funding and the labor of millions of people, active-duty service personnel and civilians alike. Inescapably, this arrangement creates economic winners – groups that have direct material incentives to uphold or expand America's sprawling overseas presence.

The "Gunbelt"

Perhaps the most obvious set of interest groups with a stake in US primacy are those connected to the so-called "military-industrial complex." Coined by President Eisenhower in his Farewell Address, this term is meant to describe those economic, bureaucratic, and political interests that benefit from high defense spending.[1] The economic elements of the military-industrial complex can be thought about in sectoral terms, with certain industries benefiting more than others from the steady flow of defense dollars. The arms industry, of course, receives much of its revenue from the Department of Defense (in addition to certain foreign governments, with the approval of Washington). But other industries also receive large quantities of defense dollars for the purposes of research, development, innovation, and manufacturing. Such industries include aerospace, engineering, microelectronics, information services, and more.

In the past, the federal government controlled most of the arms manufacturing that took place in the United States.[2] But over the past fifty years, the trend has been toward privatization and consolidation.[3] Today, there are five big defense contractors: Lockheed Martin, RTX, Northrop Grumman, Boeing, and General Dynamics. Smaller firms include L3Harris Technologies, HII, Leidos, Amentum, and Booz Allen Hamilton. These firms – or, people connected with them – contribute nontrivial amounts of money to politicians' campaign funds. In 2020, for example, the defense sector poured around $50 million into candidates' war chests. The top recipient was Mike Rogers (R-AL), then the ranking member on the House Armed Services Committee. The second-top recipient was Ken Calvert (R-CA), chair of the Committee on Appropriation's subcommittee on defense. That year, the defense industry spent an additional $125 million on lobbying.[4]

But arms manufacturers and associated industries wield most of their power indirectly – such as by creating jobs and generating tax revenue for local communities – rather than via direct campaign contributions, which are comparatively small when judged against the political donations made by other sectors of the economy. As Michael Brenes has noted, during the Cold War, both of America's political parties came to view high levels of defense spending as a way to spur economic growth and bolster the fortunes of localities around the United States.[5] An enlarged defense budget became one of the federal government's favorite instruments for redistributing wealth among US citizens. This was a shift from past practice. Before World War II, presidents had usually been pressured to rein in federal spending. From the 1950s onwards, however, the prevailing economic orthodoxy ("military Keynesianism") became that spending on the military – even during peacetime – would expand economic opportunities for ordinary Americans. This attitude was encouraged at the local level by "boosters" for communities across the United States, who petitioned for defense dollars to be invested in their region. Whole cities were built on the back of high government spending – a patchwork of defense-dependent communities that stretched across almost the entire country.[6]

Viewed from this perspective, America's "gunbelt" can be mapped geographically as well as sectorally. Some regions benefit handsomely from high levels of military spending whereas others receive no or only modest investment from the Department of Defense. Those who miss out on defense spending tend not to be aware of their status as relative "losers." But the "winners" are clear-eyed about how much they benefit from the Pentagon's largesse. Indeed, some towns and cities are now almost entirely dependent upon direct or indirect funding from the Department of Defense. In places like Colorado Springs, for example, military spending accounts for as much as 40 percent of the local economy.[7] In 2020, defense dollars accounted for 11.3 percent of Virginia's GDP. The figure was 8.5 percent for Hawaii, 8.2 percent for Connecticut, and 7 percent for Maryland. The largest absolute dollar amounts were spent in Texas ($83 billion), Virginia ($64 billion), and California ($61 billion).[8]

Bureaucratic Interests

The bureaucracy constitutes another powerful set of interests that are heavily biased against retrenchment. The Department of Defense is the largest employer in the world, with just under 3.5 million employees as of 2020.[9] This means that the US military pays the wages of around 1.5 percent of America's adult population. Although workers at the Department of Defense have a wide range of political opinions, what unites them as government employees is an overall interest in maintaining the status quo as it relates to their livelihoods – especially at the highest levels of decision-making. There is nothing inappropriate about bureaucrats being disposed toward the status quo. Scholars of public choice have long shown that policy insiders tend to have a strong preference for things to continue as they are. "Almost by definition," explains Dan Drezner, "bureaucrats are uncomfortable with radical deviations from their standard operating procedures."[10] Those who have trained their whole careers for a job inside the US foreign policy bureaucracy obviously have a vested interest in securing the health and vitality of their workplace and its core mission.[11] It would be irrational for America's army of national-security bureaucrats to support a radical and unpredictable overhaul to the defense establishment.

At the highest levels of government, primacist bureaucrats and their like-minded interlocutors in civil society are sometimes referred to as "the Blob."[12] Coined by former Obama administration official Ben Rhodes, the idea of the Blob is that there is an amorphous – but sticky, stubborn, and overwhelming – grouping of political operators in Washington that pushes for hawkish foreign policies. Members include high-level appointees, other political advisers, military officials of all ranks, and permanent members of the defense and diplomatic bureaucracies – all people whose training and intellectual milieus lead them to reflexively latch onto primacist solutions to foreign policy problems. The realist scholar Patrick Porter frames this impulsive gravitation toward primacism as "habit," which he defines as "collective ideas that come to seem obvious, axiomatic choices made from unexamined assumptions."[13] In no small measure, the foreign-policy and defense bureaucracies are the institutions within which these habits inhere; they are the repositories of primacist policies and stables for the training and incubation of primacist personnel.

The impact of bureaucratic politics is particularly evident when it comes to alliance politics. The United States was once wary of entering into permanent alliances with foreign nations. In his Farewell Address, George Washington had warned against exactly this sort of behavior. Even America's first military pact – with France, inked during the Revolutionary War – proved to be relatively short-lived. But since 1945, it has become verboten for US officials to discuss ending treaty-based alliances. In the abstract, this makes little sense. As Washington understood, basing foreign policy on "habitual fondness" is rarely a good idea. Far better for promises of mutual aid to be given as needed, in response to pressing emergencies and only under circumstances where the United States and a foreign nation share common interests. Yet bureaucrats today seem to be wedded to existing alliance structures for reasons of inertia rather than a hard-headed analysis of US national interests. It is a cardinal norm that America's bilateral alliances and collective security obligations can never be junked, regardless of what these institutions might contribute to US national security. As a result, the United States is hobbled from even *rebalancing* its existing obligations (such as by shifting focus from the Middle East to the Indo-Pacific, as so many analysts think necessary), let alone contemplating *cuts* to its overseas commitments – further evidence that America's strategic posture has become fastened in place due to inertia. Such attitudes fit Porter's definition of "habit" down a tee: an axiomatic and unflinching belief that the United States cannot justifiably shed alliance commitments in the modern age. As will be discussed in chapter 5, America's foreign-policy bureaucrats routinely intervene to uphold these norms and otherwise ensure that extended deterrence as a standard operating procedure goes uninterrupted.

Economic Internationalists

In all countries, there are sectional interests whose economic prosperity depends upon access to international markets. These stylized "internationalists" can be contrasted with sectional interests whose economic fortunes depend more upon domestic markets ("nationalists"), and who might even stand to suffer from too much integration into the world economy. In general, internationalists include export-oriented industries, firms that depend upon access to cheap imports and globalized supply chains, and investors who have an interest in maintaining favorable political and security conditions wherever their overseas investments might be located. Nationalists, on the other hand, tend to be those sectors of the economy that are import-competing, sell their wares primarily to domestic consumers, or prefer to see capital invested at home rather than abroad.[14]

All things being equal, economic internationalists have much more of a stake in their government using its power and influence to bring about favorable conditions abroad. In most countries, this does not mean much because the overwhelming majority of governments do not have the capacity to dictate what happens beyond their borders. In the US case, however, the state has enormous influence over what happens overseas. Since World War II, America's economic internationalists have supported using the power of the federal government to exert influence over foreign lands. Economic interests help to account for the Cold War strategy of containment, for example, which was waged for the express purpose of preserving an open world economy at the behest of groups inside the United States.[15] At every juncture during the Cold War, the maxim was that domestic prosperity would suffer if the United States did not use the power of its government to ensure favorable political and security conditions abroad – in Europe and East Asia at first, but later in the Persian Gulf as well.

This long stretch of internationalist domination over the US government is somewhat anomalous. In the past, internationalists and nationalists were more evenly split in terms of their influence over the federal government. This led to leaders in Washington sometimes adopting foreign policies that served the interests of economic internationalists but at other times placing strict limits on the exercise of state power abroad. The US government waged the so-called Banana Wars in defense of the economic interests of firms such as the United Fruit Company, for example, yet President Harding won election in 1920 on a platform of opposing the occupation of Haiti and the Dominican Republic – a more restrained foreign policy that cannot be understood outside of the context of nationalist influence over US foreign policy. As late as the mid-twentieth century, in fact, nationalist-oriented coalitions served as a serious counterweight to internationalists in Washington.[16]

Beginning in the 1940s and 1950s, the domestic balance of power shifted decisively in favor of the internationalists. One reason for this is that America's traditional economic rivals in Western Europe and East Asia were devasted by World War II, leaving US-based manufacturers with little competition from foreign firms. At the same time, American companies were eager to sell abroad: having benefited from high domestic demand during the war years, US producers needed foreign consumers to purchase their goods once wartime demand began to slacken. Another reason is that the economic aid dispensed to Western Europe in the late 1940s as part of the Marshall Plan was "tied" in the sense that recipients were required to spend much of it on US goods. This, too, created opportunities for US firms to focus on exports. As well, the postwar economic environment created lucrative investment opportunities for holders of capital in the United States, who anticipated high returns from participating in the rebuilding of allied economies. In short, a broad cross-section of the American economy stood to gain from Washington's active participation in the reconstruction of an open world economy during the early postwar period, a constellation of interests that helps to explain the Truman administration's decision to pursue rearmament and "deep engagement" with European and East Asian allies in the late 1940s and early 1950s.[17]

For the most part, economic internationalists have remained preponderant in US domestic politics since the early Cold War – although, as Peter Trubowitz has illustrated, the geographic heartlands of the internationalist coalition has shifted over time from the industrial Northeast to the so-called "Sunbelt" in the southern and western portions of the United States.[18] There is nothing inevitable about economic internationalists being dominant in US politics, however. Indeed, in recent decades, their influence has been called into question as domestic attention has shifted to focus on the negative consequences of globalization: import-competition, deindustrialization, deunionization, environmental challenges, the vulnerabilities posed by integrated global supply chains, and so forth. The perilous position of economic internationalists was laid bare during the Trump era, with Trump making opposition to globalization (or "globalism") a central plank of his successful 2016 presidential campaign. In office, Trump initiated a costly trade war with China, pulled out of negotiations to form megaregional trading blocs in Europe and the Asia-Pacific, condemned companies who invested abroad, and otherwise rejected the central tenets of economic openness and internationalism. Even President Biden, who appointed a team of policy advisers much closer to the political center ground than the Trump administration, rejected the idea of all-encompassing free trade agreements in favor of promoting targeted instances of economic coopera-tion that would bolster the fortunes of workers and consumers.

The Ideational Foundations of Primacy

In addition to these material interests in favor of military pri-macy and international activism, a potent constellation of ideas has emerged to undergird America's global garrison state. To be clear, these ideas are not divorced from ("exogenous to") the interests described above – that is, they do not exist in the ether, unmoored from material concerns. On the contrary, some ideas about US power and purpose are closely related ("endogenous") to perceptions about America's core interests. Analytically, it can be hard to separate the two. But whatever their precise relationship, it seems clear that material interests and ideational factors have become reinforcing pillars of the grand strategy of primacy.

Ideas about Security: Horizontal and Vertical Expansion

Consider, first, the evolution of ideas about US national security. In the mid-twentieth century, national security was defined in relatively narrow terms to mean the freedom of the nation-state from armed attack by a rival power. Over the course of the Cold War, however – and even more so since the 1990s – the United States has tended to conceptualize security in broader terms. This stretching of security as a concept has coincided with an expansion of America's perceived security interests – and, in turn, an enlargement of the universe of issues for which US leaders reach for military solutions. This expansion has been both horizontal and vertical.

The horizontal expansion of security as a concept refers to the identification of security concerns over space and place. The geographic limits of US security interests were vigorously debated in the post–World War II era, with some such as Herbert Hoover and Robert Taft calling for hemispheric defense ("fortress America") and others such as Arthur Vandenberg insisting that, because the Pacific and Atlantic oceans had "ceased to be moats," the United States must maintain forward deployments to keep America safe. In other words, leaders disagreed on whether the United States could ensure national security by simply guarding the country's borders and immediate neighborhood, or whether the pursuit of national security led inexorably to Washington adopting an active interest in the stability of regions far from America's shores. As described in chapter 1, postwar internationalists like Vandenberg ultimately won this debate in the sense that Washington came to define its security interests as extending halfway across the European continent and all along the maritime rim of East Asia.

During the Cold War and after, analysts and officials continued to expand the horizontal definition of America's security interests. Concepts like the Domino Theory were invoked to convey the idea that national safety depended upon whether South Vietnam and other small countries could be kept free from communism. In 1980, President Carter declared that the security of the Persian Gulf region was a "vital interest" of the United States. Today, Ukraine's defensive against Russia is viewed as a national security exigency by many US leaders, while others insist that a Chinese invasion of Taiwan would similarly imperil America's national security despite Taiwan being more than 6,000 miles away from the continental United States. The language of national security is also invoked to justify the never-ending counterterrorism missions formerly grouped together as the Global War on Terror, from Niger in West Africa to Yemen on the Arabian Peninsula and beyond.

The horizontal expansion of US national security echoes the concept of "turbulent frontiers" once used to describe the paranoia of British imperialists about the security of their colonial holdings.[19] Even though the homeland is safe and secure, America's overseas garrisons face grave danger on an almost continual basis – and it is these forces that require defense from hostile actors. Small wonder, then, that people in the United States feel insecure: their armed forces have been deployed abroad across an immense geographic expanse, deliberately placed in the vicinity of wrongdoers whom the US military has been ordered to kill, contain, suppress, or deter. In short, the United States has arrogated to itself the responsibility of policing insecurity on a constant basis – in Europe, the Asia-Pacific, Central Asia, Middle East, and North Africa – and, in doing so, has chosen to place its personnel in or adjacent to active warzones. It is impossible to understand the US perception of national insecurity today outside of this context.

To be clear, this perpetual state of confronting insecurity is fully endorsed by members of the US political class. America's global military footprint was long ago normalized as a feature of the nation's foreign policy. Moreover, there is at least some evidence that the general public has bought into America's horizontal redefinition of its national security interests, too. One paper by Paul Musgrave and Steven Ward, for example, found that the American public has internalized the necessity of alliance commitments, viewing such international security obligations as evidence of national interests being at play rather than, say, a policy choice that could be made differently. In their words, "security commitments and forward-deployed military assets may *produce* ideas about what constitutes the national interest – which raises serious ethical and strategic questions about their use."[20]

The vertical expansion of security interests refers to the redefinition of security to include nonmilitary threats.[21] In the mid-twentieth century, the logic and language of security was reserved for discussing how a nation-state could be kept free from armed attack. But in recent decades, the concept of security has been applied to make sense of other issues, too, such as the health of America's relationship to world markets ("economic security"), reliable access to sufficient quantities of fuel ("energy security"), human rights at home and abroad ("human security"), and ecological challenges ("environmental security"). According to Andrew Butfoy, some of the loudest proponents of expanding the concept of security to include nontraditional security issues were motivated by a desire to "rein in" military planners and emphasize that nonmilitary tools of statecraft were essential to improving America's external environment. Ironically, however, the result was the opposite: "Since more things could now be given a security label, it was easier to think the occasions for utilizing defence assets could be multiplied."[22]

Today, then, the term "national security" refers to a blurry and ill-defined range of threats to the United States that exist across space and a multitude of dimensions. There is still a focus on deterring aggression against the homeland, of course, but America's national-security state is also charged with making the nation resilient against "new" security challenges such as hostile nonstate actors, failed states, errant WMD programs, organized crime, environmental degradation, public health, drugs, human trafficking, human rights abuses, democratic erosion, and all manner of other issues. As Butfoy explains, this shift in ideas about national security – essentially, a broadening of the term to capture a limitless range of dimensions along which the United States wants to order the rest of the world – has happened alongside a parallel shift in how America fights its wars. With the rise of remote warfare ("smart weapons"), leaders in Washington find it easier to order the US military into action because they anticipate a much lower likelihood of being accused of recklessly putting American lives in harm's way.[23] The advent of drone warfare only worsens this problem.

What concrete influence does the horizontal and vertical expansion of ideas about security have on US foreign policy? For one thing, the horizontal expansion of security creates "rhetorical traps" to prevent instances of retrenchment from coming to fruition or even being suggested in the first place.[24] Once overseas territories have been brought under the purview of "national security," it follows that support for retrenchment is tantamount to endangering the homeland itself. The distinction between the United States proper and its allies and partners abroad is effectively erased; defending a US garrison in Niger is described in the same language as the defense of Guam or Hawaii. In effect, overseas deployments have been rendered as extensions of the US state. As such, these garrisons must be protected as a matter of core national security. Whereas it might otherwise have been possible to construe attacks on US forces abroad as predictable outcomes of deploying to (or adjacent to) warzones – that is, the fault of bad policy – the language and logic of national security encourages people to view them as unjustifiable assaults on the United States, period. There is little room for nuance, and even less space for debating whether retrenchment (the removal of overseas forces from threatening situations) might be a better solution.

The vertical expansion of security interests, meanwhile, serves to affect US foreign policy by creating a logic for the national-security state to assume ever more responsibility for keeping America "safe." In recent decades, the military and cognate organs of government – for example, the Department of Homeland Security – have annexed new issue areas to their area of expertise, ensuring that everything from human rights and economic development to disaster relief and democracy promotion are now central tasks of the US military. The armed forces have been used in response to migration "crises" on the US–Mexico border and are regularly touted as a viable means by which the United States could end the problem of drug trafficking from Mexico. This expansion of the military's *raisons d'être* serves to insulate the military against cuts, of course, but also helps to cement the grand strategy of military primacy in the sense that the national-security state is in control of policy domains that otherwise could have been left to nondefense bureaucracies more agnostic about the overall grand strategy of the United States. As it is, the Department of Defense has acquired legions of new personnel, all with specialist expertise, who have been charged with the development of security policy across all manner of policy areas.

The Moral Movements

Not all proponents of military primacy are motivated by security concerns, however. Others are interested in manipulating the outside world for ideological reasons. These are what I call the "moral movements" in favor of primacy – groups that argue for the US government to use its enormous power and influence to promote certain values abroad, such as democracy, human rights, freedom of religion, or anticommunism. Ideas about the ethical dimensions of US foreign policy are held and propagated by a wide range of groups, from loose elite-level assemblages such as liberal internationalists and neoconservatives to more tightly organized grassroots movements and nonprofits.

Ideology played a major role in the foreign policies of the Progressive Era. The Progressives envisaged a grand purpose for the United States – an activist world power capable of spreading freedom, democracy, and self-determination to white Europeans, while also bringing "good governance" to nonwhite populations. To be sure, Progressives like Woodrow Wilson were opposed in domestic politics by those who abjured global ambitions, thought the peoples of the Caribbean and Pacific should be free to determine their own fates, and preferred that America remain apart from the corrupt "Old World." And not all Progressives were imperialists: the Women's Peace Party and Women's International League for Peace and Freedom, for instance, are examples of reformist movements in the Progressive tradition that did not call for the United States to extend political control over other territories and peoples. But what united all Progressives was their internationalist, civilizing, and messianic bent – a robust faith in the power of the US government to do good in the world.

Other moral movements have emerged on a more ad hoc basis. Before World War II, for example, antifascists clamored for the United States to engage in the war in defense of core US values.[25] They faced off against America First organizers, who also saw World War II through the lens of morality but thought the United States could best uphold its ideals through strict neutrality. During the Cold War, anticommunism became a powerful ideological force in US politics. And from the 1970s onwards, human rights groups have emerged to promote relief efforts in specific cases (e.g., the American Committee to Keep Biafra Alive) or more generally (e.g., the Children's Defense Fund and Helsinki Watch/Human Rights Watch).[26] Meanwhile, Christian internationalists have always been involved in shaping public opinion on the proper application of US influence abroad.[27] Of course, these groups do not have (and have never had) total influence over US foreign policy; America deals with nondemocratic regimes on a routine basis and has a checkered record of its own when it comes to upholding human rights.[28] But the United States is unique in having a powerful set of domestic actors who are willing to insist that their country can – and should – be a force for good on the world stage, including via the force of arms, *while at the same time* condemning Washington for grossly unethical and inhumane acts of its own. These moral movements can exert real power and influence at key moments.

To be clear, moral movements are not defined by shared values that all (or even most) people in the United States would regard as "moral" in the sense of good, right, or ethical. For example, America's past imperialists were guided by values that many people today would find utterly abhorrent – and, indeed, which offended the consciences of people at the time – yet holders of imperial and colonial ideas certainly viewed themselves as moral agents. From their perspective, it was the duty of white, Protestant, English-speaking Americans to settle North America and bring other ("lesser") peoples under their tutelage, including via overseas imperial expansion. These were outright racist, imperial, and colonial attitudes – but they were nevertheless the animating ideas behind US foreign policy for generations. The same goes for moral movements today: some people will agree with their values and others might vehemently oppose them, but all that matters for these groups to be considered "moral" agents is that they consider themselves to be motivated by an ideational (nonmaterial) cause of some description.

Ethnic Internationalists

Finally, there is some evidence that certain ethnic minority groups in the United States can be effective lobbyists for interventionist foreign policies. This is a controversial topic, and it would be wrong to overstate the influence of any ethnic lobby group on US foreign policy. But common groups mentioned in this regard include Cubans Americans, those of Eastern European descent, and members of the so-called Israel Lobby – recognizing, of course, that the latter label does not refer to a strictly *ethnic* lobby, but rather a posited aggregation of pro-Israel groups in American society who work (whether in isolation or in concert with one another) to pressure the US government to support the Israeli government on a range of issues.[29]

The power of these lobbies on US foreign policy is likely weak when viewed in the overall context of foreign policymaking. But it would be imprudent to ignore them altogether. Cubans in Florida, for example, have disproportionate influence over the politics of that state and have worked to oppose the normalization of relations between Washington and Havana. Meanwhile, there is some evidence that US politicians pushed for NATO enlargement during the 1990s in part because they wanted to attract the support of voters in the Upper Midwest with Eastern European heritage.[30]

To be sure, there are some cases of ethnic lobbies pushing for retrenchment or restraint. This was the case with Sudanese Americans during the Darfur conflict, who argued strongly against the US government using force to defend the Fur people, who were being persecuted by Khartoum and government-backed *Janjaweed* militia. For whatever reason, however, such instances of ethnic groups lobbying the US government to exercise restraint seem to be less frequent. It seems to be more commonly the case that ethnic lobbies argue for the United States to intervene abroad on behalf of coethnics in other countries. That said, there has never been any study to ascertain the overall influence of ethnic lobbies on US foreign policy in this regard, and so the relevance of ethnic groups should not be exaggerated.

America's Militarist Identity

Ideas about national security and values tend to influence foreign policy insofar as they are held by elites. But other ideas about US power and purpose are more popular in nature. As I have argued elsewhere, America's national identity has been remade by the experience of being massively forward deployed for eighty years.[31] Even if the United States initially went abroad for reasons of material self-interest, its citizenry has since accepted an array of ideas and narratives to make sense of and justify its continued forward deployments. Over time, the routinized performance of military primacy has engendered nothing less than a shift in America's sense of self. Simply put, the country's national identity has come to depend upon its overseas presence and expansive global role.[32]

Deference to Military Leaders and Veterans

As one illustration of this, consider the treatment afforded to US service personnel and veterans – America's warrior class. It is right and proper that military veterans are held in high regard for their service, of course, but there is a problem when trust in the military far exceeds trust in the elected institutions of government. Never in its history has the United States been seriously vulnerable to a military coup or dictatorship; civil–military relations have always been tilted in favor of the country's civilian leaders. But this should not be taken for granted. In one recent poll, 40 percent of Americans supported the idea of a "coup" in the United States in the event of there being "a lot of corruption."[33] Other data show that around 20 percent of millennials and adults in Generation Z believe that "dictatorship could be good in certain circumstances."[34] These are troubling findings, even more so in the context of the public having robust faith in the military.

As Peter Feaver has shown, the high levels of trust that Americans place in the military is largely explained by social desirability bias. That is, respondents to surveys *claim* to have confidence in the military because they think *other people* would disapprove if they expressed a contrary opinion.[35] In a sense, this is an even more troubling finding because it suggests that US citizens feel uncomfortable disclosing their true beliefs about the military; there is social pressure to conform as someone who is supportive of the country's armed forces.

A culture of uncritical respect for the military as an organization can be abused by politicians to generate support for interventionist policies. Research by Christopher Coyne and Abigail Hall suggests that the US government has, in the recent past, engaged in outright propaganda to build public support for the military and its overseas missions.[36] It is also a problem when serving or retired military personnel are afforded certain privileges that civilian leaders are not. Peter Feaver and Jim Golby highlighted this problem in a 2019 article that recalled a public spat between the Trump administration and journalists in the White House press corps. The episode involved John Kelly, a retired general and then President Trump's chief of staff, who had given a fiery press conference to excoriate journalists for criticizing the President's interactions with a fallen soldier's family. Kelly blasted the press corps, suggesting that those who had never served in the military had no right to criticize those who had. According to Feaver and Golby, Kelly's line of reasoning was pernicious: people associated with the military should not be exempt from political criticism, and any claims that military status ought to confer extra rights and privileges must be rejected as undemocratic.[37]

The United States used to have a strong antimilitarist tradition. But this is no longer the case. Now, former military leaders like James Mattis and Lloyd Austin are highly respected as leaders precisely because of their military bona fides. Despite some recent signs of decline, public trust in the military remains high with 60 percent of people having "a great deal" or "quite a lot" of trust in the armed forces.[38] It is possible that public support for the military will erode in line with demographic shifts or because of partisan attacks on the Pentagon's top brass – Republican displeasure at so-called "woke" practices becoming pervasive in the military, for example. But for now, America's overarching national identity still seems to be one that elevates the military above politics, much to the detriment of the country's democratic and republican credentials.

American Irridentism

Consider, too, a feature of US political culture that I call "American irridentism." Traditional irredentism is about the reclamation of "lost" territory or populations. The English word comes from the Italian phrase *Italia irredenta* ("unredeemed Italy"), a concept developed by Italian nationalists who dreamt of bringing all former Italian lands under the jurisdiction of Rome. For more than a century, the term has been used to describe the revanchist territorial claims of states and nationalist movements. The United States has no irridentist movement in this strict sense of the term. That is, there are no "lost" American territories that nationalists in the United States clamor for reincorporation into the US republic.

American irredentism is different. It lays claim not to foreign territory nor to overseas peoples based on kinship, but rather posits the *entire unfree world* as unredeemed and awaiting liberation. In this sense, it is a far more expansive version of irredentism than seen in any other country. American irredentism has no territorial bounds. All peoples languishing under the yolk of authoritarianism are deserving of incorporation into the US-led, enlightened, and "civilized" international order. Why do Americans think in this way? One explanation is that Americans benefit from believing the unfree world is yearning for liberation because such a narrative helps to justify the gargantuan and never-ending series of military interventions that their country has waged over the past eighty years or so.[39]

To help illustrate the power of American irredentism, it is instructive to imagine what lessons future leaders will draw from President Joe Biden's historic decision to pull US troops from Afghanistan in the summer of 2021. While it is impossible to know precisely how the Afghan exit will be viewed in years to come, one thing has already been made clear: that foreign policies of retrenchment must be handled with extreme caution, and perhaps are best avoided altogether. As late as June 2021, aspirants to political office in the United States would have been forgiven for believing that ending "forever wars" – especially the war in Afghanistan – was a good and popular position for them to take.[40] Of course, there were obvious political risks to supporting a withdrawal from Afghanistan due to the widespread expectation that the US-backed government in Kabul would fall to the Taliban without American forces on the ground. But few in the United States – whether in the political class or country at large – seemed to support pushing the Afghan War into a third decade of existence.

Yet as the late political scientist V.O. Key once argued, what matters most in politics is not current public opinion but future public opinion. And while pulling the plug on the Afghan War might have been popular during the early months of Biden's presidency, it did not remain popular for long. Even before Kabul fell to the Taliban on August 15, 2021, Biden was variously accused of ceding Afghanistan to Russia, China, and Iran; undermining America's credibility as an ally; giving a free pass to terrorists; and condemning Afghan women and girls to a life of hell.[41] Once the withdrawal was put into action, Biden's approval rating plunged below 50 percent for the first time in his presidency. Some legislators went so far as to call for his resignation or removal from office.[42] As the US editor for the *New Statesman*, wrote: "Is this a stain on Biden's presidency? Of course it is. Afghanistan saw a 47 per cent increase in civilian deaths in the first half of 2021. Afghan people are dying because the US is leaving."[43]

On the second anniversary of the pullout, the Republican Party posted on the social media site X [Twitter]: "Never forget President Biden is to blame for the Taliban's takeover of Afghanistan. No one else."[44] This was American irredentism in action – tropes about the tragic "loss" of a foreign country and the abandonment of a foreign population. Watching this unfold, tomorrow's leaders will have been given ample reason to reconsider whether forever wars are quite as intolerable as they had been led to believe. Indeed, a large slice of the US commentariat and political class seemed to be outraged that America's participation in the Afghan War had been ended. Why? At least part of the answer is that President Biden's Afghan exit fell afoul of the uniquely American form of irredentism – that is, the idea that foreign countries to which the United States has no territorial claim can nevertheless be lost and thus go "unredeemed" unless Americans are courageous enough to act in their defense.

As a brief aside, it is worth considering that American irredentism helps account for why so many governments around the world see the United States in threatening terms. Quite unabashedly, leaders in Washington view the citizens of foreign countries as not truly belonging to those other states; rather, the quintessential American view is that all human beings are united in a way that supersedes their national allegiance. America claims an implicit right to act in the interests of foreign populations even if it does not lay claim to sovereignty over them. From this view, there are universal values that trump principles such as national citizenship and loyalty to the state, and it is the right and proper responsibility of the United States to uphold these values in the face of oppressive (and illegitimate) foreign powers. To people around the world, this is an offensive way of thinking, little better than an imperial or colonial mindset. But to people in the United States, it has become hardwired into the national consciousness.

Signs of Erosion

The underpinnings of primacy described in this chapter are a powerful concoction of domestic interests, ideas, and identities. Taking stock can be sobering and discouraging for those who oppose military primacy. But as in chapter 3, there is normative value in seeing the domestic political landscape for what it is. For one thing, it is only once the domestic foundations of military primacy are known and understood that analysts can hope to discern whether, when, and why those foundations might be showing signs of cracks.

In fact, there are some indications that the domestic bases of primacy are beginning to wear thin. For one thing, there is growing skepticism about trade liberalization. This matters because the foundations for the entire edifice of US primacy were put in place in the 1940s and 1950s precisely to create the conditions for an open world economy. If economic integration is no longer something Americans value, then the question arises: Why are US forces still forward deployed for the purposes of defending economic partners, securing the freedom of the seas, and upholding a "rules-based" international order?

To be clear, my argument is not that US leaders should abandon economic globalization. On the contrary, as I explain in chapter 7, an open world economy is essential to American power, prosperity, and purpose in the twenty-first century. Those who call for protectionism are wrong about what is needed to help struggling workers and their families. But it is still the case that skepticism about economic openness could evolve into more general opposition to America's overall grand strategy, including militarism and interventionism. I discuss this more in chapter 6.

At the same time, there are some signs that people in the United States are losing trust in the military as an institution. This is important because no move toward downsizing the military can happen so long as the armed forces are an untouchable third rail in US politics. Ordinary people must believe that there is some merit to trimming the size of the military, that the various military branches "deserve" to be reduced in size, and that recalibrations of the military are not tantamount to being anti-American or some other such slur. As research by Golby and Feaver (cited earlier in this chapter) clearly suggests, there are some indications that these prerequisites are falling into place as trust in the military dwindles for a variety of reasons. Helping matters, no doubt, is the fact that increasing numbers of people associated with the military – especially organized groups such as Concerned Veterans for America – now appear to be more interested in retrenchment and restraint than they were in the past. This is partly because of the military's negative experience of the wars in Afghanistan and Iraq, which some veterans' groups now regard as follies (in 2019, a poll for Pew Research Center found that clear majorities of veterans believed both wars had been "not worth fighting").[45]

Finally, it is important to stress that ideas about America's national identity are not permanent. Rather, ideas inhere within populations, and populations shift over time. This means that demographics can play a role in what America thinks about itself and its proper relationship to the rest of the world. Generations such as the Greatest Generation (people born between 1900 and 1925), the Silent Generation (born between 1926 and 1945), and the Baby Boomers (1946 to 1964) grew up during eras defined by US interventions abroad – whether World War I, World War II, or the Cold War. They became accustomed to the United States fighting and winning wars against enemies that were incontrovertibly dangerous and tyrannical. These generations tended to have positive views of the military, and, if not veterans themselves, they likely had friends and family members who had served in the military given that each of these generations experienced compulsory military service at some point or another.

Today, however, not even all octogenarians were alive when the Japanese attacked Pearl Harbor. Only America's dwindling number of nonagenarians and centenarians will have any serious recollection of what life was like before World War II. This amounts to a vanishingly small segment of the US population. The overwhelming majority of Americans have grown up in a world where global military primacy is the norm, but without any direct recollection of how the condition of primacy came about, or for what purpose. For Americans born since the late 1980s, the most visible threats to US national security have been nonstate actors such as al-Qaeda, the Islamic State, and so-called "lone wolf" terrorists. What is more, the largest of America's wars since 1991 have been judged as failures. The war in Iraq became unpopular among a majority of Americans around 2006, and even the war Afghanistan – fought in response to the 9/11 terrorist attacks, and which enjoyed overwhelming public support at the outset – was regarded as a failure by the war's end.[46]

Against this backdrop of ignominious and unpopular wars, it seems highly likely that America's national identity will change again – especially in terms of the country's relationship to militarism and interventionism. Born between 1981 and 1996, for example, millennials have few (if any) childhood memories of the Cold War, having become adults around the time of 9/11. In 2016, researchers at the Hoover Institution found that, despite having lived through the wars in Afghanistan and Iraq, millennials had a very poor understanding of the US military and tended to be skeptical of the military "as an institution."[47] According to some commentators, Generation Z is even more opposed to militarism, much preferring diplomatic solutions to international problems.[48]

Taken together, these demographic shifts provide some reasons to believe that America's citizen-army of primacists might yet give way to a more pluralist domestic landscape. To be sure, the domestic foundations of military primacy are still strong: the state apparatus is robust and there is a powerful assemblage of people who benefit from primacy's continuation. Dislodging primacy will not be easy. But for all the reasons outlined above, the project of retrenchment and restraint is not altogether a lost cause.

Conclusion

When restrainers try to change the grand strategy of primacy, they must be clear about what they are up against: a
well-entrenched, well-networked set of interests, ideas, and
identities that have colonized the entire span of the US political system. There are groups who have material interests in
primacism – economic groups, bureaucratic groups, and so
forth. There are those who are driven to use US military power
to advance their own ideological agendas. And then there is
a broad constituency of Americans who have simply become
accustomed to US primacy and would be confused about
America's role in the world in the absence of an activist foreign
policy. While not immovable, this coalition of primacists is
formidable for the time being. In the next chapter, I turn to
discuss how groups with a vested interest in military primacy
hobble attempts to reform US foreign policy in practical terms.

5

Unfit for Peace

This chapter applies what has been covered in the previous chapters to shed light on some concrete examples of the United States failing to retrench. Drawing on the concepts of stateness and path dependence, in particular, I aim to illustrate my argument that the American state has developed in ways that make it wholly unsuited to adopting policies of retrenchment. On the contrary, the foreign-policy organs of the US government are hardwired against retrenchment. While there have been some high-profile instances of retrenchment in recent years, state structures and core personnel have stymied other proposals for retrenchment before they could get anywhere close to adoption. The result is inertia – the broad continuation of a grand strategy held over from the Cold War era.

Most examples of the "automatic rejection" of retrenchment likely go unobserved because outsiders are not privy to ideas that are never conceived, are not discussed, or are squashed behind closed doors. Sometimes, however, the process of ruling out retrenchment plays out in public. Such cases can be scoured for evidence of what might be causing the US political system to reject policies of retrenchment in a general sense. The evidence presented here – imperfect and illustrative as it might be – suggests that there is no single mechanism via which the state blocks proposals for sizable retrenchment. There is a constellation of forces at work, ranging from institutional design to bureaucratic politics to electoral incentives and more.

To impose some analytic order onto the varied and overlapping processes by which proposals for retrenchment are suppressed, I organize the chapter according to five stylized, ideal-type barriers to retrenchment that exist in US domestic politics: (1) the uneven distribution of authority between the legislative and executive branches, which affords wide-ranging war powers to the president at the expense of Congress; (2) electoral incentives, which more often encourage officials to maintain, expand, and use America's overseas garrisons rather than bring them home; (3) the influence of permanent bureaucrats and political appointees, who are much more likely to be invested in a perpetuation of the status quo than radical strategic adjustment; (4) the long shadow of forward-deployed military forces, which I argue makes it more tempting for presidents to use force than would otherwise be the case; and (5) the influence of nongovernmental actors (think tanks, academics, retired officials, and so forth) on the thinking of policy insiders.

The chapter concludes by arguing that all of these institutional factors function in concert to constitute a militarist "redoubt" inside the US political system – that is, a well-entrenched set of ideas, institutions, and personnel that serve to protect military primacy as an overarching grand strategy.[1] Few other policy positions are so well fortified inside government. Militarism is special in this regard. Even those proposals for retrenchment that are permitted to become policy are almost always met with political backlash at home. In any event, the larger issue is that the American state is most certainly not configured to permit the systematic and wholesale drawdown of overseas forces. In short, proposals for broad-based retrenchment are repugnant to the US state as currently constituted. The state's outward-facing organs were built to sustain primacy – not oversee its dismantlement.

Congress and the Imperial Presidency

The "imperial presidency" is the first and most obvious way that the US state has been restructured to support the foreign-policy superstructure that is military primacy. Developed by Arthur Schlesinger, Jr. in the 1970s, the concept of the imperial presidency captures the idea that the White House has amassed far more powers than the framers of the Constitution ever intended, especially in the realms of foreign policy and national security.[2] As described in chapter 3, there are several reasons for this shift in power from Congress toward the executive branch. Part of the explanation is that national security policy (as with other areas of public policy and administration) has become much more technical as time has worn on, and so requires the specialist expertise that only professional bureaucracies in the executive branch can offer. Another reason is that some elements of national security policy (especially when it comes to intelligence) are thought to necessitate secrecy, which, again, the executive branch is better placed to provide relative to the legislative branch. Finally, however, there is a prevalent argument that successive generations of legislators have intentionally ceded authority over security policy so as to relieve themselves of having to make difficult decisions over war and peace.[3]

In the past, Congress was not shy of restraining the presidency when it came to defense policy. In the 1930s, for example, the Neutrality Acts significantly reduced President Franklin D. Roosevelt's freedom of maneuver in the run up to World War II. There was certainly no prospect of FDR taking the United States into the war without congressional approval. But the Korean War was a turning point in the history of executive–legislative relations. When President Truman ordered US troops to defend South Korea against communist North Korea in June 1950, he did so without consulting Congress. What is more, most members of Congress acquiesced in the President's decision, with only a handful of legislators protesting about executive overreach.[4] The President, his advisers, and close allies in Congress are on record as discussing whether a congressional resolution might have strengthened the war effort in some way. But in the event, Truman's team settled on the argument that the President was authorized to fight a war on behalf of the United States if the military action in question had been approved by the newly created United Nations Security Council, of which the United States was a permanent member.[5]

Partly because there was so little pushback from Congress, the Truman administration's paltry justification for the extra-constitutional deployment of US forces to Korea was allowed to stand as a precedent. To be sure, lawmakers have since been called upon to authorize military action in Lebanon (twice), Vietnam, Iraq (twice), and Afghanistan, for example.[6] In 1973, Congress adopted the War Powers Act to insist that presidents must notify Congress about any decision to send US forces into battle and must also obtain legislative authorization in the event of such forces being militarily engaged for sixty days or more. But the Korean War nevertheless stands as a watershed moment in the history of US foreign policy. Since Korea, military actions without legislative approval have become the norm. As Charles Stevenson explains, "in the cases of military intervention in Somalia, Haiti, Panama, Bosnia, Kosovo, Libya and Syria, Congress failed to muster majorities for any decisive action for or against those conflicts," but the sitting president ordered the US military into action regardless.[7] On at least one occasion – during the Kosovo War in 1999 – a president has ordered the use of military force even when Congress has appeared to vote against it.[8] No president has ever recognized the constitutionality of the War Powers Act.

The formal institutions of the US government are clear: Congress has the power to declare war. It also has the authority to regulate the size of the armed forces and must approve all appropriations to fund the military. But as the case of the Korean War shows, the willingness of domestic actors to actually uphold the formal institutions of government is a variable. One of the most pernicious ways that officials have undermined the intent of the Constitution is when it comes to the definition of "war" itself. In 2011, for example, President Obama argued that he did not require congressional approval to wage a large-scale military intervention in Libya (which resulted in the overthrow of Muammar Gaddafi) because US forces would not be taking fire from an enemy force, but rather would be responsible for bombarding Libyan military positions from afar.[9] It was the same story in 2017, when President Trump ordered the military to bomb targets in Syria as punishment for the al-Assad regime's use of chemical weapons. Because the US military would not encounter any resistance from Syrian forces, the Justice Department reasoned, the airstrikes ordered by President Trump could not be considered an act of war.[10] The same legal advice holds that the president can order military action in cases where a clear national interest can be shown to exist.

By definitional fiat, then, the government has manipulated the constitutional order of the United States such that congressional approval is not required to authorize military engagements abroad so long as such interventions do not become sustained military campaigns that involve exchanging fire with a capable enemy, and do not exhibit a reasonable probability of escalation. If the president of the day expects that military force could be applied quickly, in a one-sided fashion, and without escalating into an uncontrollable conflagration – then such military actions are not considered "war" for constitutional purposes. This is a problem for several obvious reasons, not least of all because it opens the door to the presidency waging a never-ending series of military interventions across a limitless geographic expanse. Under a more common-sense definition of war – something like "the existence of a state of armed conflict between two or more sides," for example – the United States has been at war almost continuously since 1950, and never without a formal declaration of war from Congress, only a smattering of AUMFs.

What about those cases where the Congress has debated the wisdom of military action and lent its approval? Even here, the balance of power between the legislative and executive branches has been visibly lopsided. America's participation in the Vietnam War was authorized (from 1964 onwards) via the Gulf of Tonkin Resolution, for example, but this resolution placed no limits on what Presidents Johnson, Nixon, and Ford could do in pursuit of military goals in Southeast Asia. The text of the resolution bluntly stated that "Congress approves and supports the determination of the President, as Commander in Chief, to take all necessary measures to repeal any armed attack against the forces of the United States and to prevent any further aggression."[11] As such, it amounted to little more than a preemptive rubber stamp of future presidential decision-making.

The post-9/11 AUMF, too, was another blank check from Congress. Mirroring the language found in the Gulf of Tonkin Resolution, the text adopted on September 18, 2001 affirmed that "[t]he President is authorized to use all necessary and appropriate force against those nations, organizations, or persons he determines planned, authorized, committed, or aided the terrorist attacks that occurred on September 11, 2001, or harbored such organizations or persons, in order to prevent any future acts of international terrorism against the United States by such nations, organizations or persons."[12] For more than twenty years, presidents have relied upon this single sentence to justify the legality of warfighting from West Africa to Central Asia, including against terrorist groups that did not even exist at the time of the 9/11 attacks. Despite its fading relevance to contemporary security policy, Congress has never moved to repeal the AUMF passed in September 2001. Nor has Congress otherwise taken measures to restrict presidential authority in this area.

Finally, it is worth noting that the imperial presidency has a trump card when it comes to the implementation of military primacy – namely, the constitutional authority of the commander in chief to deploy and redeploy US troops abroad during times of peace. While it is unquestioned that the White House can order troop movements large and small so long as they do not constitute a declaration of war, there is often a fine line between *moving* troops abroad and *maneuvering* those forces into a conflict. At the time of the Gulf of Tonkin Resolution, for example, the United States had already placed more than 11,000 military advisers in South Vietnam, in addition to hundreds of Special Forces and a naval contingent in the South China Sea. Without US forces operating in the region, it would have been impossible for the USS *Maddox* to have encountered North Vietnamese naval forces in August 1964 (the incident that led to the Gulf of Tonkin Resolution being passed).

In January 1991, too, Congress voted to authorize the use of force against Saddam Hussein's Iraq – but only after President Bush had sent more than 500,000 US troops to the region in preparation for the war. Under such conditions, it was hardly likely that Congress would decline to authorize a war that the President had already begun fighting for all intents and purposes. More recently, the Bush, Obama, Trump, and Biden administrations have deployed increasing numbers of US troops to Eastern Europe and the Indo-Pacific in hopes of deterring Russian and Chinese aggression against US allies and partners, never with the express authorization of Congress (although lawmakers could always move to restrict funds for such missions if it was determined to do so). This practice of sending troops to friendly countries is never criticized as illegitimate or unlawful, yet arguably puts US forces in harm's way and opens up the possibility of conflict by daring adversaries to attack US personnel that have been placed in their vicinity. If violence is ever visited upon American forces deployed overseas, the president has absolute authority to use the full might of the US military to defend them.[13] This blurs the distinction somewhat between the movement of troops during times of peace and the act of joining or precipitating a conflict: sometimes, forward-deployed troops come under fire and the United States thus becomes embroiled in an armed conflict against its will. Does it not make some sense, then, for Congress to be involved in these decisions?

The framers of the Constitution intended that the chief executive should be able to respond with energy to external crises. Legal scholars mostly accept that the presidency even has a valid claim to extraconstitutional powers during moments of severe crisis and national emergency. But on everyday matters of national security policy, it strains credulity to suggest that the Constitution is supposed to authorize what has been described above: an unlimited right of the president to move hundreds of thousands of troops around the globe with the stroke of a pen, including to regions adjacent to active warzones; presidential authority to order targeted military strikes at will, so long as these are not expected to provoke a major conflagration; and a legislative body more accustomed to delegating war powers than playing a serious role in defining the purpose of military engagements. This is an institutional setup designed to make presidential warfighting easy. It bears little resemblance to the original constitutional design, which was meant to render wars of choice difficult for a president to undertake, and charged Congress with helping to ensure that this would be the case.

Elections and Party Politics

The distribution of war powers between the presidency and the Congress is an insufficient explanation for why the US government is set up to reject policies of retrenchment. After all, the expansive powers of the presidency could theoretically be used to reduce the US military footprint. No occupant of the White House has done this, however, because the prevailing set of political incentives encourage the exact opposite behavior. This is also why returning authority over defense policy to the legislative branch would not automatically mean fewer military interventions: members of Congress are just as often enthusiastic about overseas interventions as presidents. The challenge, then, is to understand the incentive structure that drives the behavior of elected officials and probe what might be done to encourage a different set of actions.

Electoral incentives are a major factor. In short, America's domestic political system promises handsome rewards to politicians who embrace status quo-oriented militarist policies while offering fewer incentives for elected officials to support a radical overhaul to US grand strategy. The electoral cycle even helps to explain presidential decision-making during conflict, with commanders in chief sometimes choosing to extend wars (and forgo opportunities for retrenchment) due to fear of losing votes.[14] Partly, this is a function of the two-party system. National security is a valence issue – that is, an issue upon which all sides agree, and over which political parties compete for reputations of resolve, robustness, and reliability. It would be far too risky for one political party to take a general stance against militarism or interventionism because doing so would expose them to being outflanked by their rivals, who would reap the electoral benefits of being made to look more hawkish ("stronger") as a result. They are thus heavily pressured to avoid making missteps that could be construed as anything approaching weakness.

More than anything else, America's political parties care about capturing the elected branches of the federal government. This requires them to be national organizations in search of votes from across the United States. To remain viable contenders for power in Washington, the parties must serve as interest-aggregators, knitting together broad-based coalitions from disparate groups located in every region of the country. The requirement to have pancontinental appeal all but ensures that the two political parties will be disposed toward high military spending and, by extension, inclined to accept the expansive foreign-policy ends that America's defense budgets are geared toward enabling. This is because – as has already been described at length in this book – the existence of a strong and well-resourced military establishment provides so much of America with economic benefits and a strong sense of national pride. Simply put, it is impossible to get elected to office in much of the United States without declaring fidelity to the national security state and its strictures.

Driven by the pursuit of power, America's political parties are loath to adopt platforms that would risk them being portrayed as anything less than supportive of the nation's military. They promote members from within their ranks who stand a chance of winning elections, and work to marginalize those who would struggle to triumph over the other side in a binary contest. For the most part, genuine antimilitarists are "organized out" of the Democratic and Republican folds because they represent unsafe bets when it comes to winning seats in Congress or states in presidential elections. Obviously, this was not always the case. When America's political economy was less connected with militarism (pre-1945), the two political parties had concomitantly fewer incentives to promote candidates that would appeal to the militarized sectors of society. Now that the military-industrial complex is so endemic, however, the two parties have no option but to adopt platforms and back candidates that are consonant with the country's overall bias in favor of militarism.

To be sure, individuals can sometimes rise to the top of America's political parties by voicing antimilitarist policies. In Congress, this can happen most easily in safe districts, where a party's primary electorate does not have to worry about nominating a candidate for office who can secure the backing of "moderates" and "independents." But in presidential politics, too, it is possible for individual candidates to secure their party's nomination on platforms that call for significant retrenchment. Both Barack Obama and Donald Trump ran as somewhat proretrenchment candidates in 2008 and 2016, respectively, with Obama calling for an end to the Iraq War and Trump promising to downsize America's overseas commitments in a less specific but arguably much more fundamental sense.

But there are hard limits to how far antimilitarist ideas can influence America's political parties. The occasional election to Congress of antiwar candidates such as Rand Paul (R-KY) or Dennis Kucinich (D-OH) does little to shift the overall makeup of the political parties to which they belong. Not even the election of a "disruptive" president implies that a party organization is about to change its overall platform when it comes to foreign policy and national security. This was certainly the case with Obama and Trump. In due course, the parties were able to rein in both presidents' more radical positions (such as they were) to the extent that, once in office, neither was able to implement anything even barely resembling an antiwar agenda. Both behaved in a manner more or less consistent with their predecessor, including the horizontal and vertical escalation of overseas military engagements.

Without a transformation of America's party system, the prospects for a new and different conversation over foreign policy are dim.[15] Consider, for example, President Obama and his continuation of the Bush-era Global War on Terror.

Obama had based much his election campaign upon vocal
opposition to the Iraq War – a clear (even if narrow) antiwar
position. Yet he coupled his pledge to drawdown US forces
in Iraq with a promise to renew the focus on Afghanistan.
Whereas Obama called Iraq a "dumb war," he made clear that
the war in Afghanistan was different. Drawing this distinction
allowed Obama to benefit from widespread opposition to the
Iraq War while insulating himself against accusations that he
was soft on terrorism. In short, it was possible (and prudent)
for Obama to oppose the Iraq War, but it would have been
impossible (unthinkable) for Obama to oppose the War on
Terrorism altogether.

Obama's support for the Afghan War on the campaign trail
created some problems once he assumed office. One of the
President's first actions was to order an immediate review
of Afghan policy, asking his military to prepare options for a
withdrawal. As the review proceeded, it became clear that the
war in Afghanistan could not be "won."[16] But at the same time,
Obama felt under enormous pressure to "not lose." In the end,
the President chose a bifurcated approach: a decision to surge
US forces in the country (raising the number from around
68,000 to over 100,000) coupled with an announcement that
the United States would begin withdrawing in July 2011.[17] The
decision to announce a timetable for withdrawal was a telltale
sign that Obama was operating according to a political calculus,
not a military one. It made no strategic sense to announce that
the United States was intent on leaving Afghanistan by a fixed
date because doing so would simply encourage the Taliban
and other insurgent groups to wait for America's exit before
launching a bid for control over Afghanistan. But domestic
politics were not conducive to retrenchment, and so the war
dragged on.

In the event, Obama never secured a withdrawal from
Afghanistan during his time in office. Security conditions never
improved to the point where a military exit could take place

without being portrayed as a defeat by the President's critics. Obama therefore bequeathed a troop presence of around
9,800 to his successor, Donald Trump. Like Obama, Trump
had been elected on a promise to end the war in Afghanistan.
It was a surprise, then, when Trump ordered his own surge of
troops to Afghanistan – sending an additional 7,000 troops
to bolster the existing force.[18] For the next four years, Trump
made periodic claims that he intended to end US participation
in the war, even arranging an aborted meeting with the Taliban
at Camp David, but he always made a withdrawal dependent upon an improvement in security conditions (as Obama
had done). This was, perhaps, a necessary face-saving measure
– that is to say, Trump can be forgiven for not wanting to
exit Afghanistan if it meant getting blamed for a worsening
security environment[19] – but it made a pullout impossible to
implement in practice, given that the Taliban could hardly be
expected to stop fighting just so that the United States could
withdraw from the country triumphant.

Before he left the White House, Trump did manage to
conclude a deal with the Taliban that paved the way for a
US military exit. However, Trump's timetable for withdrawal
only allowed for a reduction of US forces to begin *after* the
November 2020 election. This was revealing, suggesting that
the President was unwilling to run for reelection with an exit
having been implemented. Just as Obama had not wanted
to suffer the political consequences of exiting Afghanistan
without having won, neither did Trump. He rightly perceived
that running for reelection in November 2020 with the pall of
"losing Afghanistan" hanging over his campaign would have
been an electoral disaster. As a result, his plans for a withdrawal never came to fruition during his time in office.

What can be learnt from Obama and Trump's failures to exit
Afghanistan despite overwhelming evidence of the war's folly?
The obvious conclusion is that, in today's America, politicians
must guard against accusations of weakness because to be

tarred with the brush of pusillanimity is to empower domestic rivals, alienate political allies, and offend the sensibilities of voters at large. This gives presidents strong incentives to err on the side of militarism for electoral purposes – even when militarist policies make little strategic sense.

America's Army of National-Security Bureaucrats

So far, I have argued that Congress has ceded too many war powers to the presidency, and that officials in both branches of government have formidable incentives to reject major instances of retrenchment. But there is another force at work: the power of the permanent bureaucracy. After all, elected officials do not make or implement policy alone. They are supported by armies of policy advisers – political appointees and a much larger number of career bureaucrats – whose job it is to empower elected officials to make sound decisions about national security.

As noted in chapter 4, the national-security-focused organs of the US government employ hundreds of thousands of citizens. These masses of people have been given the job of understanding how the United States can apply its preponderant power to shape conditions abroad. For the most part, they do not work for agencies whose mission is to reduce the size of America's overseas footprint. On the contrary, bureaucrats in Washington are charged with finding ways to use US power assets to advance some set of international goals. This is most obviously true of military bureaucrats, but pressure to implement interventionist foreign policies does not only come from the Pentagon. There is evidence, for example, that the institutionalization of human rights reporting in the State Department is related to humanitarian interventions, too.[20] The causal mechanism seems to be that, once the US government has devoted time, energy, resources, and political capital toward defining an overseas problem as severe – and especially if this issue is subject to the language of securitization – then it becomes more likely that those same officials, or their colleagues in government, will recommend that Washington "do something" to solve the problem. This often means the application of military force.

It is not surprising that bureaucrats and advisers accept the naturalness of militarist solutions. As described in chapter 4, there are powerful selection effects governing who takes on these jobs. People who favor restraint and retrenchment are simply very unlikely to become part of the Department of Defense, Central Intelligence Agency, or Department of Homeland Security workforce. Those who are optimistic about the potential for the United States to force policy solutions upon the rest of the world, on the other hand, are much more likely to be attracted to these jobs. For eighty years, the culture of the US government has been centered on the assumption that America can and must lead the world. The bottom line is that the existence of a permanent, professionalized, and activist-minded directorate heavily biases the US government's conversation in favor of interventionism and primacism.

Even the president, the most powerful individual in government, is vulnerable to the influence of national-security staffers because of a severe imbalance in expertise. In the journalist Peter Baker's account of President Obama's decision-making when it came to the "surge" in Afghanistan, national-security officials played a major role in convincing the President to commit more forces to the warzone. Baker's reporting shows how military and political advisers can combine to pressure a sitting president to commit blood and treasure to a distant warzone despite the odds of victory being decidedly long.[21] President Trump, too, swiftly reached a decision to expand the US military presence in Afghanistan once he took office in 2017, despite an unambiguous campaign pledge to exit the war. Explaining his choice to reverse course on the Afghan

War, Trump confided to the American people that things
"look different from behind the desk of the Oval Office" – an
admission, perhaps, that he had felt pressure to accept the
recommendations of his advisers, who exert powerful sway
over presidents by virtue of their special expertise, control of
information, and the social status afforded to security professionals in US politics and society.[22]

When Trump suggested pulling US forces out of Syria in
2019, the militarist state similarly swung into action. Trump
was condemned in the Senate, denounced in the media, and
the Democratic Party castigated him for a reckless and ignoble
foreign policy. But perhaps most damaging of all to Trump
was the fact of his Secretary of Defense James Mattis resigning
in disgust. As a profile in *The Atlantic* later explained, the
decision to withdraw from Syria "posed a dire challenge to
Mattis's beliefs" because it involved abandoning America's
Kurdish allies in the region.[23] More than any other modern
president, Trump relied upon his role as commander in chief
as a source of legitimacy. He had put enormous stock in Mattis
in particular, owing to Mattis's position as a respected former
general.[24] Mattis's resignation was thus a significant blow to
Trump. In the event, advisers convinced the President not
to withdraw US troops from Syria altogether, and to merely
relocate around 1,000 troops from the north of the country
(where Turkey was then planning an imminent invasion) to
the southern areas bordering Iraq.

Michael Glennon's concept of a double government is
instructive in this regard.[25] There are only 537 elected officials in
the federal government: 435 members of the House, 100 members of the Senate, and the president and vice president. These
representatives are nominally in charge of deciding all matters
of federal policy, and so are asked to be knowledgeable about
an impossible array of policy domains, foreign and domestic.
Given that it would be impracticable for these elected officials
to match the permanent bureaucracy in terms of expertise,

it is inevitable that they delegate most decision-making and agenda-setting to bureaucrats. Once this unavoidable bargain has been struck, however, principal–agent dynamics ensure that the elected institutions of government face enormous difficulties exercising effective control over (or even barely comprehending the work of) the unelected organs of government. Sometimes, the unelected institutions of government triumph – including over highly consequential matters of war and peace.

To be sure, Aaron Friedberg is correct that the United States has avoided the fate of becoming a totalized "garrison state."[26] National security professionals have an enormous amount of sway over the federal government, but civilians have retained overall control of the military and the intelligence community. American citizens enjoy more civil liberties than those of almost any other nation, including the freedom to criticize their government and its armed forces. But at the same time, the operation of US government and politics is heavily conditioned by the existence of a vast army of civilian and military technocrats whose expertise is geared toward the management of violence in overseas settings. The point of the national-security state is to make policy recommendations and then organize to get these recommendations enacted. Given that there is no counterweight to security professionals in the US system, the result is a heavy bias in favor of militarist, interventionist, and securitizing policies – that is, the continuation of a grand strategy of military primacy.

"Hail to the Fief": America's Global Garrison State

As well as heading a national security state at home, the American president also heads a parallel complex of military installations abroad – what I have called in this book the "global garrison state." This refers to the 800 or so overseas military installations that exist on foreign soil but are run from Washington as de facto extensions of the United States. Around 170,000 active-duty personnel are based in these locations, acting at the discretion of the president or his subordinates. While Congress is free to exercise oversight of these installations (and is required to fund their existence), the day-to-day running of America's overseas bases suffers from a lack of basic accountability and democratic input. For most intents and purposes, the commander in chief has autocratic powers over the management of this archipelago of far-flung US defense installations.

This global garrison state exists for a few reasons: to fight wars, coerce adversaries, and deter aggression. The waging of war is the most obvious purpose of maintaining overseas bases. It is from these staging posts that the United States can launch major ground invasions (e.g., the invasions of Afghanistan and Iraq) or carry out smaller strikes, such as counterterrorist missions and targeted assassinations. President Obama alone ordered 542 drone strikes from overseas bases during his two terms in office, killing 3,797 people (at least 324 of whom were civilians).[27] At times, the presidency's use of overseas assets to wage unrestricted and unmonitored warfare has become controversial in the United States – but only ever fleetingly. In 2011, for example, Obama ordered the CIA to kill Anwar al-Awlaki – a US citizen, Islamist cleric, and leading member of al-Qaeda – in Yemen. Two weeks later, Obama ordered the assassination of Abdulrahman al-Awlaki, the 16-year-old son who was also accused of terrorist activity. These killings were typical of Obama's approach to prosecuting the Global War on Terror in a way hidden from public view.[28] But the al-Awlaki strikes drew attention because they involved the assassination of US citizens without any attempt to apply due process.

Even here, however, the political blowback was minimal. The administration justified its actions with reference to the notion that the al-Awlakis were in rebellion against the United

States and so could be legitimate targets. Other political figures agreed with this assessment, including some of Obama's rivals for reelection in 2012,[29] and the issue eventually went away. Some years later, President Trump terminated the requirement of having to report drone strike data – a stark illustration of just how normal it has become for the US government to wage permanent, unregulated war from overseas locations.[30]

High-level strikes abroad such as targeted assassinations tend to require the approval of the commander in chief. But it would be a mistake to conclude that presidents always know what the overseas military personnel are doing, or planning. Clearly, it would be impossible for the president of the United States to understand in great detail what work is being performed on each of America's 800 overseas bases at any given time. Even when presidents are asked to authorize the use of military force, it is unclear to what extent the sitting president is able to question the advice he is being given. President Trump, for example, once boasted of having given the military "total authorization" to launch military strikes.[31] By one president's own admission, then, even the commander in chief is not always in charge of how the global garrison state chooses to mete out violence. To a large degree, it operates according to its own logic: identifying targets, developing plans to kill enemies, defending against possible attacks, and retaliating against any who succeed in inflicting damage upon America's overseas personnel.

Even if the president is assumed to be in overall control, the fundamental problem is that the Pentagon's network of overseas bases makes permanent warfighting far too easy for presidents who are, as has been discussed at length, unconstrained and incentivized to use military force. Benjamin Denison gets this right: forward deployments create an irresistible "temptation" for presidents to use lethal force as a solution to security challenges abroad that otherwise could have been dealt with via political, diplomatic, or economic means.[32] It should not be so easy for presidents or their subordinates to order the use of force. According to America's constitutional design, there should be a high bar for military action of any sort, and almost all such actions (except those taken in strict self-defense) should be subject to some form of democratic scrutiny at home. Viewed in this light, the overseas garrison state – that great enabler of permanent warfighting at the direction of the White House – is just as much a problem as the national-security state at home. It biases America in favor of military primacy and heavily against strategic retrenchment.

Societal Consent

Leaders in Washington make policy safe in the knowledge that their colleagues in government are broadly supportive of military primacy as a *modus operandi*. But what about the wider political system? After all, policymaking in a democracy is supposed to play out before an "audience" – the electorate – that has the ultimate recourse, should it so choose, to intervene in the public square and insist upon a course correction if the government is making decisions at odds with the public interest.[33] When it comes to foreign policy, however, the actors on stage have little to fear from onlookers in the galleries. On the contrary, those members of civil society who pay most attention to international affairs tend to endorse the grand strategy of military primacy just as much as government insiders.

Consider America's most prominent national-security think tanks: the Council on Foreign Relations, Brookings Institution, Hudson Institute, Center for Strategic and International Studies, RAND Corporation, Heritage Foundation, Center for a New American Security, Stimson Center, Atlantic Council, and Harvard University's Belfer Center, to name just some. For the most part, these think tanks produce research that takes the grand strategy of military primacy for granted. They are not "critical" in the sense of wanting to "[stand] apart from the prevailing order of the world and [ask] how that order came about."[34] Rather, most mainstream think tanks neatly fit the description of what Robert Cox once called "problem-solving theory," which "takes the world as it finds it, with the prevailing social and power relationships and the institutions into which they are organised, as the given framework for action. The general aim of problem-solving," Cox explained, "is to make these relationships and institutions work smoothly by dealing effectively with particular sources of trouble."[35]

To be sure, there are some think tanks that take a firm line in favor of retrenchment – the Cato Institute, Defense Priorities, and the Quincy Institute chief among them. But such organizations are in a distinct minority. The reality is that some of the biggest boosters for military primacy come from outside of government, with major think tanks and philanthropic foundations investing considerable resources into the study of how to pursue military primacy *well*, as opposed to considering how to do grand strategy *differently*.[36] At certain moments, this high degree of consensus between government insiders and the external policy community can be highly consequential. For example, Joseph Stieb has shown that elite-level consensus in favor of regime change in Baghdad was essential to facilitating President Bush's successful prosecution of the Iraq War.[37]

The business community, too, has largely been supportive of – and complicit in – the foreign policy status quo. As the Secretary of War Henry Stimson is reported to have told FDR during the 1940s, "you've got to let business make money out of the process or business won't work."[38] He need not have worried, given that private corporations made enormous sums of money during World War II. As discussed in chapter 4, business groups also stood to gain from US foreign policy after the war, not only from the large amounts of money being spent by the federal government in the name of national defense but also from Washington's support for open markets abroad and the reconstruction of a vibrant world economy. Still today, many US firms benefit handsomely from the pursuit of military primacy. At least, there is no discernible movement among business groups to push for smaller defense budgets, fewer overseas interventions, and less of a world role for the United States.

Indeed, American civil society offers such overwhelming consent for the project of military primacy that the US government often avails itself of outside help when it comes to refining the approach. This includes the infamous "revolving door" relationships whereby civilian and military leaders go back and forth between government service and roles in think tanks, the corporate world, and academia.[39] But it also includes formalized partnerships between government and society. It is often overlooked that Washington is relatively porous in the sense that it is tightly integrated with civil society. The National Intelligence Council, for example, was created in 1979 as a deliberate bridge between the intelligence community, academia, and the private sector. Military organizations such as the US Strategic Command and US Northern Command have formal "academic alliances" with universities and colleges across the country. And whenever a new administration comes in, it must fill thousands of openings in the bureaucracy focused on defense and national security. These positions are sometimes filled with party loyalists but also with personnel from the business world, think tanks, and academia – a bottomless reservoir of future bureaucrats and advisers who are already well-versed in (and sympatico with) the contours of US grand strategy.

Finally, and as described in chapter 4, American culture has evolved over the past eighty years to emphasize militarism much more than was previously the case. Indeed, militarization has become a pervasive part of everyday life.[40] Having grown up with the reality of a globe-spanning network of forward deployments and owing to the experience of fighting never-ending military engagements for so long, the American public is simply no longer offended by the constant use of military force abroad. Permanent surveillance, intelligence gathering, air campaigns, drone strikes, arms sales, humanitarian interventions – all these practices have become thoroughly normalized to the point where Americans are mostly desensitized to the use of force in foreign policy.[41]

The Militarist Redoubt

For all the reasons given above, presidents, members of Congress, leading military figures, and top-level bureaucrats all operate inside a political system that provides a safe haven for primacist thinking. Military interventions can be imagined and put into action without fear of causing severe domestic blowback. Plans to intervene abroad may still be rejected, of course, but not because they violate core tenets of US grand strategy. This is why the US political system has become unfit for peace: because it is made for war. Elsewhere, I have called this a "militarist redoubt" inside the US government – a complex of primacist biases that insulates the grand strategy of military primacy from criticism, reform, or accountability.[42] Not only are the formal powers of the president expansive and largely unchecked, but there is no political counterweight to restrain the president from pursuing militaristic foreign policies, either. When was the last time that a president or other leading politician saw their reputation irredeemably sullied for promoting war? Yet whenever national leaders float proposals of retrenchment, there is always a readymade constituency poised to oppose such moves.

It is worth emphasizing that only US militarism benefits from such a political redoubt. Other facets of US foreign policy are much more vulnerable to domestic opprobrium and opposition. Take, for example, participation in international institutions. In 2017, President Trump began to administer a sledgehammer to America's involvement in multilateral organizations and to the State Department as the domestic institution responsible for overseeing such participation in international forums.[43] Trump withdrew the United States from the UN Human Rights Council, UNESCO, the Paris climate accords, Iran nuclear deal, the Trans-Pacific Partnership, and other organizations – all key arenas for amplifying the voice of the US government and America's vibrant civil society abroad. The Trump administration failed to fill key ambassador positions and oversaw a huge exodus of talent from the State Department, with an 11 percent drop in foreign-affairs officers during Trump's first year in office.[44] It was possible for Trump to reduce America's diplomatic corps in this way because, unlike the military, such bureaucrats have no political constituency in the country and no caucus in Congress to fight for their jobs. Simply put, it is much easier for a leader like Trump to govern as an "anti-internationalist" in the sense of wanting to restrict US diplomacy than it is for someone to govern as an "antimilitarist."

Attacks on free trade, too, have historically managed to pass off without major domestic backlash. From President Nixon's suspension of the dollar's convertibility into gold and his imposition of 10 percent tariffs on certain imports to President Trump's "trade war" with China, US presidents have been able to criticize the very premises of free trade and unfettered cross-border investment without jeopardizing their domestic position. To be sure, there was once a reliable protrade caucus in Congress to argue in favor of economic openness. But this group has fractured in recent years, leaving presidents significant leeway to shape economic policy in ways that cut against internationalist orthodoxies.

In short, the US government tends to permit a wide range of views on international cooperation and economic foreign policy. The state does not intervene decisively to stymie debates over such questions in the same way it prevents discussion over military retrenchment. This is for the simple reason that the US political system was never really designed to ensure close cooperative relations with the rest of the world or support the management of the world economy. Although US leaders surely desired that Washington would be a lynchpin of the incipient liberal (economic) order, the US state itself was not changed to support the existence of such an international architecture. In contrast, the US government has been retrofitted to include institutions designed for the explicit purpose of projecting military power and influence abroad. The US state and its warfighting activities have become conjoined.

Conclusion

As this chapter has sought to illustrate, there are several ways that the institutional structures and processes of the US state work against retrenchment. First, the foreign-policy executive is centered on the president, who has been empowered to make unilateral decisions over war and peace. Second, both the president and Congress – and the national political parties – face political incentives to uphold military primacy and avoid any suggestion that they favor retrenchment. Third, the US government is staffed by legions of bureaucrats who are experts in the management of violence and are disposed to recommend that their expertise be reflected in policy. Fourth, the maintenance of permanent, far-flung military deployments serves to lower the cost of intervention while raising barriers to inaction. Fifth, American civil society generally lends consent to perpetual interventionism and rarely censures leaders for pursuing militaristic foreign policies. In other words, there are significant checks and balances in the US political system when it comes to the formulation and implementation of foreign policy – but almost all of these safeguards are geared toward maintaining the status quo, not discouraging the use of force. This is the militarist redoubt – an institutionalized mobilization of bias within the US state that insulates the grand strategy of military primacy from significant challenges.

6

Domestic Renewal

So far, the focus of this book has been on why the United States has not retrenched. This chapter begins to concretize the argument for how America *could* move away from primacy toward a grand strategy of restraint – and, indeed, why the United States *must* retrench for reasons of self-interest. Part of my argument is that US foreign policy suffers from an acute case of institutional maladaptation. Its organs of government have been honed for the purpose of maintaining an enormous overseas military presence, yet the world today is becoming far less hospitable to the United States being forward deployed. As the international system becomes more multipolar, it is entirely predictable that the other poles in the system – China and Russia, to name just the ones most obviously hostile to US military primacy – will harden against US attempts to assert dominance. It is therefore becoming more costly and risky for domestic leaders to perform according to the primacist playbook. In this context, American foreign policy looks ever more wrongheaded. The times have changed, but Washington's most basic assumptions about how to interface with the outside world have not changed with them.

But it is not just the international system that is creating pressure for a strategic adjustment. America's domestic politics are also badly served by primacy. During the Cold War, a preponderant slice of the US political class believed that America's overseas commitments – including a heavily militarized foreign policy – were conducive to economic growth and social cohesion at home. The United States found purpose in its quest to defend the "free world" from communism; its domestic economy flourished because of the opportunities for international trade and investment that were facilitated by America's forward presence in Europe, Asia, and the Middle East; and the benefits of international engagement were sufficiently "socialized" such that a broad cross-section of domestic society felt invested in the status quo. Without the strategy of containment, the world might have been closed to US businesses and consumers. With it, important segments of the economy boomed because of lucrative exports, cheap and plentiful imports, and heavy government investment in the defense sector and related industries.

Notably, however, each of America's post–Cold War presidents has entered office promising to reduce overseas commitments and focus on some version of domestic renewal. In 1992, Bill Clinton promised to "focus like a laser beam" on the everyday economic concerns of ordinary Americans.[1] In 2000, George W. Bush railed against "nation-building" and campaigned on a platform heavy on domestic policy priorities.[2] President Obama ran on a pledge to end the unpopular war in Iraq and inspire change at home. Donald Trump's inaugural address laid out in grandiose terms a plan to end the "carnage" taking place in America's towns and cities in part by putting "America first" in foreign policy. And Joe Biden, too, made an explicit point of connecting domestic renewal to a reformed foreign policy.[3]

At the same time, public opinion polls show that, today, ordinary Americans are pessimistic about the country's trajectory.[4] Citizens despair that the United States is beset by political polarization, hyperpartisanship, economic inequality, violence, and racial disparities, among other problems. For years, the country has been portrayed as riven by acrimonious culture wars. None of America's governing institutions seems to command the trust and confidence of the general public. Such a lack of optimism is not altogether unheard of in the modern era; Americans were similarly downbeat about the nation's future in 1980, 1992, and 2008, for example. But there are at least some signs that gloom and cynicism are more stubborn and deep-seated today than they have been in the past. In other words, there is a pervasive feeling that presidents past and present have been right: domestic renewal *is* in order, even if Americans disagree on what the path to renewal might include and what changes to public policy (foreign and domestic) ought to be part of this collective effort.

Why has every president of the past thirty years seen fit to promote some version of strategic retrenchment and domestic reform? And why have they failed to deliver despite some evidence of domestic appetite for change? As has already been canvassed at length, the problem is that America's militarist state is not set up to permit a significant downsizing of the country's world role. Domestic politics are calibrated to reject wide-ranging alterations to the foreign-policy status quo. America's leaders find themselves fighting an uphill battle whenever they attempt to follow through on a diagnosis that defense policy must change in order for national rejuvenation to be possible. The "system" works to drive a wedge between the foreign and domestic halves of their reform agendas, with only domestic reform being allowed to move forward. Major shifts in military policy are uniformly discouraged.

However, my argument is that the United States will never be able to restore a sense of optimism at home without changing its foreign policy. So long as primacy remains fixed as the nation's grand-strategic blueprint for interfacing with the outside world, there will always be a baleful domestic underside that inhibits politicians from creating a more perfect union. Without cutting the cost of defense policy, in particular, it will be hard for Congress to devote sufficient resources toward the myriad problems facing the United States at home: high borrowing, an unraveling social safety net, insolvent social programs, a lackluster industrial policy, inadequate housing, underperforming schools, unaffordable higher education, and so forth. This is especially true given that America's wars tend to be financed via the accumulation of sovereign debt, which exacerbates the problem of wealth inequality in the United States and increases the long-term strain on the public purse.[5] In short, domestic renewal and military retrenchment must go hand in hand. One cannot proceed without the other. Wide-ranging retrenchment will never become standard practice in US foreign policy unless the domestic political order undergoes some sort of structural reform and realignment, yet domestic reform cannot happen in the absence of a revolution in foreign policy. Given this co-constitutive problem, what is to be done?

The point of this chapter is to advance a theory of victory for retrenchers that is rooted in domestic politics. I argue that changes to US foreign policy must proceed in tandem with programmatic reforms at the domestic level: political, economic, social, and perhaps even constitutional. While this might seem like a tall order, I build on three reasons for optimism. First, it is demonstrably the case that US leaders do, as a matter of regularity, arrive independently at the con-clusion that domestic renewal should be a priority. Second, there are already groups agitating for retrenchment in US politics, which indicates the existence of a nascent coalition in support of a reformed foreign policy. Third, demographic shifts seem to be moving in the direction of supporting an overall grand strategy of restraint, with growing numbers of Americans skeptical about military primacy as an approach to foreign affairs. If these domestic-level trends can be harnessed and woven together into a coherent movement for change, a broad-based campaign for a slenderer foreign policy and more democratic politics at home might just succeed.

Economic Change, War Weariness, and Flagging Support for Primacy

The connection between a primacist foreign policy and domestic flourishing has frayed in recent decades – at least in the minds of many ordinary Americans. Partly, this is driven by changes to the world economy and America's place in it. Peter Trubowitz and Brian Burgoon trace the origins of the problem to decisions made in the early post–Cold War period, when Western elites chose hyperglobalization, supranational compacts, and neoliberal social policies as the recipe for expanding the democratic-capitalist world order.[6] This bargain had much to recommend it, especially high economic growth at home and the promise of international amity abroad. But the approach failed to account for the dislocation and social decay that would come along with the unfettered movement of goods, services, capital, and jobs across national borders. The benefits of economic liberalization tended to accrue to certain sectors of the economy over others, with some domestic industries experiencing difficulty and sometimes facing outright collapse as the result of being exposed to foreign competition. Wealth concentrated at the top of the income distribution, with the gap between rich and poor widening. Meanwhile, nation-states did comparatively little to ensure the equitable distribution of economic gains. In time, such trends exacted a punishing toll on social cohesion and the public's confidence in governing institutions.

In the United States, this is close to exactly what happened during the 1990s and 2000s: a neoliberal economic model premised on deep integration with the world economy helped to drive strong economic growth, technological innovation, and vast amounts of wealth creation – but the benefits of ever deeper integration into the global economy were unevenly distributed. Over time, fault lines emerged between regions, urban and rural environments, economic classes, and racial and ethnic groups. The "winners" from globalization flourished while the "losers" languished. At first, globalization's discontents were small in number and lacked political power – radicals, mostly, on the fringes of US government and politics. But in recent years, popular and political opposition to globalization has expanded to the point where antiglobalization forces are now a significant presence in US politics.

It is feasible that growing dissatisfaction with globalization will eat into political support for military primacy. This is because America's globe-spanning world role was, in large part, a function of the political elite's commitment to resurrecting and defending an open world economy in the aftermath of World War II. During the Cold War and after, one of the central *raisons d'être* of military primacy as a grand strategy was to thwart those hostile international actors who might otherwise have endangered the globalist economic project.[7] But if Americans are no longer committed to an open world economy, this poses an obvious question: Why is their military still being used to permit such a world economy to function?

To be sure, most Americans today do not make this connection between global economics and military primacy. The US military's role has been rebranded several times over, and few ordinary Americans understand that their armed forces were sent overseas in the early Cold War for the purpose of facilitating economic openness. If they are anti-internationalist in any sense, US citizens' ire tends to be directed more at the draftsmen of economic globalization ("globalists") than the architects of military intervention. In time, however, ebbing faith in America's economic leadership could be converted into opposition to the military-industrial complex. The politics of resentment are never far from the surface. Why are US tax-payers paying for the defense of economic competitors such as Japan, South Korea, Taiwan, and Germany? Why do America's wealthiest allies not finance their own defense (and the collective defense of others) in full? To be clear, there are some good-faith and compelling ways to answer these questions – but such answers are not intuitively obvious to most ordinary Americans, who could easily be turned against the notion of defending wealthy foreign nations if opposition to extended deterrence were cast in self-interested economic terms.

If Americans do not make these connections by themselves, it seems likely that entrepreneurial political leaders will make the case to them. Indeed, this is what happened with President Trump, who politicized trade to great effect and often suggested a need for the United States to cut back its overseas obligations to countries that are America's economic competitors. It warrants emphasis that Trump's occasional (albeit inconsistent) antiprimacist rhetoric in this vein likely "landed" with so much of the electorate because he connected criticism of America's alliance commitments to domestic economic grievances.

At the same time, there is the clear potential for political leaders to seize upon war weariness in America. This has already started to happen to a degree, with politicians routinely pledging to end so-called "forever wars." Conspicuously, however, political leaders are almost always reluctant to be specific about the wars they intend to end, how, and why. The domestic circumstances are ripe for someone to adopt a bolder approach. War-weariness is real. Americans can be persuaded that the enormous sums of money spent fighting wars abroad could be better spent on domestic priorities. Ordinary citizens could be made angry that the overmilitarization of US foreign policy has played a significant role in militarizing police forces at home.[8] And most importantly of all, America's recent wars have resulted in massive loss of life, with over 7,000 US service personnel dying in the line of duty and hundreds of thousands of foreign fighters and civilians dying with them – and for what? Now that the wars in Afghanistan and Iraq have been identified as unalloyed failures, a sizable slice of the US electorate seems primed to question whether permanent warfighting has made them (or anyone else) safer. Perhaps overseas meddling is a cause of enmity toward the United States rather than a way of disarming potential threats?

In the past, the negative consequences of military primacy could have been overlooked or justified because the economic benefits were so large. This, in effect, was the bargain struck in the late 1940s and early 1950s: Americans were willing to set aside core principles and place civil liberties in jeopardy, but only in exchange for a grand strategy that a bipartisan group of leaders insisted was necessary to rescue the world economy and, with it, US economic security. That bargain made sense for a long time. To many Americans today, however, it no longer does. For all these reasons, the domestic landscape is perhaps more ready for arguments in favor of retrenchment and restraint than it has been for generations. All that is needed is someone to make them cogently.

The Partisanship Problem

If all this is true, however, then why has no political entrepreneur succeeded at combining economic discontent with war weariness to create a unified platform against US primacy? One problem is that, as discussed in chapter 2, proponents of restraint are divided among several different camps that have little in common with one another beyond opposition to an overly militarized foreign policy. On the left, opposition to orthodox foreign policy has taken the form of anticapitalism and anti-imperialism, with the United States often cast in the role of imperial oppressor. This brand of politics has no chance of being adopted by the wider American public or political class. Progressives such as Elizabeth Warren and Bernie Sanders have done better at giving voice to the more mainstream antiwar views that inhere among the general public, forging a case for retrenchment that is more palatable and broadly acceptable as a foreign-policy agenda. But their ideas for remaking foreign policy and US domestic society are still viewed as too radical by centrist voters, not to mention those on the right.

Among Republicans, meanwhile, there are two noticeable splits within the party. In economic terms, libertarian-leaning free-traders differ from more populist protectionists on the question of economic integration. The Republican Party was traditionally in favor of free trade but has drifted more in the direction of antiglobalization since Donald Trump's anointment as head of the party. In military terms, the party is divided between traditional Republicans who are staunchly supportive of high military spending, robust commitments to America's overseas alliances, and hawkish stances toward potential adversaries versus a newer, Trump-inspired wing of the party whose members sometimes express support for shrinking the US military footprint.

The more fundamental barrier to the emergence of a unified "retrenchment caucus," however, is that debates over foreign policy tend to be refracted through a lens of hyperpartisanship. Even though the two political parties are divided on foreign policy, they reserve their more stinging attacks for the opposing party – not politicians on their own side.[9] In recent years, Democrats have slammed the Republican Party for recklessness (e.g., the assassination of Iranian general Qasem Soleimani) but also timidity (e.g., Trump's alleged failures to "stand up" to Putin's Russia). Republicans, too, have sensed more to gain from demonizing the Democratic Party than from pursuing bipartisan solutions. To be sure, there are some instances of bipartisan cooperation in recent US history – congressional attempts to limit US support for Saudi Arabia's war in Yemen, for example, or the bipartisan funding packages to bankroll Ukraine's resistance to Russian aggression in 2022 and 2023.[10] But such instances of cross-party cooperation are becoming less visible than in the past, and almost never move the United States in the direction of retrenchment.

Elsewhere, I have written that polarization and hyperpartisanship make it harder for presidents to wage programmatic foreign policies characterized by broad-based intervention.[11] But domestic dysfunction makes it hard for leaders in Washington to implement policies of retrenchment, too. The result is a sort of limbo: the United States is stuck with a grand strategy of military primacy that increasing numbers of Americans have come to doubt, but which the country's leaders are incapable of reforming in a programmatic fashion. Actors on both sides agree that the never-ending wars of the post-9/11 era have done little to advance the causes of freedom, liberty, justice, and democracy for people overseas, let alone contribute to the economic and physical security of people at home. There is shared dissatisfaction with the ways in which globalization has affected Americans' economic opportunities. But the two parties seem to be incapable of finding common ground, each afraid to take the first meaningful steps toward retrenchment for fear of being outflanked by the opposition. Primacy lingers by default.

The Case for Systemic Reform

Overcoming the problem of partisanship will be difficult, however, and points to a more ambitious reform that proponents of retrenchment ought to consider embracing as part of their political agenda: electoral reform in the United States. In the final analysis, changes to America's election laws are the only way to truly manipulate the party system and allow

Americans to share in a broader conversation over politics and policy, including foreign relations. At present, America's political parties function as quasi-public bodies: their existence is enshrined in state law, states tend to be responsible for running and regulating what should be the parties' internal elections (primaries), and the parties play a large role in gathering personnel to serve in civil service roles. As noted elsewhere in this book, this is a problem for US foreign policy because the two main parties in the United States also happen to be heavily biased in favor of militarism and overseas interventionism for reasons of political self-interest.

In part, the Democratic–Republican duopoly is due to the electoral dynamic known as Duverger's Law, whereby voters in a single-member plurality election have incentives to rally behind the two candidates with the highest chances of success; votes for unelectable, fringe, or protest candidates are regarded as "wasted." But lest it be forgotten, the present system is also the product of deliberate lawmaking by Democrats and Republicans. As Lisa Disch has convincingly shown, the major political parties have collaborated to design a system of electoral laws that make it much harder for third parties to get on the ballot and register support.[12] In the past, the United States did see some level of third-party success: the People's Party won several seats in Congress during the period 1890–1902, for example, as well as the governorships of at least nine states. Other countries with first-past-the-post electoral systems (e.g., Canada and the United Kingdom) also prove that multiparty competition is possible (even if somewhat discouraged) under such conditions. What distinguishes America today from its past self and from its international peers is the extent to which the Democrats and Republicans have become "established" in the sense of being fused with the state itself.

How could election rules be changed to encourage the emergence of a new and better party system? One idea that has been floated is to move toward open primaries, which would theoretically make it easier for a wider range of voices to be heard inside the established party organizations.[13] This would be a step in the right direction, but the bolder option is to pass laws that encourage a multiparty system. At minimum, this should mean state governments relinquishing control of the primary process altogether. Political parties should be private members' clubs, responsible for maintaining their own membership rolls[14] and conducting their own internal elections. Parties should be required to register with state authorities to qualify for participation in general elections, but the barriers to entry in this regard should be low. In one fell swoop, disestablishing America's political parties would remove some of the privileges currently afforded to the Democrats and Republicans, and open the door to a more pluralistic political system.

As well, the United States should move toward a system of proportional representation, whereby seats in the House of Representatives are allocated to parties based upon their overall vote share rather than their ability to muster a plurality of votes in single districts.[15] Moving toward proportional representation would be good for democracy in the United States because it would give Americans more opportunities to elect representatives that share their political preferences. It is an open secret that partisan gerrymandering has resulted in elected officials from the Democratic and Republican parties choosing their voters rather than the other way around. This would be harder to accomplish if the United States were divided into larger, multimember districts.

Proportional representation and a multiparty system would undoubtedly be good for the cause of retrenchment. According to Trevor Thrall, around 37 percent of the US public can be categorized as belonging to a "restraint constituency."[16] Yet neither of today's parties represents their views. As Ben Friedman has argued, "A multiparty system might include dovish or isolationist parties with an interest in downplaying the danger to appeal to supporters' antiwar positions. In the

United States, the [Democratic and Republican] parties engage in competitive threat inflation. Neither sees advantage in helping Americans perceive their safety. Both parties are generally hawkish."[17] This dynamic cannot be undone without changes to the rules.

Proportional representation in Congress would also make it less likely that any single party could control a majority of the House or Senate, let alone a majority in both chambers. In turn, this would make it less likely that the United States would ever experience unified government, when the executive branch and both chambers of Congress are under the control of the same political party. Again, this would be good news for proponents of restraint given that, as William Howell and Jon Pevehouse have shown, conditions of divided government are exactly when the US Congress tends to exercise the most constraints over the presidency.[18] To be clear, the point is not that the United States should choose whatever electoral system would advantage restrainers. Rather, it should choose a fairer system that gives representation to all prominent viewpoints, which is not presently the case.

Reforming America's electoral system would be challenging. For a start, it is more accurate to talk of electoral *systems* (plural) rather than an electoral *system* (singular). This is because the US states each control the means of electing representatives to Congress and nominating electors to the Electoral College, all subject to oversight by the Supreme Court. But the decentralized nature of US elections also creates opportunities: it means that those interested in political reform have fifty venues for trying to pass laws that would disestablish the main political parties and move toward greater political pluralism. It would only take a handful of states to adopt new and better laws for others to see the advantages in doing so (in 2020, Alaska switched to a ranked-choice voting system for its general elections, including the presidential election). Crucially, altering America's electoral system in this manner does not require a constitutional amendment: the Elections Clause of the US Constitution explicitly gives authority over the conduct of elections to the states.

Executive–Legislative Relations

Electoral reform and the disestablishment of the main political parties would give greater say to a wide range of voices in the country. But once elected representatives arrive in Congress – no matter what party they belong to – they still need the authority to affect change. This is not possible in today's Washington. As discussed elsewhere in this book, the national security state is too vast, impenetrable, and secretive for Congress to have much of an impact upon its everyday operations. The presidency has become too powerful – and Congress too accustomed to impuissance – for the legislative branch to exert a meaningful say over either the broad contours of US grand strategy or the specifics of foreign policy. It is therefore imperative that proponents of retrenchment support meaningful reforms to the federal government, especially in the realm of executive–legislative relations.

The centerpiece of this agenda must be to return powers over foreign policy, especially war powers, to the Congress. This means control over arms sales, intelligence, military deployments, and more. Congress must always insist on authorizations for the use of military force. Institutional mechanisms to encourage such behavior would be welcome, such as legislation that would require any given AUMF to be renewed on a regular (annual or biennial) basis. As well, Congress could move to deprive the president of unilateral authority to orchestrate large movements of troops overseas – a sort of Peace Powers Resolution, designed to exert greater influence over preparations for war rather than just entries into war, at which point it is often too late to rein in a president's war plans.

Congress must also wrest powers away from the national security state and assert its authority to conduct proper oversight. The maximal approach would be to repeal the National Security Act and design a new bureaucratic framework that involves less secrecy, fewer national-security technocrats, and a greater emphasis on ensuring that the legislature is at least coequal with (preferably dominant over) the executive branch when it comes to setting defense and intelligence policy. It would be welcome for Congress to produce its own strategy documents to complement or replace the executive branch's National Security Strategy, National Defense Strategy, Nuclear Posture Review, and so forth.

Congress can also reform how the budget process works. Legislators could require that a certain proportion of defense spending be spent in the United States, not in foreign lands. This would benefit the constituents of lawmakers, perhaps creating incentives for Congress to shift resources away from overseas operations and toward homeland-based defense forces. It might also be possible for Congress to mandate that military spending not exceed a certain proportion of spending on domestic programs; or that defense spending must be "paid for" via taxes rather than through borrowing.[19] In the past, domestic battles between "economizers" and "national security managers" resulted in some significant wins between those who expressed concern about runaway government spending.[20] This might be replicable today given that budgets are a uniquely valuable mechanism for exposing the rivalrous relationship between defense outlays and other national priorities. Budgetary politics is thus an indispensable (and proven) way to limit the foreign-policy ambitions of America's leaders, not to mention an area where Congress has a clear upper hand vis-à-vis the presidency.

To bolster its effectiveness relative to the White House, Congress could take several actions to reform its institutions and procedures. It is imperative, for starters, that Congress dispense with the filibuster in the Senate,[21] which severely hampers the legislature from being an active and energetic body. As well, both chambers should be expanded in size to give better representation to the people and to stop local-level differences from being elided. Members of the House of Representatives are responsible for representing around 750,000 people on average. In the Senate, just two legislators from each state is inadequate for representing the views of electorates that can number in the tens of millions. In short, the views of too many Americans are simply not represented in Congress – a problem that can only be addressed by shrinking the size of congressional districts and expanding the number of legislators. Enlarging the House and Senate – and abolishing the abjectly undemocratic Electoral College – would go a long way toward better connecting the American people with their leaders in Washington.

As Congress becomes bigger, so should its staff. According to the Federal Managers Association, something like 31,000 people currently work for members of Congress, legislative committees, the Library of Congress, or the Government Accountability Office.[22] This is not enough to rival the manpower and expertise that the executive branch has at its disposal. Put bluntly, Congress needs help to conduct better oversight, write more effective laws, and demonstrate true leadership when it comes to setting the direction of US foreign policy. Raising the number, quality, and remuneration of congressional staffers on Capitol Hill ought to be something that the legislative branch can fix relatively easily. Relevant for this book, improving the country's systems of representation would give voice to a much wider spectrum of interests when it comes to foreign policy – a critical democratizing move that would likely strengthen the hand of America's proretrenchment constituencies, which are badly underrepresented under the current system.

Finally, it would behoove Congress to consider creating new states out of America's existing nonsovereign territories – or, at the very least, exploring creative ways to incorporate the territories into existing states. It is indefensible for the US territories to be excluded from foreign-policy decisions. Their people fight and die in America's wars. They should have a say over them.

Making Retrenchment Salable

Beyond institutional reforms to the government (some of which might seem far-fetched in the present context), there are a number of strategies that proretrenchment figures could implement in order to give politicians a self-interested reason to move away from the primacist consensus. Proponents of retrenchment must make sensible choices regarding how to establish their preferred foreign policies as attractive in political terms. Drawing on E.E. Schattschneider, the key is to focus on the scope of political conflict by bringing forward the domestic cleavages that ought to exist when it comes to US foreign policy but have for too long been papered over.[23]

As has been discussed, not everybody in the United States benefits from military primacy. Those who do benefit tend to know about it and organize in support of it – but those who "lose out" from US foreign policy are mostly ignorant of the costs they have been forced to bear. The focus of restrainers should be to publicize the very real distributive implications of military primacy and encourage America's politicians and political parties to see the advantage in representing the losers as well as the winners, not least of all because the former group might very well now be more numerous. Per Schattschneider, the goal of proretrenchment actors must be to enjoin the "audience" (presently disengaged citizens) to become "participants" in the political process (voters and candidates for office), thus expanding the scope of the conflict over foreign policy and broadening the range of interests being represented. In short, retrenchers need to pick a series of fights over US foreign policy – fights that all Americans will want to join.

This idea is similar to what the political scientist William Riker called "heresthetic" – the strategic manipulation of dimensions, frames, and other facets of the decision-making process for the purpose of engineering a desired outcome.[24] Riker agreed with Schattschneider that political actors do not engage in a free and equal exchange of ideas, but rather that the business of politics tends to be heavily influenced by agenda-setting and the elevation of some dimensions of political disagreement over others, control of the size of the electorate, and so forth. As the British social theorist Stuart Hall once wrote: "Politics does not reflect majorities; it creates them."[25]

When it comes to manipulating the debate over foreign policy, several obvious ways forward present themselves. First, restrainers would be well advised to reframe foreign policy away from *international* security – which has a vague and overly broad meaning – toward *national* self-defense, economic security, and social cohesion. At the present time, it is all too easy for supporters of military primacy to cast retrenchment as an existential threat to global stability. This is not true, but it is an effective device at shutting down discussion over alternative foreign policies. If the stakes of foreign policy were reframed, the perceived costs of retrenchment might be lowered, and the manifold benefits of retrenchment would become more easily intelligible. It is especially important that foreign policy be portrayed in terms of the economic security of ordinary Americans, perhaps, given that economic policy is something that all citizens have a view on. Framing foreign policy in terms of domestic prosperity rather than international crises, then, would be one way of ensuring that a more diverse array of ideas and opinions are brought to the table than is presently the case.

Some politicians have had success in this regard. The concept of a "peace dividend," the slogan "America First," and the pledge to build a "foreign policy for the middle class" – all of these framings are ways to foreground the domestic implications of foreign policy and, by extension, invite a focus on how foreign policy can be reoriented for the benefit of ordinary Americans. But more can be done. After all, a foreign policy is only ever defensible in a democratic context if it makes people feel as though their interests are being served. Restrainers should therefore develop credible domestic plans to connect retrenchment with improved economic fortunes. This might mean finding ways to insulate communities against the vagaries of the world economy via a robust welfare state and redistributive policies. Or it might mean offering the voting public a literal dividend in the form of tax cuts or rebates. The point is simply that the case for retrenchment could and probably should be made in terms that convey the tangible benefits that might exist for ordinary Americans.

How much money might be available for such giveaways? In 2012, Ben Friedman and Justin Logan estimated that a radical program of retrenchment would save the United States around $900 billion over the course of a decade.[26] Adjusted for inflation, this would be equal to around $1.3 trillion in 2024, or around $130 billion per year. This is a significant amount of money – more than enough, for example, to extend pandemic-era rules on Child Tax Credit in perpetuity, a move that has the potential to end child poverty in the United States.

As it shifts its focus from international order-building to domestic priorities, the United States also needs an industrial policy that works. This will be crucial for reassuring Americans that their government puts domestic interests over the interests of the global economy. Toward this end, Charles Kupchan and Peter Trubowitz have called for workers to have a greater say in trade negotiations, with the secretary of labor becoming a member of the National Security Council, for example, and Washington creating programs to assist communities negatively impacted by trade.[27] Such moves to conciliate labor would certainly help to create a more inclusive and equitable industrial policy for the United States.

Second, proponents of restraint should insist upon a reframing of US foreign policy toward a focus on US soldiers' lives. The success of American foreign policy should be measured in blood. The avoidance of bloodshed should be a hallmark of an unimpeachable defense policy. Any loss of life should be regarded as a failure, especially when American lives are being lost in pursuit of interests divorced from core US national interests. Viewed in this light, much of contemporary US foreign policy begins to look unconscionable. Consider the ethics of US deployments in Europe and East Asia, which are essentially commitment devices meant to convince America's adversaries that Washington would (or might) intervene militarily on its allies' behalf. Because such extended deterrence commitments are inherently difficult to make credible, US leaders have drawn on Thomas Schelling to make threats that leave something to chance.[28] The idea here is that, if US troops are killed in the line of duty, the sitting US president will lose some degree of control over how to respond; domestic revulsion at American soldiers being killed by an enemy aggressor will introduce an element of passion, chance, and unpredictability into US decision-making.

On paper, this is a good way to make alliance commitments seem more credible: even if an adversary doubts that the United States would be *eager* to defend an ally, that same adversary can more easily be made to believe that the United States *might* fight for an ally once an element of chance has been introduced into the equation. But it is also a fundamentally problematic means of deterrence in the sense that it holds US soldiers' lives hostage. The American people might be receptive to arguments in favor of retrenchment if it is pointed out to them that current US defense policy is based upon the callous instrumentalization of service personnel's lives.

Third, restrainers should invoke the language of multilateralism and burden-sharing when explaining alternative foreign policies. These words resonate with ordinary Americans. What is more, they militate in favor of a more restrained foreign policy when used in conjunction with one another. While some in the United States are comfortable with a unilateralist foreign policy and chafe at the idea of Washington being constrained by external actors, most Americans are actually in favor of the United Nations, NATO, and other multilateral organizations. The problem is that, in the recent past, multilateralism has been more fiction than reality. US leaders have sought international support for interventionist foreign policies, but they have shouldered most of the burden of carrying out these interventions. If multilateralism could be coupled with a true focus on burden-sharing (or better yet, *burden-shifting*) then it should follow that the United States will be less involved in overseas military operations even when these enjoy international backing. This is something that most Americans would support.

Fourth, proponents of retrenchment should make every effort to appeal to America's environmentalists – a powerful political movement, especially among younger voters. Without doubt, a militarized foreign policy is bad for the natural environment. Preparing for war is a heavy industry, responsible for consuming massive amounts of raw materials and fossil fuels. Fighting wars is even worse, given that armed conflict invariably entails the total devastation of the natural world. And then there are the opportunity costs of spending eyewatering sums of money on warfare each year instead of investing those resources in the planet's future by developing green energy sources, installing home insulation, funding just transitions, or bankrolling other public policies designed to promote conservation and sustainability. Another opportunity cost of excessive militarism is the alienation of foreign powers whose cooperation will be essential to finding common solutions to problems such as climate change and biodiversity loss, but who are desperately unlikely to work closely with the United States so long as Washington remains dedicated to maintaining military primacy.

Finally, instead of calling for cuts to the defense budget, restrainers should call for freezes.[29] This is a sensible proposition because it avoids giving primacists an open goal. Calling for *cuts* to defense expenditure would invite obvious political attacks; it would be too easy to construe restrainers as antimilitary and ignorant about national security issues. But calling for *freezes* to defense expenditure is much more defensible. It shifts the burden onto primacists to argue for why more spending is required and allows restrainers to don the mantle of economic competency without being lampooned for illiterate security policies.

These five attempts to manipulate the dimensionality of the foreign policy debate – focus on economic security instead of national security, elevate concerns for the lives of US service personnel, insist upon true multilateralism and burden-shifting, embrace the environmental movement, and call for freezes in defense spending – are relatively hard to argue against. None of them carries the baggage of isolationism or appeasement. Each is consistent with core tenets of US political culture and can find support in recent opinion polling. In short, they constitute a firm foundation from which to argue for a more restrained foreign policy; a set of heresthetic maneuvers that promises to reframe the debate over foreign policy on terms more favorable to restrainers than primacists. The point is to break the temptation of one party to punish the other for attempting broad-based retrenchment. For policies of restraint and retrenchment to be feasible, politicians and their parties will need political cover. By reorienting policy debates along the lines laid out above, such cover might be manufactured.

Empowering a Restraint Coalition

How can restrainers build support in the country? Part of the answer can be found in the heresthetical approach described above – that is, making retrenchment more salable in political terms. Restrainers need to find salient issues that will mobilize the American people to join the conversation over foreign policy and insist upon alterations to the status quo. This might be a generational task – yet it can be done. But in the meantime, supporters of retrenchment should also rethink their target audiences if they are to conjure a restraint coalition. Elites in Washington will be most easily persuaded if they can be sandwiched between compelling arguments and grassroots political pressure. To this end, proponents of retrenchment should aim to both expand their influence in the nation's capital while also strengthening local-level institutions, interests, and associations.[30]

In terms of the former, the goal must be to "alter the intellectual and ideational fabrics of US government and society."[31] This means developing new and better-resourced think tanks dedicated to fleshing out the projects of retrenchment and restraint; funding the creation of new academic centers; publishing websites and print magazines that challenge the naturalness of the foreign-policy status quo; providing advice, briefing documents, and perhaps even political contributions to candidates for office; and otherwise offering an alternative point of view to the hegemonic discourse that normalizes America's militarist approach to foreign affairs. Much has been done in this regard already, of course, but there is still a great deal more that could be achieved.

Looking beyond Washington, the goal of foreign-policy reformers should be to identify those regions that lose from high military spending, as well as those that might benefit from a smaller defense budget. Reforms could even be introduced to *require* the US government to provide local governments with the costs of war – and the opportunity costs of war – with a view to democratizing foreign policy and empowering parts of the country that are not used to having their interests represented in the national-level conversation over grand-strategic ends and means.

Moving beyond geography, however, restrainers should also make a bargain with younger voters whose fortunes are not served by overseas interventionism. Housing shortages, expensive education, student debt, inaccessible healthcare, fewer economic opportunities, the cost of raising a family – all these problems are common complaints of young people in America, who feel as though they have had a raw deal in comparison to their older counterparts. It should be possible to convince younger voters (who already trend toward being skeptical of the military) that, instead of increasing defense spending year on year, the federal government ought to fund investments in social programs to help those who are struggling. In short, young voters are perhaps "persuadable" when it comes to foreign policy; they could feasibly be enjoined to back a grand strategy of restraint en masse if such a foreign policy was coupled with a clear and compelling domestic agenda. From this view, the future is on the side of those who are willing to imagine a more inclusive and egalitarian America.

The cause of retrenchment would also be served by political reforms to empower women in government and politics. To be clear, the argument is *not* that women's political empowerment would change US foreign policy into something more pacifist. Nor is the argument that women are essentially different from men in some way, whether because of biological differences or inflexible social roles. And nor is the argument that women's political empowerment should be valued only because it holds promise of advancing the cause of retrenchment. Rather, the point is that the inclusion of women in the foreign-policy process – which should be done anyway, for reasons of basic political equality – would almost certainly produce more peaceful outcomes. This is a fairly stable finding in political science literature, but one which restraint-minded scholars have tended to overlook.

For example, some researchers have found that women tend to negotiate international agreements that are more equitable and thus more stable.[32] This is true across country cases, but has specifically been shown to hold in the case of the United States. Other scholars have found that female peacekeepers have greater success at upholding basic human security than male counterparts.[33] And an overwhelming corpus of scholarship indicates that countries that safeguard women's rights tend to be more peaceful on the world stage, whereas societies that devalue the lives of women and girls are reliably more likely to use violence as an instrument of statecraft.[34] Overall, the consensus seems to be that empowering women at home and abroad is an essential prerequisite to formulating better foreign policies and reducing overseas tensions. This makes sense when it is considered that the opposite of female empowerment is female disempowerment, something only possible in the context of misogyny, marginalization, and outright repression – hardly the hallmarks of peace-loving societies.

For centuries, of course, the United States marginalized the views of women when it came to foreign policy.[35] This long period of male-dominated foreign policy no doubt resulted in a pattern of US foreign relations that was more militaristic and antagonistic than the population as a whole – that is, women and men combined – would have preferred if given the chance to weigh in. In other words, the disenfranchisement of half of America's adult population had an effect on the country's trajectory. Now, a course correction is long overdue.

How could women's empowerment be achieved? Options include passing the Equal Rights Amendment,[36] developing cadres of women foreign-policy leaders inside the major political parties, and moving to a system of all-women shortlists for elected offices. But whatever the solutions, it is clear that

the United States urgently needs more women in top leadership positions, women staffing the permanent bureaucracy,
and more women in the military. Women comprise just 28
percent of Congress as of 2023, a paltry proportion that could
be enhanced through electoral reform and outreach.[37] Women
hold just 30.7 percent of "senior pay level" positions in the
intelligence community.[38] And only ten women have ever held
the rank of four-star general or admiral, compared to hundreds of men who have held the same position. This imbalance
of achievement must be addressed as a basic issue of equality
and equitable access to the levers of power. But at the same
time, any reform that makes foreign policy more democratic,
inclusive, representative, and egalitarian is likely to result in
a more restrained foreign policy than is presently the case –
women's political empowerment being certainly no exception.

Conclusion

The grand strategy of military primacy can count on legions
of supporters inside the United States. But it is not good for
the country as a whole. This chapter has begun the process
of identifying which segments of society might be mobilized
against primacy and in favor of a new foreign policy. But as has
been discussed, moving toward a grand strategy of restraint
will require more than just convincing people. It will also likely
depend upon some set of domestic reforms – e.g., changes
to the electoral system – that could loosen the stranglehold
of primacists over the US government and politics. These
reforms might sound ambitious or unrealistic at first blush,
but America has changed before. It can change again.

   To be sure, it will take bold political entrepreneurs to begin
the work of changing the national conversation around foreign
policy. Most obviously, restrainers must focus on widening and deepening the cadre of retrenchers in government,

politics, society, and the economy. This is already being carried out, of course, with think tanks like the Cato Institute, Quincy Institute, and Defense Priorities doing admirable work to assemble groups of policy experts and intellectuals capable of offering insightful commentary on the full range of foreign policy and national security issues. In time, this might translate into restrainers securing toeholds in the permanent bureaucracy and as political advisers to mainstream leaders, as well as having a greater number of restrainers elected to national office in their own right.

7

Internationalism Anew

The United States must retrench – but retrenchment does not mean retreat.[1] In this final chapter, I explain how domestic renewal and military retrenchment can be pursued in tandem to produce a new version of international engagement that is more capable of advancing US interests in an uncertain world. My argument, in brief, is that the United States must reduce its reliance on hard power and instead leverage a range of nonmilitary tools of statecraft that exploit America's geographic, technological, and soft power advantages. The US military does not need to be massively forward deployed for the United States to be safe and secure. On the contrary, vast overseas deployments likely worsen US national security. Nor does the United States need to be militarily preponderant in order to inspire change overseas. In a multipolar world, there are better and safer ways to promote international change than primacy.

What I propose, then, is not retreat or isolation – but a brand of overseas engagement that differs from the current grand strategy of military primacy. In concrete terms, what I call "internationalism anew" has six components. The most important of these is military retrenchment. Without doubt, the United States must shrink the size of its global military footprint. This means reducing the number of US forces that are stationed in the Middle East, Europe, and East Asia – no matter what crises might be plaguing each of these regions. I argue that military retrenchment will make the United States more secure (by reducing the risk of the US military becoming embroiled in foreign wars), that it will enhance international security (by making others more responsible for deterring aggression in their respective regions), and that it will help to restore US soft power.

Second, the United States should move toward a smaller military that is designed primarily for the purposes of direct deterrence and national self-defense. In terms of conventional forces, this means investing in the Navy and the Air Force over the Army and Marine Corps. Washington should also invest heavily in intelligence and cybersecurity. Having a smaller Army and reducing the number and size of overseas bases will result in cost savings that, over time, will allow for the gradual redeployment of resources toward the home front. But nothing should be done to weaken America's ability to deter attacks on itself. To this end, I support the maintenance of a strong nuclear deterrent.

Third, the United States should implement a strategy of offshore balancing. This means making foreign allies and partners more robust against external aggression rather than shouldering the burden of their defense. Offshore balancing could take the form of offering America's allies generous amounts of military aid, economic backing, and intelligence-sharing, as well as support for regional security pacts – but it should not involve the assumption of more security obligations by the United States. The key point is that regional allies have more of a stake in their own security than does Washington, and so it is these regional actors that have the best chance of upholding the international status quo by making credible threats against would-be aggressors.

Fourth, Washington should continue to invest in international institutions. Organizations like the United Nations are important for facilitating international cooperation, advancing arms control agreements where appropriate, and amplifying America's voice on the world stage. Global governance has great potential to solve pressing challenges facing the world today, and the United States has self-interested reasons to play a leading role in these institutions. Washington should be a standard-bearer for the causes of international law, peaceful resolution of disputes, arms control, and universal human rights. Wherever possible, the United States should push for international institutions to have broad memberships – preferably universal membership – rather than being restricted to those countries that are already favorable to the United States.

Fifth, I argue for the United States to invest heavily in economic and humanitarian aid, with a special focus on women's rights and political empowerment. Political scientists have demonstrated a clear and compelling connection between the treatment of people (especially women) in domestic politics and the behavior of states on the world stage. The conclusion is that the world will be safer and more secure if it is more equal and humane. These are conditions that the United States can harness its awesome material wealth and soft power advantages toward bringing about.

Finally, the United States must remain in favor of an open world economy. Even though trade liberalization has lost some support in recent decades, it is still the best available means that humankind possesses to reduce poverty, increase life expectancy, and promote just and lasting peace. What is more, globalization is actually the best way to make states resilient to the sorts of international economic disruptions that many commentators fear will be the hallmarks of the coming multipolar world. The United States and its allies should therefore reembrace globalization for reasons of geopolitical self-interest.

Pulling Back

The cornerstone of America's next strategic adjustment must be a drawing down of forward-deployed forces.[2] These garrisons, most of which originate from World War II and the early Cold War era, have long since passed their expiration date. Perhaps they once were necessary to maintain regional security in Europe, East Asia, and the Persian Gulf – but they no longer are. On the contrary, they make the United States less safe. Not only do garrisons make it too easy for presidents to launch wars and other military strikes,[3] but they are targets for hostile powers – tripwires that, if activated, could plunge the United States into devasting and unwanted foreign wars. It is already the case that America's garrisons in places like Iraq and Syria have become punching bags for Shia militias backed by Iran. In East Asia, US forces are highly vulnerable to a Chinese surprise attack. And in Europe, the United States occupies some of the wealthiest countries in the world, who also happen to be adjacent to an active warzone in Ukraine. Europeans could easily defend themselves if they spent enough on defense, yet they rely upon American forces to deter Russian aggression.[4] In each of these regions, retrenchment is essential to avoid the United States being dragged into a war at a time of an adversary's choosing.

It is worth emphasizing that the whole logic of overseas deployments is that they are *supposed* to ensnare the United States in wars that US leaders would otherwise rather not fight. As described in chapter 6, the logic of "tripwire" forward deployments is best understood in the context of what Thomas Schelling called "the threat that leaves something to chance."[5] Writing in the context of the Cold War, Schelling recognized that it was inherently difficult to threaten to fight against a nuclear-armed adversary because, if push ever came to shove, no rational leader would follow through on such a suicidal threat. He argued that one way to make such threats credible is to take decision-making out of the hands of political leaders. Putting forward deployments in the line of fire serves this purpose: if US soldiers are killed in battle, nobody can say for sure what leaders in Washington would do in response. Emotions would take over. Would the United States stay out of a conflict that could go nuclear, even if it meant uproar at home? Or would American leaders feel compelled to fight back, even if this meant escalating an unwinnable war? Would leaders in Washington even be in control of events at that point, once passions were so high? None of these questions can be answered with certainty in advance – and it is exactly this unpredictability that is supposed to make America's commitments to its allies more believable than would otherwise be the case.

In an age of multipolarity, however, it is incredibly risky to leave America's string of overseas garrisons intact. Too many US soldiers are exposed to attacks from Russia, China, Iran, North Korea, and other adversaries for tripwire forces to be worth the gamble. What if a stray rocket hits US forces? What if a mercenary group like Wagner or a proxy like Hezbollah launches an unauthorized assault? What if American forces themselves provoke an incident with a hostile power? There is no telling how these scenarios could end. The sitting US president might feel compelled to mobilize the United States for all-out war, even though the costs and consequences would be unfathomably bad. Or future leaders might decide to back down in the face of foreign aggression, causing irreparable harm to America's reputation. Either way, leaving the United States so broadly exposed to such enormous risks makes little strategic sense at a time when America's allies could simply engage in direct deterrence to defend themselves rather than relying on US-led extended deterrence.

Retrenchment should therefore be sold to the US public as a means of making Americans more secure. As described in chapter 6, the voting public cares about the lives of service personnel. To ordinary Americans, it makes little sense why US troops continue to die in places like Iraq, Niger, Somalia, Syria, and Yemen. If there is a need for counterterrorism operations in a place like Niger, why can local actors (or adjacent states) not undertake these missions? If the security of Taiwan is at stake, why should the Taiwanese and their nearest neighbors not be responsible for deterring a Chinese invasion? It is unconscionable, unstrategic, and unnecessary to continue using US forces as hostages. Most overseas garrisons should be brought home. The American people will understand these arguments, especially given that retrenchment need not mean abandonment: the US should still focus on making its partners resilient to aggression, even as it declines to assume the burden of fighting on their behalf.

As well as making Americans safer, retrenchment would be good for the United States at home. As noted in the previous chapter, it would allow for money that would otherwise have been spent on increasing the defense budget to be reallocated toward other budget items, whether social programs or tax cuts. Retrenchment would also allow US political culture and national identity to evolve in a positive direction. As Andrew Bacevich has argued, overseas deployments have led America's elites to think like imperialists.[6] To shake this imperious mindset, obviously detrimental to the health of the US republic, some degree of retrenchment is essential.

Abroad, retrenchment will almost certainly help to restore US soft power. Some countries will be sad to lose US garrisons – and perhaps these overseas deployments could be the last to go – but in the long term, it will serve America well to reorient its external engagement away from militarism. From Okinawa to Morocco, local people are resentful about US troops being based on their soil. Soldiers should not be ambassadors for the United States; that is the job of diplomats.

Direct Deterrence and National Self-Defense

Of course, Americans will not support policies of retrenchment if such policies will leave the country less secure. Nor should they. Proponents of retrenchment must therefore be clear that overseas retrenchment (the withdrawal of forces from foreign soil) need not come at the overall expense of US national security. They must explain how, on the contrary, retrenchment can be pursued in tandem with a strengthening of the US military in terms of its core functions: direct deterrence and national defense.

What will this look like in practice? First, it requires an appreciation that the United States is already secure. It has two friendly neighbors to the north and south, and benefits from the vast Atlantic and Pacific oceans as "moats" to the east and west. Of course, America's geographic remoteness is no guarantee against external threats; Pearl Harbor and 9/11 are evidence enough for this point. But the country is not at risk of invasion. By investing in the right kind of military – one that boasts a formidable Navy and Air Force, especially – the United States can leverage its geographic advantages and ensure that North America remains more or less impregnable to conventional military attack for the foreseeable future. No other great power enjoys such a fortuitous geopolitical setting.

To be sure, investing in a strong Navy and Air Force means that the United States will (and should) retain power-projection capabilities. But the ability to bomb targets from a long range is different from the ability to fight multiple simultaneous ground wars. The United States should strengthen the former sort of capability but relinquish the latter. The United States needs long-range bombers, missiles, and stealth ships that can operate far from America's shores and defeat threats as they emerge – but it does not need an enormous Army capable of fighting pitched battles in Europe, Asia, or the Middle East.

The ability to fight and win such wars has little to do with national self-defense in the twenty-first century.[7]

Given America's formidable strategic depth and power-projection capabilities, it would be safe for leaders in Washington to reduce the size of the Army and Marine Corps, with a particular focus on shrinking the Army. As described in the previous chapter, the US should freeze its defense budget and gradually shift resources from the Army (overseas garrisons being the first to be cut) toward air, naval, and nuclear forces. If US strategists fear the onset of a major land war in Europe or Asia, it should be the policy of the United States to encourage America's allies to take primary responsibility for preparing to fight and win such wars – which, presumably, would concern their own national self-defense much more than America's. In short, the United States does not need hundreds of thousands of troops who can deploy at a moment's notice, and it certainly does not need these troops to be forward deployed on foreign soil. Kyle Haynes is right that "leading from behind" remains a viable strategy for the United States in most conceivable contexts.[8] The Libya debacle has unfairly tarnished what is, at its core, a good *modus vivendi* for helping allies achieve their own regional security goals. And in the unlikely event that the United States ever needs to mobilize an expeditionary force in the future, it could surely do so, just as it has done before.[9]

Of course, nuclear weapons remain the ultimate defensive tool. The United States must maintain a sufficient nuclear arsenal to deter aggression. For maximum deterrence, the United States should maintain the full nuclear triad of strategic bombers, intercontinental ballistic missiles, and submarine-launched ballistic missiles, but the focus ought to be on building advanced submarines given the greater secrecy that they afford. In all likelihood, America's nuclear arsenal could be reduced in size without harming the nation's ability to engage in deterrence – but Washington must always invest in nuclear modernization. The safety and security of the US nuclear arsenal must be a priority.

The United States does not need to spend more money on defense – it just needs to spend its money more wisely. Most obviously, resources could be spent on developing high-tech, advanced weapons focused on defensive operations. Money could also be spent on veterans' affairs – rewarding those women and men who have served their country with honor but are too often forgotten upon return to civilian life. Investing in this way would be good strategy and the ethical thing to do, but it would also be good politics in the sense that all Americans desire to see the nation's service personnel and veterans being treated with dignity and respect.

Overhauling America's military in this way will be difficult in political terms. But it is an essential task. The United States does not need to disarm, but it does need to adopt a defensive posture. It does not need to abandon its allies, but it does need to rebalance those alliances and refrain from creating new ones. It does not need to sacrifice a strong defense, but it can do without formidable offensive (expeditionary) capabilities. In sum, America's hard power should be used for the primary purpose of deterring great-power rivals.

At the same time, internationalism anew means remaining attuned to foreign threats. This, in turn, means a huge role for intelligence. Edward Luttwak argues that the Byzantine Empire relied heavily on espionage as a means of ensuring external security.[10] The United States today can learn from this. Washington should strive to have the best intelligence services in the world, and should continue to ally itself with others in the Five Eyes (an intelligence-sharing compact between the United States, Britain, Australia, Canada, and New Zealand) as well as developing similar such arrangements with other allies and partners. Intelligence-sharing will help the United States to be a good ally to its partners around the world given that such cooperation can save lives and prevent wars.[11]

As well as investing in intelligence, the United States must also maintain a robust capability to defend itself in the cyber realm. The United States must invest in deterrence by denial (the ability to stop hackers and others in their tracks) as well as deterrence by punishment (the ability to inflict terrible consequences upon hostile powers in response to cyberattacks). Washington should engage in "persistent engagement" rather than waiting for an attack to happen. Again, this is a way that the United States can protect itself and serve its allies, as an arsenal of digital democracy. For this to be successful, however, Washington will have to forge real partnerships with academia and the private sector – investing significant amounts of money in research, development, training, and the rollout of best practices – recognizing that the private sector has an interest in being resilient against cyberattacks, too, but needs significant government backing to become so.

Offshore Balancing

If the United States exchanges its global military footprint for a focus on direct deterrence and national self-defense, what does this mean for the security of other regions? In particular, how will the United States ensure that no hostile power is ever positioned to dominate Europe or East Asia (or both), which has long been a cardinal objective of US foreign policymakers? My argument is that the United States should move to offshore balancing as a means of ensuring security in overseas regions.[12] I recognize that the United States will always have a national interest in ensuring that Europe and East Asia remain outside of the control of a hostile power, but aver that overseas garrisons are not the best solution anymore even if they might have been during the Cold War. In today's context, Washington can best ensure the security of its friends and allies via the provision of arms, economic support, military intelligence, and political cooperation – not the direct deployment of US troops.

What is offshore balancing? In a nutshell, it is the strategy of asking US allies to prepare their own means of deterrence and national defense.[13] It is based upon an assumption that other countries have the strongest interest in their own self-preservation, and so can be relied upon to take measures to deter adversaries and, if necessary, fight wars of national survival. Where allied capabilities are lacking, offshore balancing dictates that the United States should intervene to help strengthen its partners' military capacity and training[14] – but should not deploy its own troops except as a last resort.

Of course, the point that Europeans and East Asians are capable of defending themselves has been made time and again by restrainers. It is accurate. So, too, has it been pointed out that the United States always meant for its garrisons in East Asia and Europe to be temporary measures. But the problem is that America's allies will not begin to spend more on their own militaries so long as they have the option of sheltering beneath the US security umbrella. This means that US retrenchment must happen first. It must be announced and begun to be implemented before America's allies will move to make up the shortfall. This should begin with the issuing of private warnings to close US allies but should ultimately include public announcements about the US intention to reduce its overseas military footprint. If handled correctly, shifting the burden of security onto America's allies need not create an opening for insecurity; and, in the end, will actually result in more credible regimes of deterrence in both Europe and East Asia.

What will a strategy of offshore balancing look like once it has been fully implemented? To be clear, it will still require a highly active United States on the world stage – but the forms of international engagement being pursued by Washington will be very different from the permanent military occupation of foreign lands. Offshore balancing means a hypervigilant role for the United States in terms of developing and providing arms, rendering military training, gathering and sharing intelligence, engaging in political cooperation, gifting economic support, and working to create regional security pacts that do not depend upon the United States. Offshore balancing is thus a strategy aimed at upholding the status quo and preventing any major territorial revisions that would benefit US adversaries; it is not a strategy of retreat, isolation, or disinterest. The goal is to make US allies and partners resilient to coercion – that is, more able to conduct deterrence autonomous from the United States – rather than assume that only US security guarantees can keep the world safe.

Can offshore balancing work? The answer is yes. Across the Atlantic, the nations of Europe have the economic and military potential to defend themselves and deter aggression from Russia. Washington should support the formation of a European Army if this is what Europeans decide is best, but should not make retrenchment contingent upon a European Army. Strong national militaries working in concert with one another will be enough to deter aggression from Russia and other hostile powers. The United States should not leave NATO in the near term, but should gradually move toward a posture where European security depends much less upon the credibility of the US threat to intervene on Europe's behalf. In time, the NATO alliance could be renegotiated to clarify America's role in transatlantic security, emphasizing that Europeans are primarily responsible for the maintenance of international security on their continent. Toward this end, Washington should encourage the creation of British, French, and German bases in Poland and the Baltics. London and Paris might even be enjoined to extend their nuclear umbrellas over the rest of Europe.

In Asia, it is unlikely that an analog to NATO will emerge. Regional security will not be ensured via a collective security pact like in Europe. Instead, the United States must focus on encouraging regional allies and partners to spend more on self-defense and to invest in the right kinds of weaponry to deter aggression. To be clear, the US garrisons in South Korea and Japan should ultimately be withdrawn. Those nations can deter Chinese, North Korean, and Russian aggression via strong conventional deterrents.[15] The US will retain a sizable presence in Guam, Hawaii, Alaska, and its other Pacific states and territories, of course – whatever is necessary for strict national defense – but its focus in Asia must be on making others resilient to aggression. The United States should maintain its commitment to nuclear nonproliferation. Enlarging the club of nuclear-armed states will do nothing to make Americans or the rest of the world safer. Instead, Washington and its allies should turn to conventional military deterrents – plus threats of economic punishments and political sanctions – to dissuade revisionist powers from attempting to overturn the territorial status quo in East Asia.

The current grand strategy of military primacy is a recipe for conflict with China. It is a false choice to say that the United States must choose between military primacy and Chinese domination. This denies agency to East Asian states, who have a self-interest in their own survival and can be relied upon to balance against China if it were ever to appear as though Beijing was intent upon regional hegemony. America's biggest interest in East Asia is to avoid a war with China. This is not best achieved through military primacy, but through diplomacy and political accommodation – to which US militarism is a barrier, not an asset. Of course, the United States does not want East Asia to fall under the control of Beijing and should work with its regional partners to make the region robust to Chinese coercion. But this is an achievable goal. The United States should not be fatalistic.

In the Middle East, there is already widespread recognition that the United States must withdraw from the region. Washington should start by ending its wars in Syria, Iraq,

Somalia, and elsewhere. This is the low-hanging fruit. But it must follow up with reducing its garrisons in the Persian Gulf states, too. There is no feasible scenario in which the United States should want to wage another land war in the Middle East. Over the medium to long term, then, America's focus should be on reducing its ability to deploy land power across the Middle East as a means of tying the hands of future leaders who might otherwise have been tempted to use such forces in battle – a capability that is unnecessary to secure US interests and has led to misadventures in the recent past. As in the Asia-Pacific, the United States must remain committed to nuclear nonproliferation in the Middle East. There is the risk that existing strategic partners such as Saudi Arabia will threaten to "go nuclear" in response to a US withdrawal from the region. It would be wrong to minimize this risk, which would imperil security in the Persian Gulf. But at the same time, the United States cannot allow itself to be held hostage: if forward-deployed forces are unnecessary to uphold US national security then they should be brought home.

Russia's invasion of Ukraine in February 2022 offers an illustrative example of how to (not) engage in offshore balancing. For years after the Russian annexation of Crimea in 2014, the United States refused to send lethal aid to Ukraine. It should have. Nor did Washington do enough to encourage European militaries to increase their spending between 2014 and 2022. This was another major mistake. Economic support for Ukraine was lacking, and the United States did far too little to ensure that Ukrainian forces were ready to repel a Russian armed assault. The question is: Would Russia's leaders have invaded Ukraine in 2022 if they had known that (1) Ukraine was poised to fight back and (2) European members of NATO would mobilize to support Ukraine and help it avoid defeat? This must be considered uncertain at best. The lesson of this counterfactual is that the best way the United States can secure

Europe and Asia is to lay plans for how its allies and partners can be made obviously resilient to coercion and armed
attack.

International Organizations and Arms Control

Military retrenchment does not mean isolationism. As it pur-
sues retrenchment, the United States must engage with and
revitalize the world's most important international organizations. These forums matter because they can amplify America's
voice and serve as venues for the organization of like-minded
coalitions on topics such as climate change, arms control, and
economic development. In no small measure, global governance
can serve to alleviate international problems that otherwise
would go unsolved. Of course, international institutions can
disappoint. They do not always live up to expectations. But
in world politics, there is rarely an alternative to talking with
allies and adversaries alike. It is a good thing that international institutions exist to lower the transaction costs for such
dialogue, routinize diplomatic engagement, and provide focal
points for essential intergovernmental cooperation. If they did
not exist, they would have to be invented.

All of these advantages of international organizations will
matter more than ever in a post-American world. There is
no chance of mounting effective responses to climate change,
transnational public health crises, human rights abuses, and
economic underdevelopment without resort to international
organizations. If the United States wants to see these challenges overcome – which it should, out of self-interest if not
altruism – then it has no option but to participate in the
world's panoply of international organizations. America has
enormous soft power, moral authority, and diplomatic heft. It
should make every effort to leverage these assets rather than
walk away and cede international forums to others.

The United States should continue to be a leader in the realm of arms control and nonproliferation of WMD. This means backing the work of organizations like the International Atomic Energy Agency, the UN Institute for Disarmament Research, the UN Office for Disarmament Affairs, and other relevant agencies. The United States should collaborate with foreign governments to fund and insist upon reciprocal monitoring regimes, and ought to push for stronger and more expansive controls on inhumane weapons. Cooperation with Russia and China will be critical in this regard. It is true, of course, that the United States today does not support all arms control initiatives. The Pentagon has shown no inclination to give up cluster munitions, for example. But even in areas such as this, Washington could announce an intention to destroy its stockpile of cluster munitions contingent upon others doing the same. This might never happen, but it would be a relatively cost-free pledge, and would be consistent with America's long-term interest in supporting arms control. When it comes to managing emerging threats, Washington has an opportunity to be a leader in developing common standards regarding the use of artificial intelligence, robotics, and cyberwarfare.

To be sure, critics might wonder why the United States should put faith in multilateral organizations given that, in the past, such institutions were ineffective at upholding international law and order. This is a fair criticism. One needs to look no further than the interwar years – an era during which the United States embraced multilateralism as a means of lessening the risk of conflict – to find evidence of what happens when states expect treaties to do things like limit the size of national militaries, establish laws of war, or even prohibit war as a tool of statecraft. But the policies pursued by the interwar presidents were appropriate given America's place in the distribution of power during the 1920s. International agreements such as the Covenant of the League of Nations (which the United States never ratified), Kellogg-Briand Pact,

Washington Naval Treaty, and Geneva Protocol were imperfect, but they were useful improvements to the pre–World War I international architecture and almost certainly served America's interests. They might have worked even better had Washington joined the League.

Today, organizations like the UN Security Council, World Trade Organization, and World Health Organization are just as imperfect as their predecessors. There is little prospect of the United States, China, Russia, and other major powers cooperating on major questions of international security. Global governance is not a substitute for a strong national defense and does not relieve national governments of having to pursue vigorous bilateral and multilateral diplomacy outside of the confines of formal organizations. But there is much to gain and little to lose from participation in international forums, and the likelihood of the great powers finding common ground will be increased if the United States drops military primacy as its approach to international affairs. Active participation will play well at home and abroad, might result in some nontrivial policy achievements that advance the US national interest, while costing Washington almost nothing in return.

As it engages with international organizations, the United States should try strenuously to avoid carving the world into blocs. Of course, taking soft power seriously means that the United States will not be able to avoid picking fights with the world's most unsavory undemocratic regimes. Washington should continue to condemn human rights abuses abroad, as well as giving vocal support to democratic movements resisting tyranny. This is consistent with US values, and nobody will be surprised to hear such positions coming from America's leaders. But from Germany to Japan and South Africa to South Korea, America's democratic allies are not asking for a global coalition to contain Russia or China. They want the United States to help facilitate a peaceful transition to multilateral order, not a freefall into another Cold War. This means investing in broad-based, inclusive multilateral organizations; not trying to bypass global institutions via exclusive, "minilateral" groupings such as the Quadrilateral Security Dialogue, AUKUS Pact, or even the G7 and G20.

Overseas Development and Women's Empowerment

America spends an enormous amount on humanitarian and economic aid – around $58.5 billion in 2022.[16] But it should spend even more. Overseas aid is one of the best ways that the United States can ameliorate problems in foreign countries and stop overseas crises from metastasizing into security problems that one day impinge upon the United States. This is what Tocqueville called "self-interest properly understood" – the quintessential American view that people thrive most easily when those around them are thriving, too.[17] Applied to foreign policy, self-interest properly understood means promoting the economic development of poorer nations, their integration into the global economy on favorable terms, debt relief, and generous aid packages meant to spur sustainable growth and human development.

The United States should focus its economic and humanitarian aid in a way that promotes women's political empowerment. Scholars such as Robert Trager and Joslyn Barnhart have persuasively shown that women's inclusion in the political process helps to promote peace.[18] This complements earlier work in International Relations that demonstrated a strong link between misogynistic societies and violence.[19] While it is not going to be possible for an outside power like the United States to coerce foreign societies to adopt more inclusive social attitudes when it comes to sex and gender, there is evidence that foreign aid can help to move the needle on these issues.[20] If it wants to inhabit a safer international environment, then, the United States could do far worse than prioritize aid projects that have the potential to create a more gender-equal world. In fact, it is no exaggeration to say that the world will likely never become appreciably more secure (either *within* foreign societies or *among* the world's nations) without making significant progress in terms of sex and gender equality. This should be an absolute priority for every US administration.

An Open World Economy

In the economic sphere, the United States should promote a world economy that is free and fair. This means serving as the world's most vocal defender of free trade, capital account liberalization, and the mobility of labor. Along with the political empowerment of women overseas, free trade is still one of the best ways to promote peace among nations and relieve human misery. Free trade is a progressive idea, with enormous potential to improve the living standards of working people around the world, including in the United States. In fact, Washington should consider reducing tariffs and nontariff barriers on foreign imports even absent the expectation of reciprocity. This would be good for US workers and consumers.

Of course, globalization comes with strings attached. Washington must balance support for economic openness with recognition that national governments have a role to play in safeguarding the interests of their citizens and natural environments. Dani Rodrik is right: the downsides of hyperglobalization are too high to justify untrammeled economic integration.[21] This means Washington must take action to establish a strong social safety net that will protect those most vulnerable to the vagaries of international markets. It should support others in doing so, too, but in a way that promotes the harmonization of social policies rather than the obliteration of the nation-state. If it leads by example in this way, the United States can help to ensure the long-term survival of the global capitalist system by showing other countries how to enjoy the benefits from economic integration in a sustainable, equitable fashion.

At least since Donald Trump's election as President in November 2016, free trade has not been perceived to be a popular issue for US politicians to run on. But in fact, research suggests that Americans reacted with skepticism to Trump's trade war with China, punishing him at the polls.[22] There is still significant potential to mobilize voters in support of free trade if it can be coupled with workers' rights and environmental protections, and if it is framed in the right way – that is, as an effective tax cut, as a way to reduce consumer prices, and as a way to create jobs. Most evidence indicates that American voters are "sociotropic" when it comes to trade issues – that is, they formulate their views on trade policy with reference to how they perceive their fellow citizens to be faring rather than focusing on their own individual circumstances.[23] The implication is that trade policy must be contextualized as a means to improve the lot of average Americans – not a tall order, by any stretch.

At the same time, America should do its best to preserve the role of the dollar. As Carla Norlöff explains, "Americans benefit from the ease and convenience of transacting in dollars, seigniorage, monetary flexibility, and being the world's safe haven in times of crisis. For the US government, it serves as a non-military instrument of coercion with which to police the world, as well as a source of prestige."[24] The more transactions are denominated in dollars the world over, the more liquidity exists in the US economy – making it far easier for America's firms to access capital. The dominance of the dollar also keeps the dollar high, allowing US consumers to purchase goods from abroad at lower costs than would otherwise be the case. These are advantages worth preserving. This means using financial sanctions judiciously (lest foreign countries try to reduce their reliance on the dollar),[25] ensuring political stability at home, reducing the size of America's budget deficits, and working with others to uphold the conditions that make an open world economy possible.

The United States must resist the temptation to "weaponize" its central and dominant position in the world economy. It is tempting for US leaders to use economic tools of statecraft such as sanctions, export controls, and even trade wars to coerce its foreign rivals. In the recent past, the United States leveraged its enormous economic power to punish Russia for its invasion of Ukraine, heap pressure upon the North Korean and Iranian economies, and isolate China from high-end semiconductors. These are all defensible policies – but the cumulative effect of too much "weaponized interdependence"[26] might be to dissuade foreign nations from participating in the US-led international economy altogether, for fear of having their vulnerabilities exploited in the future. This would be a tragic outcome. Global interdependence is good for the United States and it is good for the cause of world peace. Instead of exploiting economic power for short-term advantages, leaders in Washington should prioritize upholding a world economy that incentivizes long-term peace by providing all stakeholders a reasonable expectation of benefiting from mutual cooperation long into the future.

Retrenchment without Retreat

The forward posture inherited from the World War II and Cold War eras constitutes a material substrate – a hulking set of extraordinary physical circumstances – that still conditions US foreign policy in important ways.[27] First, the fact of never-ending forward deployments has made overseas interventionism a central part of the US national identity. Not everyone in the United States agrees that being beached on the Eurasian landmass is a right and proper world role, of course. But among the political class, narratives to make sense of America's legacy forward deployments invariably draw upon (and, in turn, help to reinforce) deep-seated ideas about national uniqueness, omnipotence, and benevolence – a *language* of overseas intervention that normalizes and legitimizes the indefinite garrisoning of foreign territories.

Second, the physical presence of so many military personnel and power assets overseas exerts a gravitational tug on politics at home, biasing US leaders in favor of activism over restraint. For decades, leaders have found that they can more easily derive political benefits from using forward-deployed military force to solve, forestall, or otherwise "deal with" foreign crises than by pursing policies of restraint or disengagement.[28] Indeed, US officials can often face stiff penalties for appearing inactive or inattentive when threats emerge along the turbulent frontiers of the Greater United States[29] – a *logic* of overseas intervention that leaders of all political stripes have found difficult to ignore.

The point is that America's large and long-term forward presence in Eurasia has rewrought politics on the home front such that the United States has become hardwired to accept indefinite overseas entanglements. Over time, a common script has emerged for national leaders to follow, one based upon the assumption that the US military can and must continue to occupy countries in Europe, East Asia, and the Middle East. There have been leaders who deviated from this script at times, but they have done so at their own political peril, and rarely successfully. Those who challenge the naturalness of America's indefinite overseas presence tend to find themselves on the wrong side of a hegemonic discourse that stresses US exceptionalism and indispensability. Proposals for retrenchment and nonintervention invite a disproportionate amount of punishment in domestic politics in comparison to policies that are consonant with the idea of enlightened overseas activism.[30]

This gross case of institutional maladaptation cannot stand. The world is no longer safe for a grand strategy of military primacy. Nor does primacy serve the everyday interests of ordinary Americans. The country clings to a set of international policies that were designed for a different era but cannot be changed because of inflexible domestic politics. This would be bad enough if the policies in question were merely suboptimal or anachronistic, but today the problem is far worse. Military primacy is deleterious to domestic society and heightens the risks of the United States sleepwalking into a disastrous confrontation with a great-power rival.

In the abstract, America's leaders have no shortage of options when it comes to foreign policy. There is a wealth of academic literature and policy explainers that outline the alternatives to a grand strategy of military primacy. But theoretical substitutes for primacy are of little practical value if they stand no chance of being adopted by policymakers. In the final analysis, this is what prevents the United States from considering different configurations of grand strategy: a domestic political system that is hardwired to support primacist foreign policies and reject programmatic attempts at retrenchment. The conclusion is obvious. America must reform its domestic politics.

Reforming the United States to permit a move away from military primacy will have the added benefit of empowering America's leaders to address a host of domestic afflictions that can hardly be dealt with absent changes to the nation's self-harming foreign policy. Each year, the federal government appropriates $850 billion and ploughs this money into regions of the country that are already doing well in social and economic terms. America's defense budget is a grand exercise in wealth redistribution from the "have nots" to the "haves." This does nothing to address the very real problems that blight the US polity: wealth inequality, racial and gender disparities, housing shortages, unaffordable education, unsustainable debt, substance abuse, and so much more.

Meanwhile, young Americans continue to be sent abroad for dubious purposes. Garrisons in Europe, East Asia, and the

Persian Gulf exist in a constant state of insecurity. Their exposure to lethal risk is by design. Leaders in Washington want
their own citizens to be placed in harm's way as a costly signal
of the nation's support for its allies and partners around the
world. If these service personnel are attacked and killed, their
deaths will be used to spur the United States into a military
response meant to avenge their loss. Why? Why can other
nations not engage in direct deterrence and self-defense just as
the United States does? Why do the lives of US soldiers need
to be put on the line to secure distant regions of the world?
If the answer is that America's allies are too poor or weak to
defend themselves, perhaps the solution is to make them more
resilient rather than keep them dependent upon the United
States for security in perpetuity.

In this book, I have outlined a grand strategy of domestic renewal and international anew that has the potential to
restore US vitality and soft power at home while wielding new
and better tools of statecraft abroad. I have argued that the
United States should implement a grand strategy of enlightened international engagement that will preserve national
security, promote domestic wellbeing, and help to guide the
world toward a more stable form of multipolar coexistence
than will ever be possible under conditions of US pretenses to
primacy. The key pillars of this new grand strategy are military retrenchment, a focus on direct deterrence and national
self-defense, offshore balancing, vigorous participation in
international organizations, generous amounts of overseas aid,
and support for an open world economy.

Domestic renewal and internationalism anew must go
hand in hand; one cannot exist without the other. Not only
must America undertake a wide-ranging strategic adjustment,
exchanging faith in military power for fidelity to the principles
of restraint, but the country must also undertake a series of
political reforms that will make such an adjustment possible.
Some scholars will disagree with the specific ideas for domestic

reform outlined in the book. This is to be expected. But the point is that any grand strategy for the United States must be suited to current and future conditions at the domestic and international levels. It is clear that military primacy is suited to neither. If analysts dispute the arguments made here, then the onus is on them to put forward what a better mix of policies might look like.

America must retrench. But it cannot retreat. Its people must find a way to engage with the outside world in a sustainable fashion. To do this, some form of domestic reform and realignment will be essential. The goal must be to create a new political equilibrium that encourages a slenderer foreign policy and a more harmonious society at home. It can be done.

Notes

Introduction

1　Daniel Immerwahr, "The Strange, Sad Death of America's Political Imagination," *The New York Times*, July 2, 2021, https://www.nytimes.com/2021/07/02/opinion/us-politics-edward-bellamy.html.

2　Doug Bandow, "750 Bases in 80 Countries Is Too Many for Any Nation: Time for the US to Bring Its Troops Home," Cato Institute, October 4, 2021, https://www.cato.org/commentary/750-bases-80-countries-too-many-any-nation-time-us-bring-its-troops-home.

3　See, for example, Chalmers Johnson, *Blowback: The Costs and Consequences of American Empire* (New York, NY: Metropolitan Books, 2000); John Glaser, "Withdrawing from Overseas Bases: Why a Forward-Deployed Military Posture Is Unnecessary, Outdated, and Dangerous," Policy Analysis no. 816 (Cato Institute), 18 July 2017, at 8–11.

4　Charles A. Kupchan, *Isolationism: A History of America's Efforts to Shield Itself from the World* (Oxford: Oxford University Press, 2020).

5　Andrew Bacevich, *The New American Militarism: How Americans*

Are Seduced by War (Oxford: Oxford University Press, 2013 [2005]).

6 Ann Markusen, Peter Hall, Scott Campbell, and Sabina Deitrick, *The Rise of the Gunbelt: The Military Remapping of Industrial America* (New York, NY: Oxford University Press, 1991), at 3.

7 Although Harold Laswell developed the concept of the garrison state before the United States entered World War II, his ideas influenced later critics of societal militarization. See Harold D. Lasswell, "The Garrison State," *American Journal of Sociology* 46, no. 4 (1941): 455–468.

8 Michael Hogan, *A Cross of Iron: Harry S. Truman and the Origins of the National Security State, 1945–1954* (New York, NY: Cambridge University Press, 1998).

9 Stephen M. Walt, *The Hell of Good Intentions: America's Foreign Policy Elite and the Decline of U.S. Primacy* (New York, NY: Farrar, Straus, and Giroux, 2018).

10 C. William Walldorf Jr. and Andrew Yeo, "Domestic Hurdles to a Grand Strategy of Restraint," *The Washington Quarterly* 42, no. 4 (2019): 43–56.

11 See, for example, Eugene Gholz, Daryl G. Press, and Harvey M. Sapolsky, "Come Home, America: The Strategy of Restraint in the Face of Temptation," *International Security* 21, no. 4 (1997): 5–48; Barry Posen, *Restraint: A New Foundation for U.S. Grand Strategy* (Ithaca, NY: Cornell University Press, 2014); John J. Mearsheimer and Stephen M. Walt, "The Case for Offshore Balancing: A Superior U.S. Grand Strategy," *Foreign Affairs* 95, no. 4 (2016): 70–83; A. Trevor Thrall and Benjamin H. Friedman, eds., *US Grand Strategy in the 21st Century: The Case for Restraint* (New York, NY: Routledge, 2018).

12 This definition follows that found in Posen and Andrew L. Ross, "Competing Visions for US Grand Strategy," *International Security* 21, no. 3 (1996): 5–53, at 32–43.

13 Walt, *The Hell of Good Intentions*.

14 Charles Krauthammer, "The Unipolar Moment," *The National Interest* 70, no. 1 (1990/1991): 23–33.

15 Peter Harris, "The Geopolitics of American Exceptionalism," *Asian Perspectives* 46, no. 4 (2022): 583–603, at 591–595.

16 Krauthammer, "The Unipolar Moment."

17 Jared M. McKinney and Harris, *Deterrence Gap: Avoiding War in the Taiwan Strait* (Carlisle, PA: US Army War College Press, 2024), at 52.

18 Van Jackson, *On The Brink: Trump, Kim, and the Threat of Nuclear War* (Cambridge: Cambridge University Press, 2018); Harris, "Trump's War of Choice with Iran," *The National Interest*, January 13, 2020, https://nationalinterest.org/blog/mid dle-east-watch/trumps-war-choice-iran-113411.

19 Caroline Vakil, "Foreign policy experts call for 'limited no-fly zone' over Ukraine," *The Hill*, March 8, 2022, https://thehill.com /policy/international/597279-foreign-policy-experts-call-for-limited-no-fly-zone-over-ukraine/.

20 Harris, Iren Marinova, and Gabriella Gricius, "War in Ukraine in a Polarised America," *LSE Public Policy Review* 3, no. 1 (2023): 1–12, at 3, citing Benjamin Friedman in Murtaza Hussain, "The war in Ukraine is just getting started," *The Intercept*, March 9, 2023, https:// theintercept.com/2023/03/09/ukraine-war-russia -iran-iraq/.

21 Bandow, "750 Bases in 80 Countries Is Too Many for Any Nation"; David Vine, *Base Nation: How U.S. Military Bases Abroad Harm America and the World* (New York, NY: Metropolitan Books, 2015).

22 In addition to the thirty allies in NATO and the seventeen members of the Rio Pact, the US has mutual defense treaties with the Philippines, Australia, South Korea, and Japan – totaling fifty-one formal treaty allies. A further fifteen states enjoy Major Non-NATO Ally status (or in the case of Taiwan, enjoy those privileges without being recognized as such).

23 See https://watson.brown.edu/costsofwar/. These are just the costs to the US homeland and the American people. The human and environmental costs of the US military presence overseas are also considerable. See Catherine Lutz, ed., *The Bases of Empire:*

The Global Struggle Against US Military Posts (Washington Square, NY: New York University Press, 2009); and Vine, *Base Nation*.

24 Posen, *Restraint*.

25 See, for example, Alan J. Kuperman, "A Model Humanitarian Intervention? Reassessing NATO's Libya Campaign," *International Security* 38, no. 1 (2013): 105–136.

26 This is what International Relations scholars call the "second image reversed" – the process of domestic politics, institutions, alignments, and identities being changed as the result of exposure to the outside world. See Peter Gourevitch, "The Second Image Reversed: The International Sources of Domestic Politics," *International Organization* 32, no. 4 (1978): 881–912.

27 Robert Kagan, *The World America Made* (New York, NY: Knopf, 2012). See also G. John Ikenberry, *After Victory: Institutions, Strategic Restraint, and the Rebuilding of Order after Major Wars* (Princeton, NJ: Princeton University Press, 2001), chapters 6 and 7.

28 Lasswell, "The Garrison State."

29 Harris, "How the attack on Pearl Harbor shaped America's role in the world," *The Conversation*, December 6, 2017; Stephen Wertheim, *Tomorrow, the World: The Birth of U.S. Global Supremacy* (Cambridge, MA: Belknap Press, 2020).

Chapter 1

1 Harris, "The Geopolitics of American Exceptionalism," at 587–588; Harris and Marinova, "American Primacy and US–China Relations: The Cold War Analogy Reversed," *Chinese Journal of International Politics* 15, no. 4 (2022): 335–351, at 336, 339–341.

2 John C. Sparrow, "History of Personnel Demobilization in the United States Army," Department of the Army Pamphlet No. 20-210, July 1952, at 301.

3 Tyler Bamford, "The Points Were All That Mattered: The US Army's Demobilization after World War II," The National WWII Museum, August 27, 2020, https://www.nationalww2museum

.org/war/articles/points-system-us-armys-demobilization. See also Michael J. Hogan, *A Cross of Iron: Harry S. Truman and the Origins of the National Security State 1945–1952* (Cambridge: Cambridge University Press, 2000), at 72–77. Dean Acheson notes that the rapid pace of demobilization was a direct response to domestic pressure. See Dean Acheson, *Present at the Creation: My Years in the State Department* (New York, NY: W.W. Norton, 1969), at 196.

4 Hubert Zimmermann, "The Improbable Permanence of a Commitment: America's Troop Presence in Europe during the Cold War," *Journal of Cold War Studies* 11, no. 1 (2009): 3–27.

5 Tim Kane, "Global U.S. Troop Deployment, 1950–2003," The Heritage Foundation, October 2004, https://www.heritage.org /defense/report/global-us-troop-deployment-1950-2003, at 2.

6 Kagan, *Dangerous Nation: America's Foreign Policy from Its Earliest Days to the Dawn of the Twentieth Century* (New York, NY: Vintage Books, 2007); George C. Herring, *From Colony to Superpower: US Foreign Relations Since 1776* (Oxford: Oxford University Press, 2008).

7 Jimmy M. Skaggs, *The Great Guano Rush: Entrepreneurs and American Overseas Expansion* (New York, NY: St. Martin's Press, 1995).

8 Herring, *From Colony to Superpower*, at 265–298.

9 Peter Trubowitz, *Defining the National Interest: Conflict and Change in American Foreign Policy* (Chicago, IL: University of Chicago Press, 1998), chapter 2.

10 Richard W. Maass, *The Picky Eagle: How Democracy and Xenophobia Limited US Territorial Expansion* (Ithaca, NY: Cornell University Press, 2020).

11 Herring, *From Colony to Superpower*, at 299–377.

12 Bartholomew H. Sparrow, *The* Insular Cases *and the Emergence of American Empire* (Lawrence, KS: University Press of Kansas, 2006).

13 Some scholars question whether the US acquisition of overseas colonies represented something qualitatively new and different

from the experience of governing the aboriginal peoples of what became the continental United States. For a detailed exposition of this view, see Katharine Bjork, *Prairie Imperialists: The Indian Country Origins of American Empire* (Philadelphia, PA: University of Pennsylvania Press, 2019).

14 Fred H. Harrington, "The Anti-Imperialist Movement in the United States, 1898–1900," *The Mississippi Valley Historical Review* 22, no. 2 (1935): 211–230, at 211.

15 In addition to occupying parts of Nicaragua proper, the United States leased the Corn Islands from Nicaragua beginning in 1914. The terms of this agreement were in force until 1970.

16 Jerry Hendrix, *Theodore Roosevelt's Naval Diplomacy: The US Navy and the Birth of the American Century* (Annapolis, MD: Naval Institute Press, 2014).

17 Jeff Frieden, "Sectoral Conflict and Foreign Economic Policy, 1914–1940," *International Organization* 42, no. 1 (1988): 59–90.

18 Frieden, "Sectoral Conflict and Foreign Economic Policy." On the general phenomenon of domestic politics constraining US expansionism, see Jeffrey W. Meiser, *Power and Restraint: The Rise of the United States, 1898–1941* (Washington, DC: Georgetown University Press, 2015).

19 Trubowitz, *Politics and Strategy: Partisan Ambition & American Statecraft* (Princeton, NJ: Princeton University Press, 2011), at 64–74.

20 Michael Holm, "Isolationism and Noninterventionism," in Mitchell K. Hall, ed., *Opposition to War: An Encyclopedia of U.S. Peace and Antiwar Movements* (Santa Barbara, CA: ABC-CLIO, 2018), at 334–335.

21 Quoted in John David Lewis, *Nothing Less than Victory: Decisive Wars and the Lessons of History* (Princeton, NJ: Princeton University Press, 2010), at 247.

22 Georg Schild, "The Roosevelt Administration and the United Nations: Re-creation or Rejection of the League Experience?" *World Affairs* 158, no. 1 (1995): 26–33, at 29.

23 Robert Rosscow, "The Battle of Azerbaijan, 1946," *Middle East Journal* 10, no. 1 (1956): 17–32.

24 Marc Trachtenberg, *A Constructed Peace: The Making of the European Settlement, 1945–1963* (Princeton, NJ: Princeton University Press, 1999), at 4–15, 79.

25 John Lewis Gaddis, *Strategies of Containment: A Critical Appraisal of American National Security Policy during the Cold War* (Oxford: Oxford University Press, 2005 [1982]), at 18–23; George Kennan, "Long Telegram," http://www.gwu.edu/~ns archiv/coldwar/documents/episode-1/kennan.htm.

26 Howard Jones, *"A New Kind of War": America's Global Strategy and the Truman Doctrine in Greece* (Oxford: Oxford University Press, 1997).

27 Paul Y. Hammond, "NSC-68: Prologue to Rearmament," in Warner R. Schilling, Paul Y. Hammond, and Glenn H. Snyder, eds., *Strategy, Politics, and Defense Budgets* (New York, NY: Columbia University Press, 1962).

28 Elizabeth Edwards Spalding, *The First Cold Warrior: Harry Truman, Containment, and the Remaking of Liberal Internationalism* (Lexington, KY: University Press of Kentucky, 2006).

29 Lester H. Brune, "Guns and Butter: The Pre-Korean War Dispute over Budget Allocations: *Nourse's Conservative Keynesianism Loses Favor Against Keyserling's Economic Expansion Plan,*" *American Journal of Economics and Sociology* 48, no. 3 (1989): 357–371.

30 Acheson, *Present at the Creation*, at 194–201.

31 U.S. Department of Defense, "Freedom Is Not Free: Take a Look Inside the Korean War Veterans Memorial," https://www.defen se.gov/Multimedia/Experience/Korean-War-Memorial/.

32 Benjamin O. Fordham, *Building the Cold War Consensus: The Political Economy of U.S. National Security Policy, 1949–1951* (Ann Arbor, MI: University of Michigan Press, 1998); Michael Brenes, *For Might and Right: Cold War Defense Spending and the Remaking of American Democracy* (Amherst, MA: University of Massachusetts Press, 2020).

33 Herring, *From Colony to Superpower*, at 651–701.

34 Kane, "Global U.S. Troop Deployment, 1950–2003."

35 Thomas M. Nichols, "Carter and the Soviets: The Origins of the US Return to a Strategy of Confrontation," *Diplomacy & Statecraft* 13, no. 2 (2002): 21–42.

36 See Michael T. Klare, "Oil, Iraq, and American Foreign Policy: The Continuing Salience of the Carter Doctrine," *International Journal* 62, no. 1 (2007): 31–42, at 34.

37 Krauthammer, "The Reagan Doctrine," *Washington Post*, July 19, 1985, https://www.washingtonpost.com/archive/politics/19 85/07/19/the-reagan-doctrine/b2a06583-46fd-41e5-b70d-c949 dd3c50c2/.

38 Markusen, Hall, Campbell, and Deitrick, *The Rise of the Gunbelt*.

39 At the time of writing, Sweden's application for membership of NATO has not been approved by all member states. If Sweden is permitted to join NATO, the number of alliance members will have doubled since 1989, from 16 to 32.

40 Joseph S. Nye, Jr., "The Case for Deep Engagement," *Foreign Affairs* 74, no. 4 (1995): 90–102.

41 Nina Silove, "The Pivot Before the Pivot: US Strategy to Preserve the Power Balance in Asia," *International Security* 40, no. 4 (2016): 45–88; Kurt M. Campbell, *The Pivot: The Future of American Statecraft in Asia* (New York, NY: Hatchette, 2016).

42 F. Gregory Gause, "The Illogic of Dual Containment," *Foreign Affairs* 73, no. 2 (1994): 56–66.

43 Muhammad Idrees Ahmad, *Road to Iraq: The Making of a Neoconservative War* (Edinburgh: Edinburgh University Press, 2014).

44 Colin Dueck, "Ideas and Alternatives in American Grand Strategy, 2000–2004," *Review of International Studies* 30, no. 4 (2004): 511–535.

45 Marc Ambinder, "McCain's '100 Years' in Iraq," *The Atlantic*, February 25, 2008.

46 See Shawn Snow, "Esper says US forces combating ISIS in Libya

'continue to mow the lawn'," *Military Times*, November 14, 2019.

47 Max Boot, "Why winning and losing are irrelevant in Syria and Afghanistan," *The Washington Post*, January 30, 2019.

48 See, for example, Michael Mandelbaum, *The Frugal Superpower: America's Global Leadership in a Cash-Strapped Era* (New York, NY: PublicAffairs, 2010).

49 Steve Holland, "Trump to West Point grads: 'We are ending the era of endless wars'," Reuters, June 13, 2020, https://www.reuters .com/article/idUSKBN23K0PQ/.

50 This might also help to explain the withdrawal of US forces from Iraq (2011) and Afghanistan (2021). With so many forward-deployed forces in the Greater Middle East – not to mention offshore bases such as Diego Garcia in the Indian Ocean – Washington could have ordered a reintervention in either country, should conditions deteriorate. This happened, of course, in Iraq in 2014.

51 The decolonization of US overseas territories has been a historically rare occurrence. The Philippines and Panama Canal Zone are the only populated territories to have ever been decolonized by the United States.

52 "Remarks by President Biden on the United Efforts of the Free World to Support the People of Ukraine," The White House, March 26, 2022, https://www.whitehouse.gov/briefing-room /speeches-remarks/2022/03/26/remarks-by-president-biden-on -the-united-efforts-of-the-free-world-to-support-the-people-of -ukraine/.

Chapter 2

1 Some post-Soviet states like Belarus and Moldova did not democratize.

2 Alvin Richman, "Poll Trends: Changing American Attitudes Toward the Soviet Union," *Public Opinion Quarterly* 55, no. 1 (1991): 135–148, at 138.

3 Today, common justifications for America's forward presence

are: to deter war, reassure allies, prevent regional arms races, dampen regional security dilemmas, and to exert geopolitical influence. See Dave Shunk, Charles Hornick, and Dan Burkhart, "The Role of Forward Presence in U.S. Military Strategy," *Military Review* 97, no. 4 (2017): 57–64. For a cogent criticism of America's forward presence, see Gil Barndollar, "Global Posture Review 2021: An Opportunity for Realism and Realignment," Defense Priorities, July 2021, https://www.defensepriorities.org /explainers/global-posture-review-2021.

4 Bill Clinton, "First Inaugural Address of William J. Clinton," January 20, 1993, https://avalon.law.yale.edu/20th_century/ clinton1.asp. Emphasis added.

5 Robert D. Kaplan, "The Coming Anarchy: How Scarcity, Crime, Overpopulation, Tribalism, and Disease are Rapidly Destroying the Social Fabric of Our Planet," *The Atlantic*, February 1994, https://www.theatlantic.com/magazine/archive/1994/02/the-co ming-anarchy/304670/.

6 Samuel P. Huntington, *The Clash of Civilizations and the Remaking of World Order* (New York, NY: Simon and Schuster, 1996).

7 Krauthammer, "The Unipolar Moment," at 29.

8 Eric S. Edelman, "The Strange Career of the 1992 Defense Planning Guidance," in Melvyn P. Leffler and Jeffrey W. Legro, *American Foreign Policy after the Berlin Wall and 9/11* (Ithaca, NY: Cornell University Press, 2011).

9 Bacevich, *American Empire: The Realities and Consequences of U.S. Diplomacy* (Cambridge, MA: Harvard University Press, 2002), at 44–46.

10 Joseph Nye, Jr., "The Case for Deep Engagement," at 90.

11 Michael McCgwire, "NATO Expansion: 'A Policy Error of Historic Importance'," *Review of International Studies* 24, no. 1 (1998): 23–42, at 23.

12 Strobe Talbott, "Why NATO Should Grow," *New York Review of Books*, 10 August 1995, cited in McCgwire, "NATO Expansion," at 24–25.

13 George Bush and Brent Scowcroft, *A World Transformed* (New York, NY: Vintage Books, 1998), at 370.

14 Richard S. Lowry, *The Gulf War Chronicles: A Military History of the First War with Iraq* (Lincoln, NE: iUniverse, 2003).

15 Joseph Darda, "Kicking the Vietnam Syndrome Narrative: Human Rights, the Nayirah Testimony, and the Gulf War," *American Quarterly* 69, no. 1 (2017): 71–82.

16 Carl Boggs and Tom Pollard, *The Hollywood War Machine: U.S. Militarism and Popular Culture*, 2nd edition (New York, NY: Routledge, 2007), at 130.

17 Douglas Brinkley, "Democratic Enlargement: The Clinton Doctrine," *Foreign Policy*, 106 (1997): 110–127, at 112.

18 The United States and United Kingdom launched airstrikes against Iraq in December 1998 as punishment for the Saddam Hussein regime refusing to grant proper access to UN weapons inspectors.

19 Madeleine K. Albright, Interview on NBC-TV "The Today Show" with Matt Lauer, February 19, 1998, https://1997-2001.state.gov /statements/1998/980219a.html.

20 Brinkley, "Democratic Enlargement."

21 Krauthammer, "The Unipolar Moment," at 26.

22 This is similar to what Stephen Wertheim has argued about the origins of the UN system in the 1940s – that liberal internationalism in the United States has always been something of a fig leaf for US dominance. See Wertheim, "Instrumental Internationalism: The American Origins of the United Nations, 1940–3," *Journal of Contemporary History* 54, no. 2 (2018): 265–283.

23 Bacevich, "Policing Utopia: The Military Imperatives of Globalization," *The National Interest* 56 (1999): 5–13.

24 Daniel Wirls, *Irrational Security: The Politics of Defense from Reagan to Obama* (Baltimore, MD: The Johns Hopkins University Press, 2010).

25 This is what Daniel Wirls calls a militarist "tilt" in domestic politics. Wirls, *Irrational Security*.

26 The Philippines is a notable exception.

27 Robert Jervis, "Understanding the Bush Doctrine," *Political Science Quarterly* 118, no. 3 (2003): 365–388.

28 Barack Obama, cited in Harris, "Why Trump Won't Retrench: The Militarist Redoubt in American Foreign Policy," *Political Science Quarterly* 133, no. 4 (2018): 611–640, at 624.

29 Wertheim, "Return of the Neocons," *New York Review of Books*, January 2, 2019, https://www.nybooks.com/online/2019/01/02/return-of-the-neocons/.

30 Abby Phillip, "Trump passes blame for Yemen raid to his generals: 'They lost Ryan'," *The Washington Post*, February 28, 2017, https://www.washingtonpost.com/news/post-politics/wp/2017/02/28/trump-passes-blame-for-yemen-raid-to-his-generals-they-lost-ryan/; Leo Shane III, "Trump: I'm giving the military 'total authorization'," *Military Times*, April 13, 2017, https://www.militarytimes.com/news/pentagon-congress/2017/04/13/trump-i-m-giving-the-military-total-authorization/.

31 Mark Katkov, Jessica Taylor, and Tom Bowman, "Trump Orders Syria Airstrikes after 'Assad Choked Out the Lives' of Civilians," NPR, April 6, 2017, https://www.npr.org/2017/04/06/522948481/u-s-launches-airstrikes-against-syria-after-chemical-attack.

32 Walt, *The Hell of Good Intentions*; Posen, *Restraint*, chapter 1.

33 Jeane J. Kirkpatrick, "A Normal Country in a Normal Time," *The National Interest* 21 (1990): 40–44

34 Patrick J. Buchanan, "America First – and Second, and Third," *The National Interest* 19 (1990): 77–82.

35 Harris, "Why Trump Won't Retrench," at 616.

36 Zachary Zwald and Jeffrey D. Berejikian, "Is There a Public–Military Gap in the United States? Evaluating Foundational Foreign Policy Beliefs," *Armed Forces & Society* 48, no. 4 (2022): 982–1002.

37 For later examples of this genre, see Roberto J. Gonzalez, *Militarizing Culture: Essays on the Warfare State* (New York, NY: Routledge, 2010); and Vine, *United States of War: A Global History of America's Endless Conflicts, from Columbus to the*

Islamic State (Berkeley, CA: University of California Press, 2020).

38 See, *inter alia*, Mearsheimer, *The Great Delusion: Liberal Dreams and International Realities* (New Haven, CT: Yale University Press, 2018); Walt, *The Hell of Good Intentions*; Posen, *Restraint*; Charles L. Glaser, "A US–China Grand Bargain? The Hard Choice Between Military Competition and Accommodation," *International Security* 39, no. 4 (2015): 49–90; Gholz, Press, and Sapolsky, "Come Home, America"; and Patrick Porter, *The False Promise of Liberal Order: Nostalgia, Delusion and the Rise of Trump* (Cambridge: Polity, 2020).

39 See, for example, Sebastian Rosato and John Schuessler, "A Realist Foreign Policy for the United States," *Perspectives on Politics* 9, no. 4 (2011): 803–819.

40 Mearsheimer, "Why the Ukraine Crisis Is the West's Fault: The Liberal Delusions That Provoked Putin," *Foreign Affairs* 93, no. 5 (2014): 77–89; and Gideon Rachman, "It makes no sense to blame the west for the Ukraine war," *Financial Times*, February 13, 2023, https://www.ft.com/content/2d65c763-c36f-4507-8a7d-13517032aa22.

41 C. Glaser, "Washington Is Avoiding the Tough Questions on Taiwan and China: The Case for Reconsidering U.S. Commitments in East Asia," *Foreign Affairs*, April 28, 2021, https://www.foreignaffairs.com/articles/asia/2021-04-28/washington-avoiding-tough-questions-taiwan-and-china; and Blake Herzinger, "Abandoning Taiwan Makes Zero Moral or Strategic Sense," *Foreign Policy*, May 3, 2021, https://foreignpolicy.com/2021/05/03/taiwan-policy-us-china-abandon.

42 For an archetypical example, see Michael Desch, *Cult of the Irrelevant: The Waning Influence of Social Science on National Security* (Princeton, NJ: Princeton University Press, 2019).

43 Walldorf and Yeo, "Domestic Hurdles to a Grand Strategy of Restraint."

44 Harris, "The Geopolitics of American Exceptionalism," at 590–591.

45 Bacevich, "Tradition Abandoned: America's Military in a New Era," *The National Interest*, no. 48 (1997): 16–25.

46 Christopher Coyne and Abigail Hall, *Tyranny Comes Home: The Domestic Fate of U.S. Militarism* (Stanford, CA: Stanford University Press).

47 Walter Russell Mead, *Special Providence: American Foreign Policy and How It Changed the World* (New York, NY: Knopf, 2001), chapter 6.

48 Mead, *Special Providence*, chapter 7.

49 Michael Clarke and Anthony Ricketts, "Donald Trump and American Foreign Policy: The Return of the Jacksonian Tradition," *Comparative Strategy* 36, no. 4 (2017): 366–379.

50 Jacob Pramuk, "US could have been rebuilt three times with leader who knew how to 'negotiate,' Trump says," CNBC, February 28, 2017, https://cnbc.com/2017/02/28/the-time-has-come-for-a-new-program-of-national-rebuilding-trump.html.

51 Buchanan, "America First – and Second, and Third," at 80.

52 Wertheim, "The Crisis in Progressive Foreign Policy: How the Left Can Adapt to an Age of Great-Power Rivalry," *Foreign Affairs*, August 24, 2022, https://www.foreignaffairs.com/united-states/crisis-progressive-foreign-policy.

53 Peter Beinart, "America Needs an Entirely New Foreign Policy for the Trump Age," *The Atlantic*, September 16, 2018, https://www.theatlantic.com/ideas/archive/2018/09/shield-of-the-republic-a-democratic-foreign-policy-for-the-trump-age/570010/.

54 Jackson, *Grand Strategies of the Left: The Foreign Policy of Progressive Worldmaking* (Cambridge: Cambridge University Press, 2023).

55 Author calculation: $1 trillion divided by 122.8 million households.

56 This comparison is for illustrative purposes only. The federal government raises revenue from sources other than households.

57 See https://www.nationalpriorities.org/.

58 Thomas Wright, "The problem at the core of progressive foreign

policy," Brookings Institution commentary, September 11, 2019, https://www.brookings.edu/articles/the-problem-at-the-core-of-progressive-foreign-policy. Such criticisms are not entirely fair. Van Jackson, for example, has identified at least three variants of progressive grand strategy: progressive pragmatism, anti-hegemonism, and peacemaking – explaining in concrete terms how each flavor of progressivism relates to the question of militarism. See Jackson, "Left of Liberal Internationalism: Grand Strategies within Progressive Foreign Policy Thought," *Security Studies* 31, no. 4 (2022): 553–592.

59 Jackson, "Toward a Progressive Theory of Security," *War on the Rocks*, December 6, 2018, https://warontherocks.com/2018/12/toward-a-progressive-theory-of-security/.

60 Jackson, "A Capital Critique: Progressive Alternatives to Neo-Liberal Economic Order," *International Journal* 78, no. 1–2 (2023): 212–231.

61 Marshall Auerback and James Carden, "The Rotten Alliance of Liberals and Neocons Will Likely Shape U.S. Foreign Policy for Years to Come," *Public Seminar*, September 1, 2020, https://publicseminar.org/essays/the-rotten-alliance-of-liberals-and-neocons-will-likely-shape-u-s-foreign-policy-for-years-to-come-biden-kagan/.

62 Daniel Bessner, "Twenty Years after Invading Iraq, American Liberalism Is Discredited Yet Still Dominant," *Jacobin*, March 20, 2023, https://jacobin.com/2023/03/iraq-war-twentieth-anniversary-liberalism-us-imperialism-hegemony-end-of-history.

63 Bessner, "The Specter of Liberal Internationalism," *Dissent*, Fall 2017, https://www.dissentmagazine.org/article/specter-liberal-internationalism-brookings-foreign-policy/. See also Bessner, "What Does Alexandria Ocasio-Cortez Think about the South China Sea?" *New York Times*, September 17, 2018, https://www.nytimes.com/2018/09/17/opinion/democratic-party-cortez-foreign-policy.html.

64 Walt, "Socialists and Libertarians Need an Alliance against the

Establishment," *Foreign Policy*, September 24, 2018, https://foreignpolicy.com/2018/09/24/socialists-and-libertarians-need-an-alliance-against-the-establishment/.

65 Inderjeet Parmar, "Washington's Newest Thinktank Is Fomenting a Revolution in US Foreign Affairs," *The Wire*, March 1, 2020, https://thewire.in/world/washingtons-newest-thinktank-is-fomenting-a-revolution-in-us-foreign-affairs.

66 Harris, "Entrenching Retrenchment: The Uphill Struggle to Shrink America's World Role, *Israel Journal of Foreign Affairs* 13, no. 2 (2019): 159–171.

Chapter 3

1 Gourevitch, "The Second Image Reversed"; Gourevitch, *Politics in Hard Times: Comparative Responses to International Economic Crises* (Ithaca, NY: Cornell University Press, 1986).

2 Kenneth N. Waltz, *Man, the State, and War: A Theoretical Analysis* (Columbia University Press, 2001 [1954]).

3 Bartholomew H. Sparrow, *From the Outside In: World War II and the American State* (Princeton, NJ: Princeton University Press, 1996).

4 J.P. Nettl, "The State as a Conceptual Variable," *World Politics* 20, no. 4 (1968): 559–592. See also David Andersen, Jørgen Møller, and Svend-Erik Skaaning, "The State-Democracy Nexus: Conceptual Distinctions, Theoretical Perspectives, and Comparative Approaches," *Democratization* 21, no. 7 (2014): 1203–1220, at 1205.

5 Nettl, "The State as a Conceptual Variable"; Ira Katznelson, "Rewriting the Epic of America," in Ira Katznelson and Martin Shefter, eds., *Shaped by War and Trade: International Influences on American Political Development* (Princeton, NJ: Princeton University Press, 2002), at 12–13.

6 Stephen Skowronek, *Building a New American State: The Expansion of National Administrative Capacities, 1877–1920* (Cambridge: Cambridge University Press, 1982), at 29.

7 Jeffrey K. Tulis and Nicole Mellow, *Legacies of Losing in American Politics* (Chicago, IL: University of Chicago Press, 2017).
8 Karen Orren and Skowronek, *The Search for American Political Development* (Cambridge: Cambridge University Press, 2004).
9 Fareed Zakaria, *From Wealth to Power: The Unusual Origins of America's World Role* (Princeton, NJ: Princeton University Press, 1998).
10 This is one reason, perhaps, that the Guano Islands Act gave private citizens responsibility for acquiring new territory: American traders, whalers, and fishermen were better positioned to go about discovering and occupying island territories than the US Navy. See Skaggs, *The Great Guano Rush.*
11 Skowronek, *Building a New American State.*
12 Will Morrisey, *The Dilemma of Progressivism: How Roosevelt, Taft, and Wilson Reshaped the American Regime of Self-Government* (Lanham, MD: Rowman & Littlefield, 2009).
13 Zachary A. Callen, *Railroads and American Political Development: Infrastructure, Federalism, and State Building* (Lawrence, KS: University Press of Kansas, 2016).
14 Zakaria, *From Wealth to Power.*
15 Sparrow, *From the Outside In*, at 4. See also his "American Political Development, State-Building, and the 'Security State': Reviving a Research Agenda," *Polity* 40, no. 3 (2008): 355–367.
16 Heidi B. Demarest and Erica D. Borghard, *US National Security Reform: Reassessing the National Security Act of 1947* (New York, NY: Routledge, 2018).
17 Sparrow, *From the Outside In*, at 24–25. This was mirrored in other policy domains too. See Bryan D. Jones, Sean M. Theriault, and Michelle Whyman, *The Great Broadening: How the Vast Expansion of the Policymaking Agenda Transformed American Politics* (Chicago, IL: University of Chicago Press, 2019).
18 Figures taken from https://www.whitehouse.gov/omb/budget/historical-tables/.
19 Federal employment statistics taken from https://www.opm.gov

/policy-data-oversight/data-analysis-documentation/federal-em
ployment-reports/historical-tables/executive-branch-civilian
-employment-since-1940/

20 Aaron Wildavsky, "The Two Presidencies," *Trans-Action* 4 (1966): 7–14.

21 Arthur M. Schlesinger, Jr., *The Imperial Presidency* (Boston, MA: Houghton Mifflin, 1973).

22 Thomas Cronin, "A Resurgent Congress and the Imperial Presidency," *Political Science Quarterly* 95, no. 2 (1980): 209–237.

23 Marcus G. Raskin, "Democracy Versus the National Security State," *Law and Contemporary Problems* 40, no. 3 (1976): 189–220, at 189.

24 Andrew Rudalevige, *The New Imperial Presidency: Renewing Presidential Power After Watergate* (Ann Arbor, MI: University of Michigan Press, 2006).

25 David Jablonsky, "The State of the National Security State," *Parameters* 32, no. 4 (2002): 4–18.

26 Karen J. Greenberg, *Subtle Tools: The Dismantling of American Democracy from the War on Terror to Donald Trump* (Princeton, NJ: Princeton University Press, 2021).

27 Michael Touchton and Amanda J. Ashley, *Salvaging Community: How American Cities Rebuild Closed Military Bases* (Ithaca, NY: Cornell University Press, 2019).

28 RAND Corporation, *The Army's Local Economic Effects* (Santa Monica, CA: RAND Corporation, 2015), at x, quoted in Harris, "Why Trump Won't Retrench," at 622.

29 See, for example, Richelle M. Bernazzoli and Colin Flint, "Embodying the Garrison State? Everyday Geographies of Militarization in American Society," *Political Geography* 29, no. 3 (2010): 157–166.

30 Katherine Schaeffer, "The changing face of America's veteran population," Pew Research Center, April 5, 2021, https://www.pewresearch.org/short-reads/2021/04/05/the-changing-face-of-americas-veteran-population/.

31 Bat Sparrow points out that an expanded degree of stateness in

the realm of military-security policy might actually have weakened the US state in other respects. He writes: "Policymakers have put the U.S. government on a less fiscally sound basis; they have reduced the administrative and regulatory capacities of the U.S. government in many non-military issue areas; and they have relied more and more heavily on a quasi-professional/voluntary armed forces – those who self-select to serve. And except for the brief period between late 2001 and mid-2004, the American public has become even more disaffected from government and less engaged with the military." See Sparrow, "American Political Development, State-Building, and the 'Security State'," at 364.

32 On path dependence, see Paul Pierson, "Increasing Returns, Path Dependence, and the Study of Politics," *American Political Science Review* 94, no. 2 (2000): 251–267; and Pierson, "Not Just What, but When: Timing and Sequence in Political Processes," *Studies in American Political Development* 14, no. 1 (2000): 72–92.

33 Pierson, "The Limits of Design: Explaining Institutional Origins and Change," *Governance* 13, no. 4 (2000): 475–499, at 488. Emphasis added.

34 Pierson, "The Limits of Design," at 491, citing Terry Moe, "The Politics of Structural Choice: Toward a Theory of Public Bureaucracy," in O.E. Williamson, ed., *Organization Theory: From Chester Barnard to the Present and Beyond* (Oxford: Oxford University Press, 1990).

35 Pierson, "The Limits of Design," at 493.

36 James Mahoney and Kathleen Thelen, "A Theory of Gradual Institutional Change," in Mahoney and Thelen, eds., *Explaining Institutional Change: Ambiguity, Agency, and Power* (Cambridge: Cambridge University Press, 2009), at 15–18.

37 Richard J. Barnet, "The Ideology of the National Security State," *The Massachusetts Review* 26, no. 4 (1985): 483–500, at 499.

38 On the difficulty of identifying shocks and junctures, see Orren and Skowronek, *Searching for American Political Development*, at 103.

39 Tyler M. Curley, "Models of Emergency Statebuilding in the United States," *Perspectives on Politics* 13, no. 3 (2015): 697–713.

40 John M. Schuessler, "The Deception Dividend: FDR's Undeclared War," *International Security* 34, no. 4 (2010): 133–165; Schuessler, *Deceit on the Road to War: Presidents, Politics, and American Democracy* (Ithaca, NY: Cornell University Press, 2015).

41 Douglas T. Stuart, *Creating the National Security State: A History of the Law That Transformed America* (Princeton, NJ: Princeton University Press, 2008), at 40–41.

42 Colin Dueck, "Ideas and Alternatives in American Grand Strategy, 2000–2004," *Review of International Studies* 30, no. 4 (2004): 511–535. See also Trubowitz, *Politics and Strategy*, at 97–104.

43 James Mann, *Rise of the Vulcans: The History of Bush's War Cabinet* (New York, NY: Penguin, 2004).

44 Hogan, *A Cross of Iron*.

45 Pierson, "Not Just What, but When."

46 Skowronek, *The Politics Presidents Make: Leadership from John Adams to Bill Clinton* (Cambridge, MA: Belknap Press, 1993).

47 Glenn P. Hastedt, *American Foreign Policy: Past, Present, and Future*, 11th edition (Lanham, MD: Rowman & Littlefield, 2018), at 87–88.

48 John Gerring, "Mere Description," *British Journal of Political Science* 42, no. 4 (2012): 721–746.

Chapter 4

1 The original draft of the Farewell Address referred to a military-industrial-*congressional* complex, with the last component of the term only removed for fear of causing offense to colleagues on Capitol Hill. I thank an anonymous reviewer for making me aware of this fact.

2 Brenes, *For Might and Right*.

3 Brenes, "How America Broke Its War Machine: Privatization and the Hollowing Out of the U.S. Defense Industry," *Foreign Affairs*,

July 3, 2023, https://www.foreignaffairs.com/united-states/how-america-broke-its-war-machine.

4 https://www.opensecrets.org/industries/indus.php?Ind=D

5 Brenes, *For Might and Right.*

6 Markusen, Hall, Campbell, and Deitrick, *The Rise of the Gunbelt.*

7 Rob Quirk, "Defense and aerospace remain an economic driver for Pikes Peak region," KOAA, September 7, 2023, https://www.koaa.com/community/uccs-economic-forum/defense-and-aerospace-remain-an-economic-driver-for-pikes-peak-region.

8 US Department of Defense, "Defense Spending by State, Fiscal Year 2020," Office of Local Defense Community Cooperation, https://oldcc.gov/sites/default/files/defense-spending-rpts/OLDCC_DSBS_FY2020_FINAL_WEB.pdf.

9 https://download.militaryonesource.mil/12038/MOS/Reports/2020-demographics-report.pdf.

10 Daniel W. Drezner, "Present at the Destruction: The Trump Administration and the Foreign Policy Bureaucracy," *Journal of Politics* 81, no. 2 (2019): 723–729, at 723.

11 Richard Hanania, *Public Choice Theory and the Illusion of Grand Strategy* (New York, NY: Routledge, 2021).

12 Porter, "Why America's Grand Strategy Has Not Changed," *International Security* 42, no. 4 (2018): 9–46, at 11, citing David Samuels, "The Aspiring Novelist Who Became Obama's Foreign Policy Guru," *New York Times Magazine*, May 5, 2016, at 27.

13 Porter, "Why America's Grand Strategy Has Not Changed," at 11.

14 Frieden, "Sectoral Conflict and Foreign Economic Policy."

15 Fred Block, "Economic Instability and Military Strength: The Paradoxes of the 1950 Rearmament Decision," *Politics & Society* 10, no. 1 (1980): 35–58.

16 Trubowitz, *Defining the National Interest*; Frieden, "Sectoral Conflict and Foreign Economic Policy."

17 Block, "Economic Instability and Military Strength."

18 Trubowitz, *Defining the National Interest.*

19 See John S. Galbraith, "The "Turbulent Frontier" as a Factor in British Expansionism," *Comparative Studies in Society and History* 2, no. 2 (1960): 150–168.

20 Paul Musgrave and Steven Ward, "The Unreality of Offshore Balancing: Security Commitments, Military Bases, and Public Support for Intervention," paper presented at the International Studies Association International Conference, Hong Kong, 2017, at 2.

21 Jessica Tuchman Mathews, "Redefining Security," *Foreign Affairs* 68, no. 2 (1989): 162–177.

22 Andrew Butfoy, "The Rise and Fall of Missile Diplomacy? President Clinton and the 'Revolution in Military Affairs' in Retrospect," *Australian Journal of Politics and History* 52, no. 1 (2006): 98–114, at 104.

23 Butfoy, "The Rise and Fall of Missile Diplomacy?"

24 According to Hélène Dufournet, a rhetorical trap "exists when the target of the actions of naming and shaming has no choice but to comply with the demands of the advocates in order to avoid contradicting the principles that the target is seeking to defend." See Hélène Dufournet (trans. Beverly Adab), "The Rhetorical Trap: A Moral Coercion Reflections on the influence of 'moral arguments' on the process of public action," in *Revue Française de Science Politique* 65, no. 2, 2015: 261–278.

25 Andrew Johnstone, "To Mobilize a Nation: Citizens' Organizations and Intervention on the Eve of World War II," in Andrew Johnstone and Helen Laville, eds., *The US Public and American Foreign Policy* (New York, NY: Routledge, 2010): 26–39.

26 Stephen Hopgood, *The Endtimes of Human Rights* (Ithaca, NY: Cornell University Press, 2013).

27 Michael G. Thompson, *For God and Grace: Christian Internationalism in the United States between the Great War and the Cold War* (Ithaca, NY: Cornell University Press, 2015); Angela Lahr, *Millennial Dreams and Apocalyptic Nightmares: The Cold War Origins of Political Evangelicalism* (Oxford:

Oxford University Press, 2007); Markku Ruotsila, *The Origins of Christian Anti-Internationalism: Conservative Evangelicals and the League of Nations* (Washington, DC: Georgetown University Press, 2008).

28 Clair Apodaca, *Human Rights and US Foreign Policy: Prevarications and Evasions* (New York, NY: Routledge, 2019).

29 Mearsheimer and Walt, *The Israel Lobby and U.S. Foreign Policy* (New York, NY: Farrar, Straus and Giroux, 2007).

30 James Goldgeier and Joshua R. Itzkowitz Shifrinson, "Evaluating NATO Enlargement: Scholarly Debates, Policy Implications, and Roads Not Taken," *International Politics* 57 (2020): 291–321, at 302, citing Goldgeier, *Not Whether but When: The U.S. Decision to Enlarge NATO* (Washington, DC: Brookings Institution Press, 1999), at 73–85.

31 Harris, "The Geopolitics of American Exceptionalism."

32 Michael S. Sherry, *The Shadow of War: The United States Since the 1930s* (New Haven, CT: Yale University Press, 1995); Charles A. Kupchan, "The Clash of Exceptionalisms: A New Fight over an Old Idea," *Foreign Affairs* 97, no. 2 (2018): 139–149.

33 Noam Lupu, Luke Plutowski, and Elizabeth Zechmeister, "Would Americans ever support a coup? 40 percent now say yes," *The Washington Post*, January 6, 2022, https://www.washingtonpost.com/politics/2022/01/06/us-coup-republican-support/.

34 Craig Helmstetter and Terrence Fraser, "Poll: Majority of Americans endorse democracy, younger generations skeptical," MPR News, January 18, 2023, https://www.mprnews.org/story/2023/01/18/poll-majority-of-americans-endorse-democracy-younger-generations-skeptical.

35 Peter Feaver, *Thanks For Your Service: The Causes and Consequences of Public Confidence in the US Military* (Oxford: Oxford University Press, 2023).

36 Coyne and Hall, *Manufacturing Militarism: US Government Propaganda in the War on Terror* (Stanford, CA: Stanford University Press, 2021).

37 Jim Golby and Peter Feaver, "Thank You For Your Lip Service?

Social Pressure to Support the Troops," *War on the Rocks*, August 14, 2019, https://warontherocks.com/2019/08/thank-you-for-your-lip-service-social-pressure-to-support-the-troops/. Golby and Feaver point to the Reagan administration as a turning point in the history of public trust in the military, citing David C. King and Zachary Karabell, *The Generation of Trust: Public Confidence in the U.S. Military Since Vietnam* (Washington, DC: AEI Press, 2003).

38 Mohamed Younis, "Confidence in U.S. Military Lowest in Over Two Decades," Gallup, July 31, 2023, https://news.gallup.com/po ll/509189/confidence-military-lowest-two-decades.aspx; Kelly Beaucar Vlahos, "Americans' trust in military hits 'malaise era' territory," *Responsible Statecraft*, August 1, 2023, https://respon siblestatecraft.org/2023/08/01/americans-trust-in-military-hits -malaise-era-territory/.

39 This is similar to the French concept of *pré carré* ("one's own little corner").

40 During the previous year's primary debates, every leading Democrat had made some sort of pledge to downsize America's military footprint, including commitments to end the Afghan War. While Republican lawmakers tended to be more tolerant of an indefinite military presence in Afghanistan, it was Donald Trump who authored the exit agreement that Biden ended up fulfilling. Opinion polls consistently showed the voting public to be exasperated with America's longest war.

41 See, for example, Peter Bergen, "The worst speech of Biden's presidency," CNN, July 10, 2021, https://www.cnn.com/2021 /07/09/opinions/biden-afghanistan-speech-malarkey-bergen/in dex.html; and Emma Graham-Harrison, "Forget the geopolitics. Let's focus on the human cost of the exit from Afghanistan," *The Guardian*, July 11, 2021, https://www.theguardian.com/com mentisfree/2021/jul/11/forget-the-geopolitics-lets-focus-on-the -human-cost-of-the-exit-from-afghanistan.

42 Andrew Solender, "GOP Lawmakers Ramp up Calls for Biden's Resignation, Removal over Kabul Attacks," *Forbes*, August 26,

2021, https://www.forbes.com/sites/andrewsolender/2021/08/26/gop-lawmakers-ramp-up-calls-for-bidens-resignation-removal-over-kabul-attacks/?sh=2f449ae039a5.

43 Emily Tamkin, "Will the US withdrawal from Afghanistan come to haunt Joe Biden's presidency?" *New Statesman*, August 13, 2021, https://www.newstatesman.com/world/2021/08/will-us-withdrawal-afghanistan-come-haunt-joe-biden-s-presidency.

44 House Republicans, "Never forget President Biden is to blame for the Taliban's takeover of Afghanistan. No one else," Twitter, August 15, 2023, https://twitter.com/HouseGOP/status/1691425504874962944.

45 Ruth Igielnik and Kim Parker, "Majorities of U.S. veterans, public say the wars in Iraq and Afghanistan were not worth fighting," Pew Research Center, July 10, 2019, https://www.pewresearch.org/short-reads/2019/07/10/majorities-of-u-s-veterans-public-say-the-wars-in-iraq-and-afghanistan-were-not-worth-fighting/.

46 Anna Shortridge, "The U.S. War in Afghanistan Twenty Years On: Public Opinion Then and Now," Council on Foreign Relations blog post, October 7, 2021, https://www.cfr.org/blog/us-war-afghanistan-twenty-years-public-opinion-then-and-now.

47 Matthew Colford and Alec J. Sugerman, "Millennials And The Military," Hoover Institution, August 2, 2016, https://www.hoover.org/research/millennials-and-military. See also A. Trevor Thrall and Erik Goepner, *Millennials and U.S. Foreign Policy: The Next Generation's Attitudes toward Foreign Policy and War (and Why They Matter)* (Washington, DC: Cato Institute, 2015).

48 See, for example, Sam Carliner, "The Anti-War Movement Could Be Reignited By Gen Z," *Teen Vogue*, January 6, 2022, https://www.teenvogue.com/story/gen-z-anti-war.

Chapter 5

1 Harris, "Why Trump Won't Retrench."

2 Schlesinger, *The Imperial Presidency*.

3 See, for example, Tom Malinowski, "Congress Has Willfully

Abdicated Its Responsibility over War," *Foreign Policy*, April 20, 2018, https://foreignpolicy.com/2018/04/20/congress-has-will fully-abdicated-its-responsibility-over-war.

4 Bruce Buchanan, "Presidential Accountability for Wars of Choice," Brookings Institution, Issues in Governance Studies, no. 22, December 2008, at 3–5.

5 Charles A. Stevenson, "The Korea War Powers Precedent," Lawfare, July 23, 2020, https://www.lawfaremedia.org/article/ko rea-war-powers-precedent.

6 Jennifer K. Elsea and Matthew C. Weed, "Declarations of War and Authorizations for the Use of Military Force: Historical Background and Legal Implications," Congressional Research Service, January 11, 2013, https://www2.law.umaryland.edu/ marshall/crsreports/crsdocuments/RL31133_01112013.pdf.

7 Stevenson, "The Korea War Powers Precedent."

8 Ryan C. Hendrickson, *The Clinton Wars: The Constitution, Congress, and War Powers* (Nashville, TN: Vanderbilt University Press, 2002), chapter 6.

9 Charlie Savage and Mark Landler, "War Powers Act Doesn't Apply for Libya, Obama Says," *New York Times*, June 15, 2011, https://www.nytimes.com/2011/06/16/us/politics/16powers .html.

10 Charlie Savage, "Trump Had Power to Attack Syria without Congress, Justice Dept. Memo Says," *New York Times*, June 1, 2018, https://www.nytimes.com/2018/06/01/us/politics/trump -war-powers-syria-congress.htm.

11 See https://www.archives.gov/milestone-documents/tonkin-gulf -resolution.

12 See https://www.congress.gov/107/plaws/publ40/PLAW-107pu bl40.pdf.

13 Even under the War Powers Act, Congress recognizes that an attack upon the armed forces of the United States abroad counts as an instance in which the president's constitutional authority to wage war is unquestioned.

14 Andrew Payne, *War on the Ballot: How the Election Cycle Shapes Presidential Decision-Making in War* (New York, NY: Columbia University Press, 2023).

15 Angelos Chryssogelos, *Party Systems and Foreign Policy Change in Liberal Democracies: Cleavages, Ideas, Competition* (New York, NY: Routledge, 2020).

16 Craig Whitlock, *The Afghanistan Papers: A Secret History of the War* (New York, NY: Simon & Schuster, 2021).

17 Obama, "The New Way Forward – The President's Address," speech at the US Military Academy at West Point, New York, December 1, 2009, https://obamawhitehouse.archives.gov/blog/2009/12/01/new-way-forward-presidents-address.

18 Daniel Byman and Steven Simon, "Trump's Surge in Afghanistan: Why We Can't Seem to End the War," *Foreign Affairs*, September 18, 2017, https://www.foreignaffairs.com/articles/afghanistan/2017-09-18/trumps-surge-afghanistan.

19 Even the suggestion of withdrawal drew rebukes from the Republican-controlled Senate, who sought (likely unconstitutionally) to protect the US deployment in Afghanistan from presidential meddling. To have withdrawn and then face the embarrassment of "losing" Kabul to the Taliban would have been even more politically dangerous for Trump.

20 Seung-Whan Choi, Youngwan Kim, David Ebner, and Patrick James, "Human Rights Institutionalization and US Humanitarian Military Intervention," *International Interactions* 46, no. 4 (2020): 606–635.

21 Peter Baker, "How Obama Came to Plan for 'Surge' in Afghanistan," *New York Times*, December 5, 2009, https://www.nytimes.com/2009/12/06/world/asia/06reconstruct.html.

22 Krishnadev Calamur, "Trump's Plan for Afghanistan: No Timeline for Exit," *The Atlantic*, August 21, 2017, https://www.theatlantic.com/international/archive/2017/08/trump-afghanistan/537474/.

23 Jeffrey Goldberg, "The Man Who Couldn't Take It Anymore,"

The Atlantic, October 2019, https://www.theatlantic.com/maga zine/archive/2019/10/james-mattis-trump/596665/. Emphasis added.

24 Harris, "Why Trump Won't Retrench," at 633–634.

25 Michael J. Glennon, *National Security and Double Government* (Oxford: Oxford University Press, 2015).

26 Aaron L. Friedberg, *In the Shadow of the Garrison State: America's Anti-Statism and Its Cold War Grand Strategy* (Princeton, NJ: Princeton University Press, 2000). See also William Inboden, "Reforming American Power: Civilian National Security Institutions in the Early Cold War and Beyond," in Jeremi Suri and Benjamin Valentino, eds., *Sustainable Security: Rethinking American National Security Strategy* (Oxford: Oxford University Press, 2016): 136–165.

27 Micah Zenko, "Obama's Final Drone Strike Data," Council on Foreign Relations, January 20, 2017, https://www.cfr.org/blog /obamas-final-drone-strike-data.

28 David E. Sanger, *Confront and Conceal: Obama's Secret Wars and Surprising Use of American Power* (New York, NY: Crown Publishers, 2012).

29 Neil Macdonald, "U.S. jeopardizes justice with al-Awlaki execu- tion from sky," CBC, October 4, 2011, https://www.cbc.ca/ news/world/analysis-u-s-jeopardizes-justice-with-al-awlaki- execution-from-sky-1.1100716.

30 Congress requires that the Department of Defense release figures on drone strikes, including fatalities, but this legislation does not apply to drone strikes carried out by the CIA.

31 Shane, "Trump: I'm giving the military 'total authorization'."

32 Benjamin Denison, "Bases, Logistics, and the Problem of Temptation in the Middle East," Defense Priorities, May 12, 2022, https://www.defensepriorities.org/explainers/bases-logis tics-and-the-problem-of-temptation-in-the-middle-east.

33 E.E. Schattschneider, *The Semisovereign People: A Realist's View of Democracy in America* (New York, NY: Holt, Rinehart, and Winston, 1960).

34 Robert W. Cox, "Social Forces, States and World Orders: Beyond International Relations Theory," *Millennium* 10, no. 2 (1981): 126–155, at 129.

35 Cox, "Social Forces, States and World Orders," at 128–129.

36 As Inderjeet Parmar has shown, some of America's biggest philanthropic foundations were always concerned with overseas interventionism. See Parmar, *Foundations of the American Century: The Ford, Carnegie, and Rockefeller Foundations in the Rise of American Power* (New York, NY: Columbia University Press, 2012).

37 Joseph Stieb, "The Regime Change Consensus: Iraq in American Politics, 1990–2003," PhD dissertation, University of North Carolina at Chapel Hill, 2019.

38 Quoted in Stuart, *Creating the National Security State*, at 43.

39 Thomas K. Duncan and Coyne, "The Revolving Door and the Entrenchment of the Permanent War Economy," *Peace Economics, Peace Science and Public Policy* 21, no. 3 (2015): 391–413; Dror Etzion and Gerald F. Davis, "Revolving Doors? A Network Analysis of Corporate Officers and US Government Officials," *Journal of Management Inquiry* 17, no. 3 (2008): 157–161.

40 Cynthia Enloe, *Maneuvers: The International Politics of Militarizing Women's Lives* (Berkeley, CA: University of California Press, 2000).

41 Patrick Deer, "Mapping Contemporary American War Culture," *College Literature* 43, no. 1 (2016): 48–90.

42 Harris, "Why Trump Won't Retrench."

43 Robbie Gramer, Dan De Luce, and Colum Lynch, "How the Trump Administration Broke the State Department," *Foreign Policy*, July 31, 2017, https://foreignpolicy.com/2017/07/31/how -the-trump-administration-broke-the-state-department.

44 Jack Corrigan and Government Executive, "The Hollowing-Out of the State Department Continues," *The Atlantic*, February 11, 2018, https://www.theatlantic.com/international/archive/2018 /02/tillerson-trump-state-foreign-service/553034/.

Chapter 6

1 Aubrey W. Jewett and Marc D. Turetzky, "Stability and Change in President Clinton's Foreign Policy Beliefs, 1993–96," *Presidential Studies Quarterly* 28, no. 3 (1998): 638–665, at 638.

2 Simon Chesterman, "Bush, the United Nations and Nation-Building," *Survival* 46, no. 1 (2004): 101–116, at 102; John D. Graham, *Bush on the Home Front: Domestic Policy Triumphs and Setbacks* (Bloomington, IN: Indiana University Press, 2010).

3 In August 2021, Secretary of State Antony Blinken gave a speech that called for "domestic renewal as a foreign policy priority." See Antony J. Blinken, "Domestic Renewal as a Foreign Policy Priority," speech at University of Maryland A. James Clark School of Engineering, College Park, MD, August 9, 2021, https://www .state.gov/domestic-renewal-as-a-foreign-policy-priority/.

4 See, for example, Alexandra Cahn and Kiley Hurst, "Americans are more pessimistic than optimistic about many aspects of the country's future," Pew Research, September 18, 2023, https:// www.pewresearch.org/short-reads/2023/09/18/americans-are -more-pessimistic-than-optimistic-about-many-aspects-of-the -countrys-future.

5 Rosella Cappella Zielinski, *How States Pay for Wars* (Ithaca, NY: Cornell University Press, 2016).

6 Peter Trubowitz and Brian Burgoon, *Geopolitics and Democracy: The Western Liberal Order from Foundation to Fracture* (Oxford: Oxford University Press, 2023); Brian Burgoon, Tim Oliver, and Peter Trubowitz, "Globalization, Domestic Politics, and Transatlantic Relations," *International Politics* 54, no. 4 (2017): 420–433; and Trubowitz and Burgoon, "The Retreat of the West," *Perspectives on Politics* 20, no. 1 (2022): 102–122.

7 Block, "Economic Instability and Military Strength"; Bacevich, "Policing Utopia."

8 See Coyne and Hall, *Tyranny Comes Home.*

9 Kenneth A. Schultz, "Perils of Polarization for US Foreign Policy," *The Washington Quarterly* 40, no. 4 (2017): 7–28.

10 Jordan Tama, *Bipartisanship and US Foreign Policy: Cooperation in a Polarized Age* (Oxford: Oxford University Press, 2023).

11 Trubowitz and Harris, "The End of the American Century?"; Harris and Trubowitz, "The Politics of Power Projection: The Pivot to Asia, Its Failure, and the Future of American Primacy," *The Chinese Journal of International Politics* 14, no. 2 (2021): 187–217.

12 Lisa Jane Disch, *The Tyranny of the Two-Party System* (New York, NY: Columbia University Press).

13 Kupchan and Trubowitz, "The Home Front: Why an Internationalist Foreign Policy Needs a Stronger Domestic Foundation," *Foreign Affairs* 100, no. 3 (2021): 92–101.

14 In the United States, voters do not "join" political parties but rather register their party affiliation with the state or local government.

15 The obvious system would be "single transferable vote," also known as "proportional ranked choice voting," which is used in some local elections in the United States. Senators should be elected via an "instant-runoff" system (known elsewhere as the "alternative vote"), which is also used in some US elections.

16 Thrall, "Primed against Primacy: The Restraint Constituency and U.S. Foreign Policy," *War on the Rocks*, September 15, 2016, https://warontherocks.com/2016/09/primed-against-primacy-the-restraint-constituency-and-u-s-foreign-policy/; see also Thrall, "Identifying the Restraint Constituency," in Thrall and Friedman, eds., *US Grand Strategy in the 21st Century: The Case for Restraint* (New York, NY: Routledge, 2018), chapter 12.

17 Friedman, "Managing Fear: The Politics of Homeland Security," *Political Science Quarterly* 126, no. 1 (2011): 77–106, at 92.

18 William G. Howell and Jon C. Pevehouse, *While Dangers Gather: Congressional Checks on Presidential War Powers* (Princeton, NJ: Princeton University Press, 2007).

19 The insight from political science is that spending-through-borrowing is bad for constraining foreign policy. See Sarah Kreps, *Taxing Wars: The American Way of War Finance and the*

Decline of Democracy (Oxford: Oxford University Press, 2018); and Zielinski, *How States Pay for Wars.*

20 Hogan, *A Cross of Iron.* It may also be possible to explore alternative budget models, such as devolving budgetary authority more to the individual services, given that there is some historical evidence of the US Navy having more success negotiating lower prices for naval hardware than the larger Department of Defense. See Daniel Carpenter, "The Evolution of National Bureaucracy in the United States," in Joel D. Aberbach and Mark A. Peterson, eds., *The Executive Branch* (Oxford: Oxford University Press, 2005): 41–71, at 56, citing Sparrow, *From the Outside In: World War II and the American State* (Princeton, NJ: Princeton University Press, 1996), at 161–257.

21 Kupchan and Trubowitz, "The Home Front."

22 See https://fedmanagers.org/Legislative-Branch.

23 Schattschneider, *The Semisovereign People.*

24 Riker contrasted *heresthetic* (political manipulation) with *rhetoric* (political persuasion). See William H. Riker, *The Art of Political Manipulation* (New Haven, CT: Yale University Press, 1986).

25 Stuart Hall, *The Hard Road to Renewal: Thatcherism and the Crisis of the Left* (London: Verso, 1988), at 273, 274, and 266, quoted in Wendy Brown, "Resisting Left Melancholy," *boundary 2* 26, no. 3 (1999): 19–27, at 24.

26 Friedman and Logan, "Why the U.S. Military Budget Is 'Foolish and Sustainable'," *Orbis* 56, no. 2 (2012): 186–187.

27 Kupchan and Trubowitz, "The Home Front." On the role of labor in the past, see Rhodri Jeffreys-Jones, "Organized Labor and the Social Foundations of American Diplomacy, 1898–1920," in Andrew Johnstone and Helen Laville, eds., *The US Public and American Foreign Policy* (New York, NY: Routledge, 2010), chapter 4.

28 Schelling, *Arms and Influence.*

29 Stephen Moore, "If Congress Won't Cut the Budget, Then Freeze It," Cato Institute Commentary, January 13, 1997, https://www

.cato.org/commentary/congress-wont-cut-budget-then-freeze
-it.

30 Nina Hachigian, "Why U.S. Cities and States Should Play a
Bigger Role in Foreign Policy," *Foreign Policy*, April 19, 2021,
https://foreignpolicy.com/2021/04/19/american-cities-states-
local-foreign-policy-role-domestic-biden-sullivan/.

31 Harris, "Entrenching Retrenchment," at 166.

32 Joslyn N. Barnhart, Robert F. Trager, Elizabeth N. Saunders, and
Allan Dafoe, "The Suffragist Peace," *International Organization*
74, no. 4 (2020): 633–670.

33 Olivera Simić, "Does the Presence of Women Really Matter?
Towards Combating Male Sexual Violence in Peacekeeping
Operations," *International Peacekeeping* 17, no. 2 (2010):
188–199.

34 Valerie M. Hudson, Mary Caprioli, Bonnie Ballif-Spanvill, Rose
McDermott, and Chad F. Emmett, "The Heart of the Matter: The
Security of Women and the Security of States," *International
Security* 33, no. 3 (2009): 7–45.

35 For an overview of women's participation in US foreign policy
in the past, see Helen Laville, "Gender Apartheid? American
Women and Women's Rights in American Foreign Policy," in
Andrew Johnstone and Helen Laville, eds., *The US Public and
American Foreign Policy* (New York, NY: Routledge, 2010),
chapter 7; Helen Laville, *Cold War Women: The International
Activities of American Women's Organizations* (Manchester:
Manchester University Press, 2002).

36 As proposed in 1923, the text of the Equal Rights Amendment is
simply that "Equality of rights under the law shall not be denied or
abridged by the United States or by any state on account of sex."

37 Øyvind Søraas Skorge, "Mobilizing the Underrepresented:
Electoral Systems and Gender Inequality in Political
Participation," *American Journal of Political Science* 67, no. 3
(2023): 538–552.

38 https://www.dni.gov/files/documents/EEOD/FY18_IC_Annu
al_Demographic_Report_V6_ExecSec.pdf.

Chapter 7

1 Eugene Gholz, Daryl G. Press, and Harvey M. Sapolsky, "Come Home, America: The Strategy of Restraint in the Face of Temptation," *International Security* 21, no. 4 (1997): 5–48, at 5–6.

2 Posen, "Pull Back: The Case for a Less Activist Foreign Policy," *Foreign Affairs* 92, no. 1 (2013): 116–128. Cf. Stephen G. Brooks, G. John Ikenberry, and William C. Wohlforth, "Lean Forward: In Defense of American Engagement," *Foreign Affairs* 92, no. 1 (2013): 130–142.

3 Denison, "Bases, Logistics, and the Problem of Temptation in the Middle East."

4 Posen, "Europe Can Defend Itself," *Survival* 62, no. 6 (2020): 7–34.

5 Schelling, *Arms and Influence*.

6 Bacevich, "Policing Utopia."

7 Friedman and Logan, "Why the U.S. Military Budget Is 'Foolish and Sustainable'," at 185–187.

8 Kyle Haynes, "How Washington can lead from behind in Europe," *Defense News*, July 25, 2023, https://www.defensenews.com/opin ion/2023/07/25/how-washington-can-lead-from-behind-in-eu rope/.

9 That said, expanding the National Guard and providing more opportunities for citizens to participate in voluntary military training would be a good idea to make sure that America could ground troops quickly and efficiently if this ever became necessary.

10 Trubowitz, *Politics and Strategy*, at 11, citing Edward N. Luttwak, *The Grand Strategy of the Byzantine Empire* (Cambridge, MA: Harvard University Press, 2009).

11 That said, intelligence should be placed under the scrutiny of Congress rather than being left as the sole preserve of the executive branch.

12 Harris, "Moving to an Offshore Balancing Strategy for East Asia," Defense Priorities, October 31, 2023, https://www.defensepriori ties.org/explainers/offshore-balancing-east-asia.

13 See Christopher Layne, "From Preponderance to Offshore Balancing: America's Future Grand Strategy," *International Security* 22, no. 1 (1997): 86–124; Mearsheimer and Walt, "The Case for Offshore Balancing: A Superior U.S. Grand Strategy," *Foreign Affairs* 95, no. 4 (2016): 70–83.

14 As part of a strategy of burden-sharing (or burden-shifting), much of America's inventory – tanks, armored vehicles, weapons and munitions – should be gifted to allies as military aid. To incentivize this, Washington should ban military equipment being used for civilian purposes by reforming the 1033 program by which military gear is offered to law enforcement agencies in the United States.

15 For details, see Harris, "Moving to an Offshore Balancing Strategy for East Asia"; and Eugene Gholz, Benjamin Friedman, and Enea Gjoza, "Defensive Defense: A Better Way to Protect U.S. Allies in Asia," *Washington Quarterly* 42, no. 4 (2019): 171–189.

16 OECD, "ODA Levels in 2022 – preliminary data Detailed summary note," OECD Development Co-operation Directorate, April 12, 2023, https://www.developmentaid.org/api/frontend /cms/file/2023/04/ODA-2022-summary.pdf.

17 Harris, "Entrenching Retrenchment."

18 Barnhart, Trager, Saunders, and Dafoe, "The Suffragist Peace."

19 Hudson, Caprioli, Ballif-Spanvill, McDermott, and Emmett, "The Heart of the Matter." See also Hudson, Ballif-Spanvill, Caprioli, and Emmett, *Sex and World Peace* (New York, NY: Columbia University Press, 2012).

20 Byungwon Woo and Dana Parke, "Official Development Assistance and Women's Rights: How Aid Donor Characteristics Affect Women's Rights Improvement in Recipient Countries," *Asian Women* 32, no. 1 (2016): 1–29.

21 Dani Rodrik, "Globalization's Wrong Turn," *Foreign Affairs* 98, no. 4 (2019): 26–33.

22 Edward Mansfield and Omer Solodoch, "The Political Costs of Trade War Tariffs," unpublished manuscript, available at SSRN: https://papers.ssrn.com/sol3/papers.cfm?abstract_id=4516694.

23 Mansfield and Diana C. Mutz, "Support for Free Trade: Self-Interest, Sociotropic Politics, and Out-Group Anxiety," *International Organization* 63, no. 3 (2009): 425–457.

24 Carla Norlöff, "The Dollar's Full-Spectrum Dominance," Project Syndicate, September 19, 2023, https://www.project-syndicate.org/commentary/why-us-dollar-hegemony-will-survive-by-carla-norrlof-2023-09.

25 Henry J. Farrell and Abraham L. Newman, "The U.S. Is the Only Sanctions Superpower. It Must Use That Power Wisely," *New York Times*, March 16, 2022, https://www.nytimes.com/2022/03/16/opinion/us-russia-sanctions-power-economy.html.

26 Farrell and Newman, "Weaponized Interdependence: How Global Economic Networks Shape State Coercion," *International Security* 44, no. 1 (2019): 42–79.

27 On the relationship between material structure and ideas about social reality, I take inspiration from Colin Wight, *Agents, Structures and International Relations: Politics as Ontology* (Cambridge: Cambridge University Press, 2006).

28 Walldorf and Yeo, "Domestic Hurdles to a Grand Strategy of Restraint"; Miroslav Nincic, *The Logic of Positive Engagement* (Ithaca, NY: Cornell University Press, 2011).

29 The term "Greater United States" has historically been used to refer to the United States proper plus its nonsovereign territories (colonies). See Immerwahr, "The Greater United States: Territory and Empire in U.S. History," *Diplomatic History* 40, no. 3 (2016): 373–391. Today, however, it might also be used to refer to America's hundreds of overseas bases that, in some cases, have existed for well over half a century, and are de facto permanent parts of the US dominion.

30 Walldorf and Yeo, "Domestic Hurdles to a Grand Strategy of Restraint"; Wirls, *Irrational Security*.

Index